HUNGRY FOR CHANGE

FARMERS, FOOD JUSTICE AND THE AGRARIAN QUESTION

A. HAROON AKRAM-LODHI

FERNWOOD PUBLISHING
HALIFAX & WINNIPEG

KUMARIAN PRESS
STERLING, VA

Editing: Marianne Ward
Cover design: John van der Woude
Printed and bound in Canada

Published in Canada by Fernwood Publishing
32 Oceanvista Lane, Black Point, Nova Scotia, B0J 1B0
and 748 Broadway Avenue, Winnipeg, MB R3G 0X3   www.fernwoodpublishing.ca
and in the United States by Kumarian Press, an imprint of Stylus Publishing, LLC
22883 Quicksilver Drive, Sterling, VA 20166-2102   www.kpbooks.com

ISBN 978-1-55266-546-6 pb (Fernwood Publishing)
ISBN 978-1-56549-643-9 pb (Kumarian Press)
ISBN 978-1-56549-644-6 (Kumarian Press library networkable e-book edition)
ISBN 978-1-56549-645-3 (Kumarian Press consumer e-book edition)

Fernwood Publishing Company Limited gratefully acknowledges the financial support of the Government of Canada through the Canada Book Fund and the Canada Council for the Arts, the Nova Scotia Department of Communities, Culture and Heritage, the Manitoba Department of Culture, Heritage and Tourism under the Manitoba Book Publishers Marketing Assistance Program and the Province of Manitoba, through the Book Publishing Tax Credit, for our publishing program.

Library and Archives Canada Cataloguing in Publication

Akram-Lodhi, A. Haroon (Agha Haroon), 1958-
Hungry for change : farmers, food justice and the agrarian
question / A. Haroon Akram-Lodhi.

Includes bibliographical references and index.
ISBN 978-1-55266-546-6

1. Food industry and trade. 2. Food supply. 3. Agriculture--
Economic aspects. 4. Agriculture--Social aspects. 5. Farms, Small.
I. Title.

HD9000.5.A47 2013   338.1'9   C2012-908084-5

Library of Congress Cataloging-in-Publication Data has been applied for

CONTENTS

ACKNOWLEDGEMENTS

This book reflects decades of work in agrarian political economy; consequently the list of those that should be acknowledged is far too long to be elaborated. Rather, I would like to thank colleagues past and present, and generations of students, at London South Bank University in the United Kingdom, the International Institute of Social Studies in the Netherlands and Trent University in Canada. My students in particular have forced me, on a sustained and daily basis, to continually think through and rethink my ideas as well as articulate them in accessible English, and this book could not have been written without them. It was because of them that I chose to write this book as a series of factual vignettes built around people, although some of the individuals portrayed in these pages are composites of several people that I have met, and, in a few cases, the portrayals are drawn from secondary sources.

I have had the great fortune to have been taught by and work with some of the great agrarian political economists of our time. There are two people, though, without whom this book could not have been written: Terry Byres and Cristóbal Kay. For your continued critical engagement and encouragement, thank you both.

In the early stages of writing this book Raj Patel not only offered encouragement but opened a number of important doors. He did not have to do so. Thank you.

Marianne Ward has been invaluable in making this book accessible for readers. Thanks.

As anyone who has done this knows, writing a book is a collective act because it requires an immense amount of support from friends and family. Catherine, Cameron and Róisín: thanks for your patience. I hope you think it was worth it.

During the course of writing this book I lost my mother, Dorothy Miller Osborne Stewart. From her I learned that our purpose is to give of ourselves, with conviction and integrity, in order to make this world what it is capable of being. From her I learned that social justice is not an option — it is the future. To her, I dedicate this book.

THE ARGUMENT

This book explains how the creation, structure and operation of the capitalist world food system is marginalizing family farmers, small-scale peasant farmers and landless rural workers as it entrenches a global subsistence crisis. It also shows how, on the margins of that crisis, an alternative future is not only being envisioned but is being built by movements of people.

The book starts by laying out the crude numbers that express the dimensions of the global subsistence crisis: almost a billion people chronically malnourished, another billion people always unsure from where their next meal will come, 500 million that are clinically obese and 1.5 billion people that are overweight.

Chapter 1 describes how, in the contemporary global food regime, entitlements to food require money, a fundamental historical change that sustains the insecurity of contemporary access to food. Yet money and markets in access to food have been around for time immemorial: what is now different?

Chapter 2 uses a number of stories to show that family farmers and small-scale peasants live and work in an economic system that compels them to make certain decisions and that when they fail to meet the dictates of that system they are forced to quit. That economic system is capitalism, and in the last three centuries it has transformed food provisioning and farm production. To understand how, the "agrarian question" is introduced: whether or not capital and capitalist relations of production are or are not transforming agriculture, and if so, how. This transformation occurs by dispossessing farmers through outright displacement from the land or through the advent of marked differences in rural wealth.

Chapter 3 explains how this transformation began to be engineered in the developing capitalist countries. Small-scale peasant farmers around the world were drawn into the world's first global food regime, which reconfigured rural landscapes and farming systems to produce large quantities of food for export in rigged markets. This created food-based deprivation because peasant farmers needed money and therefore had to sell their crops.

Peasants resisted their incorporation into a global food regime, and Chapter 4 tells the story of this resistance as the peasant wars of the twentieth century sought to overthrow social structures by introducing pro-poor redistributive land reform. Yet socialist and capitalist land reform as it was introduced around the world failed to meet the aspirations of the peasantry, and indeed often increased the control of land by the rural elite. As such, the processes by which capitalist markets and capitalism were transforming farming and agriculture to the detriment of the peasantry was in fact broadly accelerated in many places and spaces. This anti-peasant bias was reinforced by "Green Revolution" agricultural technologies that were designed to increase farm productivity per unit of land.

As explained in Chapter 5, these technologies were developed in the 1940s, applied in the 1950s and 1960s, and resulted in dramatic increases in farm yields between the mid1960s and 1980s. However, the Green Revolution did not alleviate the increasing insecurity of peasant livelihoods in many places. No: reinforced by externally-mandated processes of economic "adjustment" the Green Revolution contributed to the ongoing and deepening differences in wealth and inequality evident across developing capitalist countries as capitalist relations of production spread through agriculture, and peasant populations, increasingly displaced from their land, were forced to migrate into urban slums. More recent efforts to use biotechnologies to bring about a "gene revolution" has the same potential to further deepen entrenched rural inequality and sustain the ongoing capitalist transformation of agriculture.

In Chapter 6 the contrasting story of two farms is used to explore the predatory role of the capitalist state in establishing a global food regime that undermined peasant and family farming in many countries, to the benefit of the large-scale capitalist farms and industrial agriculture that has consolidated its dominant position in the world food system over the last seventy-five years. The United States in particular has used its hegemonic position to suture together a contemporary global food regime that has dispossessed through displacement and differentiation small-scale farmers around the world, organizing and configuring a global food regime that is dominated by transnational agro-food capital, most particularly supermarkets.

This process is illustrated in Chapter 7, which shows how transnational agro-food capital has transformed societies in order to construct export-oriented agricultures, but in ways that deepen the global subsistence crisis.

Chapter 8 offers two contrasting visions of a way out of this crisis, namely the continued deepening of capitalism in agriculture advocated by the World Bank, or food sovereignty, which is advocated by the global peasant movement La Vía Campesina. The World Bank's vision reiterates and indeed accelerates the very processes that created the global subsistence crisis while it is suggested that behind food sovereignty lie some dilemmas that must be tackled.

So, in Chapter 9, a series of propositions are elaborated in order to show the types of changes that are needed to construct a people- and community-centred, climate-friendly, local and sustainable food system that produces abundant, nutritious, culturally appropriate and tasty food using low impact agroecological principles that work to conserve the environment. An alternative food regime is possible, and answering the agrarian question of our times and eliminating the global subsistence crisis is possible — and now — but it will require transcending capitalist social relations in farming and agriculture and instead uniting diverse food movements around an agrarian alternative that, in meeting the need for food justice, meets the aspirations of global consumers, family farmers and peasants.

"FOOD, GLORIOUS FOOD!"

DIMENSIONS OF THE GLOBAL SUBSISTENCE CRISIS

The world faces a calamity of historically unprecedented proportions. The planet produces enough food to feed ten billion people — enough for the world's population when it peaks around 2050 (Patel 2011). Yet almost a billion people are, day in and day out, chronically malnourished, and another billion people are always under the immanent existential threat of not knowing for sure where their next meal is coming from (Provost 2012). The result: every seven seconds a child under five dies somewhere because they have not had enough to eat (Sheeran 2009). This obscene, brutal picture has another side to it: the 500 million around the world who are clinically obese, the 1.5 billion people who are overweight and the astonishing acceleration in the last fifteen years of type 2 diabetes in developed and developing capitalist countries, a potentially life-threatening disease commonly associated with an unhealthy sugar-intensive diet (World Health Organization 2011). There is plenty of food to go around; and yet we see the particularly paradoxical combination of too many not getting enough of any food and too many getting too much of the wrong sort of food. Something is wrong.

There's more though. The vast majority of those that do not get enough to eat live in the countryside and work, for the most part, as small-scale peasant farmers or landless waged labourers (International Fund for Agricultural Development 2011). That's right: in the vortex that is contemporary chronic poverty, people in the countryside are the hungriest. Half the planet's population of seven billion lives in the countryside. Of these, more than three billion rely on small amounts of land — typically, two hectares or less (Food and Agriculture Organization 2002). Using land that very often they have to rent because they do not own it, using family members to work that land and using small amounts of basic tools and equipment such as hoes and sickles, such small-scale peasant farmers have to cultivate arable land, either in settled farming or the slash-and-burn techniques of shifting cultivation, and prosper

4

or go hungry on the basis of whether the land, after meeting their costs, provides them with enough farm produce so that the family can maintain a rudimentary standard of living and, if possible, some farm produce that can be stockpiled as a surplus, to be sold or saved for future use.

With so many going hungry, many small-scale peasant farmers do not prosper; they do not live an idyllic, romanticized rural life, for such a life is a populist myth; their lives are harsh, harrowing and short, and they are continually hammered by forces outside their control. Nor do peasants live in surroundings where all are united in their trying circumstances: in trying to get land, they may have to deal with landlords, whose control of land attunes their power over the impoverished; in trying to sell farm produce, they may have to deal with traders, whose mastery of the complex calculus of markets conveys a power that can wreak havoc upon those without; and in trying, when necessary, to work for others because they do not have a stockpile of food, they may have to accept what is offered by stubbornly tight-fisted employers whose ability to offer a job gives them power. Small-scale peasant farmers live in communities riddled with and permeated by a Faustian bargain of notoriously incorrigible inequalities.

These razor-sharp differences can also be found within communities, between small-scale peasant farmers who can appear, to the untrained eye, to look fairly equal. Of course, whether you are a man or a woman, whether you are younger or older, whether you are closer or more distantly related and whether you are on good or bad terms with local leaders: all continually collide to effect your position in your community, the character of the trans-actions that you undertake with others and the content and meaning of the culture within which you live. But differences can go much deeper. Having microcosmic stocks of basic tools and equipment as well as the labour-power of family members, small-scale peasants have to work, in a sense, as both a petty capitalist of little consequence and as a worker with little control. Trying to do both, within the complicated intricacies of a convoluted and often contradictory set of social and economic conditions, brings with it a set of Byzantine challenges. Most are not up to the task: needing to get es-sentials that they do not produce, they have to navigate the murky waters of ruthlessly arbitrary markets as both petty capitalist and worker, and only a few are able to solve the hard equations that define the incessantly confusing choices that have to be made. For the rest, the inexhaustible and continual judgments of the market are coldly and vigorously enforced: a continuum of polarizing processes both recapitulates and reconfigures the landscapes of the social and economic circumstances within which their all too human condition so often unhappily resides.

Incredibly, landless rural workers have it worse: lacking the existential security provided by trivial stocks of tools and equipment or access to land, landless rural workers face the never-ending appetites of the "endlessly fran-chised petty exploitation" (Davis 2006) that permeates the daily drudgery that, if they are lucky, they get from employers ranging from rapacious landlords all the way down to micro-entrepreneurs. In lurid and often dangerous working conditions they are forced to creatively improvise in order to survive on the knife-edge of subsistence. Many enter into the compulsorily forced exodus that is migration to the cities; and, of course, many do not survive at all.

Here's the rub, though: in a world where some with plenty of food cruelly collide with many that have a pittance, the way in which those have plenty is inextricably threatening those with a pittance. That's right: the way that we get our food is considerably exacerbating the increasingly dense difficulties faced by small-scale peasant farmers and landless rural workers, because the way that we get our food is directly strengthening the multiple and convoluted processes that virulently marginalize the food insecure and deepen the extent of the food-based inequality that permeates the globe. We are witnessing an unparalleled betrayal of a fundamental human right — the right to food — that is ceaselessly crushing the rural poor. There has never been anything like it.

Imagining a future that can be found in the interstices of the present, where the abandonment of the disempowered is not so, this book explains the duplicitous conditions confronting small-scale peasants and landless rural workers. This explanation is not just done to enlighten the reader, for the current crisis demands more; it is done to map out a path by which the alternative future that I envisage here could be built. The alternative future is not just presented out of a sense of the need for justice, but is also presented out of a sense that the particular and specific horror that is contemporary rural hunger cannot continue: the human and ecological misery that end-lessly erupts from the way we get our food is the ground zero of a threat that is, as I write, irresistibly undermining our very existence as a species. There is a possibility of hope, but the world cannot continue as an acutely vicious latter-day Dickensian poorhouse, with hungry children like Oliver Twist knowing that while there is a momentous abundance of "food, glorious food," they have to go to Mr. Bumble and beg, "Please sir, can I have some more?," only to be silenced by his apoplectic rage. The world is hungry for change; indeed, it demands it.

Together, we must end a global food regime in which one person's inexhaustible cornucopia requires the creation of a community of hunger, for this accurate and painful description of our world is an inexcusable act. Together, we must build a food system where everyone can get the food they need. The world's small-scale peasant farmers and landless waged workers want, as a preliminary yet extraordinarily important step toward a better life for themselves and their families, to be able to feed themselves, securely, without having to submit themselves, like vassals, to the multifariously macabre agreements and arrangements of the market. They are hungry for change. We, who are the world's wealthy, have to imaginatively transform and inventively revolutionize what we expect of our food. We have to be hungry for change. If together we engage in the direct confrontation of the sources of human degradation that we have created, there is indeed a possibility of hope, if we begin now. So let's start.

1

THE THIN
AND THE FAT

FOOD ENTITLEMENTS
IN THE TWENTY-FIRST CENTURY

Noor Mohammed was sitting in a parched field under a tall solitary tree, getting some shade from the ferocious bright sun that radiated across the cloudless, starkly blue sky. It was 1996. A tall, thin man with angular fingers, his face showed the effects of a life working out in the sun, day in, day out, for it was dark and dry; so dark, in fact, that it almost matched the colour of his black mustache and his tousled, dirty hair, and was much darker than the dirty blue of the shalwar kameez that he was wearing, with its long-sleeved shirt draping down nearly to the knee and its loose-fitting pyjama-like trousers. It was probably his only shalwar kameez.

His face was stretched taut. It was almost as if I was witnessing rage congealing with despair. He was quiet, but finally said, "I don't know what my children will eat tonight," the despair overwhelming him at last and tears welling in his fiercely proud eyes. "I am a poor *kisan* [small-scale peasant farmer]. I farm one hectare, but the land is *barani* [dry] and does not produce a good crop. The harvest was months ago, we have no money and I have nothing left to sell … I don't know what my children will eat tonight," he repeated, a haunting mantra that brought forth no hope.

I met Noor Mohammad in the middle of doing some research into the impact of a big development project that was to reclaim land for farming and, it was hoped, contribute to reducing rural poverty.[1] I knew he was very poor when I met him, and I spent some time talking to him to get a more human, more humane understanding of the terrible lived experience that was his and his family's deprivation. In the distance, I could see the hamlet where Noor Mohammed and his family lived: a small cluster of ruefully basic one-storey mud homes, reached on a jarringly disintegrating dirt road. It was, literally, the middle of nowhere. There was little there but the shocking extremities of indiscriminate poverty: a dispiriting continuum that ranged from a lack of adequate food to a lack of even the most basic education and beyond to a lack of any semblance of health care. Lacking even the dignity of a name, it went without saying that the hamlet had no electricity. Water, that most canonical of human needs, had to be carried from an open well in a neighbouring hamlet; and without water, no one had a toilet, pissing and shitting in nearby fields, as small-scale peasant farmers have done for time immemorial. I could see human excrement in the field next to the field in which we were sitting, but the micronutrients in it had had little effect; other than that below the tree we were sitting under, the soil was beige brown, dry and so crumbly that when I scooped up a fistful it ran through my fingers in small, lifeless lumps. The soil was achingly barren; without water, it would not produce anything at this time of year for Noor Mohammed and his family.

Yet I knew as he did not that a lack of water was not the critical mechanism that prevented Noor Mohammed from tilling his plots of land during the months when the rains did not darken the skies of the Peshawar valley, for there was, in truth, an abundance of water. The British, when occupying this part of the Khyber Pakhtunkhwa province of northern Pakistan, built a huge canal system, diverting the waters of several large rivers into a massive irrigation system that reshaped the landscape (Akram-Lodhi 2001a). They were trying to turn this part of South Asia into the empire's granary. Where the irrigation canals run, the Peshawar valley is, in the warmth of the summer, strikingly and relentlessly vibrant: the fruit trees are green, lush and ripe with oranges bursting with flavour; the corn stalks grow high and the kernels deliciously sweet; and the stands of sugar cane are deep, tall and so dense that it is difficult to see how someone could walk through them, a man-made jungle that at ground level can cut off the light radiating down from the sky. I didn't have to be an agronomist to see that the canals and their extensive network of tributaries could allow the small-scale peasant farmers of the Peshawar valley and beyond — people like Noor Mohammed — to produce more from their fields, in the first place by getting at least two crops a year from land that without irrigation will yield only one. Yet they did not get that second crop, which was, for Noor Mohammed and many others, the difference between destitution and decency.

I asked Noor Mohammed why he did not leave and move to the city. "I prefer half a roti [bread] in the village to a full meal in the city; but we will starve here." Noor Mohammed was an intensely unassuming and unpretentious Pakhtun tribesman, and more than most other men Pakhtun do not display their feelings easily, for it is a sign of weakness; from weakness comes dishonour, something that above all else Pakhtun do not want to show, for it makes them less of a man, and, more to the point, less Pakhtun.[2] That day, though, without water, without food, without hope, Noor Mohammed despaired, and I saw the tears. That he despaired in a land that was bountiful for some shows that his circumstances were not an inevitable outcome of

an indiscriminate set of social and economic conditions that subverted the
subsistence of his family. Rather, his circumstances were the outcome of a
fundamental and divisive state of affairs that can and must be historically
and socially explained: Noor Mohammed was unable to get irrigation water
because of his landlord, Haji Shahrukh Khan.

When I met Haji Shahrukh Khan one morning for sweet milky tea in
the comfortably furnished yet unpretentious reception room of his large
concrete and brick home, I saw that he, like Noor Mohammed, was every bit
Pakhtun: tall, with greying hair surrounding a weather-beaten face on which
a neatly-trimmed beard marked ostentatious piety. Displaying the hospitality
for which Pakhtun are renowned, his belly showed that he ate well. But it
was Haji Shahrukh Khan's white shalwar kameez that was more revealing;
to wear a white set of clothes in the dust and grime of the Peshawar valley
meant that it would quickly get dirty. That it was clean meant that it had been
laundered, that it had to be laundered every day, and so Haji Shahrukh Khan
had more than one suit of clothing. In this part of the world a white shalwar
kameez was a signifier of wealth and hence, amongst Pakhtun — with their
demandingly strict and pervasively rigorous social code, called Paktunwali
— of the independence and honour to which both Haji Shahrukh Khan and
Noor Mohammed aspired. Haji Shahrukh Khan was wealthy compared to
his neighbours, but for him his wealth was less important. More important
was that his wealth allowed him to be Pakhtun, in the same way that Noor
Mohammed's poverty did not.

Haji Shahrukh Khan owned fifty hectares of land, most of which was
irrigated by the canal system built by the British. Ask him what he does, and
Haji Shahrukh Khan, like the few others with similar quantities of land,
would be strikingly forthright: "I am a farmer." Yet you would never see
Haji Shahrukh Khan standing with a hoe, furrowing a field; you would never
see him spraying a plot with fertilizer; you would never see him driving the
tractor that he proudly owns. For Haji Shahrukh Khan's idea of farming
is to rent out most of his fifty hectares, in often miniscule plots, to men like
Noor Mohammed, who in turn have to give Haji Shahrukh Khan one half
of everything that they produce on the land as an in-kind payment for the
land they farm but do not own. This pernicious arrangement, which is as
old as small-scale peasant farming, is called sharecropping.[3]

Pakhtuns of the Peshawar valley have a saying that captures the essence
of the pervasive and perverse logic of sharecropping: "we earn only for you."
If the land is irrigated, and much of it is, it becomes capable of producing
more than one crop a year, a lot more, and Haji Shahrukh Khan coldly closes
off the opportunities for his sharecroppers by assuredly getting his share of
the crop produced on the more productive land. If the land is not irrigated,
it produces less, but Haji Shahrukh Khan still indifferently impoverishes his

sharecroppers by getting his share of the crop produced on the less productive land. In either case, nineteen families are mercilessly dependent for their livelihoods and their lives on Haji Shahrukh Khan — 171 men, women and children who earn for him, seeing half of what they produce on their farms given over to him, the brutal hardware of a ceaseless social and economic situation that allows him to have his shalwar kameez laundered.

So Noor Mohammed lacked irrigation water because Haji Shahrukh Khan only allowed him to farm unirrigated land, and Noor Mohammed had no choice in the matter. Despite the strikingly marked egalitarianism amongst men articulated in Pakhtunwali the two men are only rhetorically equal; in practice, Haji Shahrukh Khan's status was based on his ability to systematically further disenfranchise the already marginalized, forcing their continued sublimation to one who was incomparably more powerful, a power that was based, ultimately, on the control of land that they needed to farm by those who could, if and when necessary, use the force of arms to sustain their control. In this way, Haji Shahrukh Khan stood at the apex of a set of social relations that produced the poverty that crushes the rural poor.

Yet Haji Shahrukh Khan's capacity to do this was not the result of his superior entrepreneurial skill set or of his greater ability to read the market runes and understand deep-seated and elemental shifts that might be underway. No: Haji Shahrukh Khan was able to do this because the British, in their attempts in the late nineteenth century to pacify Pakhtun tribes that continually threatened the northwestern corner of the Raj, deployed a tactic used extensively throughout their empire, allocating the ownership of good farmland in the Peshawar valley to a highly select group of local leaders (Lynch 2005). In exchange for getting the security of large holdings of land, which brought with it independence, honour and a stronger capacity to be Pakhtun, these imperially-created landlords became a conservative agrarian bulwark against a potentially unruly Pakhtun peasantry. It was, in so many ways, a nefarious compact between a tiny and fractious embryonic agrarian elite and the imperialists, a compact predicated upon the sustained subordination of Pakhtun small-scale peasant farmers. And it worked. All Haji Shahrukh Khan has done is inherit his position and self-centredly reproduce, by force if necessary, the extraordinarily inequitable social and economic conditions that sustain his privilege.

Across the space of the world and a mode of life and standard of living that is, literally, centuries ahead of that of Noor Mohammed, Jessica Carson stares out of the window of her Canadian university residence room at the river that flows past. It is 2008. It has been an unusually severe winter, and with its end the river is running high and fast. Jessica Carson considers herself lucky to be able to see the river from her room, for many of her friends have windows that look out onto parking lots or the concrete monstrosities that pass for modern architecture, and the sight of the river continuously reminds her of the momentous power of nature and the sweep of the seasons.

Jessica Carson's room is a decaying box big enough to fit a single bed, a desk, some shelves, a chest-of-drawers and a closet. Inside the closet there is a small white Chinese-made refrigerator, some more shelf space — with some boxes of Kraft macaroni and cheese dinner, some white bread and some other bits and pieces — and a clothes rail full of clothes. I look inside the refrigerator: cans of diet soda and bottles of water. The walls of her room are decorated with personal mementos: photographs, hand drawings and posters that give her a sense of comfort.

I have had to go to her room because she has not given me a medical certificate that I need to properly evaluate her work, and we end up talking about something that I teach: food. From our casual conversation I realize that Jessica Carson has need of a friendly voice. Although she has a softly round face that many of her friends tell her is pretty, sharp brown eyes, skin that is admirably clear for an eighteen-year-old and long brown hair that has been hand-sculpted so that it frames her face, she is not at ease with herself. Jessica Carson is visibly overweight; her loose-fitting black blouses and long skirts do not camouflage her body any more than her facial piercings distract people's attention away from her size.

"I don't know why I can't manage," she says, with a resolute matter-of-factness that displays a gritty determination that I can only but admire. "I don't eat a lot. I don't drink a lot. I don't eat candy. I ride my bike when the weather is good, and I try to get to the gym on campus. And yet … nothing. Nada."

I ask Jessica Carson about her food choices. "I'm a student, I seem to be doing pretty good and I don't want to have to take a part-time job, which means money is tight — really tight now that the school year is almost over. So I want to eat cheaply. The campus is a long way from the supermarket, which makes it hard to get it together to have everything that I need. Besides, I don't really know how to cook! The university's food plans seem like a lot of money, and they are, but they still work out to be the cheapest way of eating on a budget when you live on campus, because I can always eat in the cafeteria. The cafeteria is easy, and my friends are there. So I mostly eat in the cafeteria," she explains.

Like many other organizations, the university contracts out its on-campus catering services to an enormous Philadelphia-based global food corporation called Aramark, whose contract gives them the exclusive right to sell food and beverages to the 80 percent of first year undergraduates that live on campus. In the final quarter of 2011 Aramark pleased its corporate share-holders by increasing its U.S. sales to $3.4 billion and increasing its operating income to $166.9 million while sitting on assets with a net worth of $10.5

billion (Thomson Reuters 2012). In seeking to sustain and indeed enhance its profits, this corporation often relies on the inertia of its customers, an inertia predicated on and maintained by a contractual lack of choice. So, as one of those millions of customers, what Jessica Carson does not realize is that her ongoing struggles over her weight are in part connected to the monopolistic position that Aramark has in the catering services that it operates and that she uses.

Here's how. Aramark is interested in selling as much food as it can to the hungry students, nurses, pensioners and others that make up its customer base. Pitas, pastas and pizzas: all have to be sold in large quantities in order for Aramark to make a profit, because the more it sells the higher its revenues will be. But Aramark is not just interested in selling any old food; Aramark has to buy all the food that it sells, so it wants the food that it buys to be cheap, in order to reduce its operating expenses. High revenues and low operating expenses are the key to its corporate profitability.

In order to buy the food it sells as cheaply as possible, Aramark heavily relies upon industrially-produced processed food made by other global food corporations that supply it with its "product": pre-prepared french fries and onion rings that don't need to be washed, peeled and sliced, and which are high in fats; hamburger patties and chicken nuggets, whose relationship to beef and poultry is tenuous, and which are also high in fats; bagels and muffins made from refined grains supplied by a global grain trader; and far, far more. The industrially-processed food that Aramark — and we — strongly rely on to meet our food needs emerged in the 1950s for a simple reason: processing dramatically simplified food preparation while increasing shelf life; the longer the food lasted on the shelf the greater the likelihood that it would be sold and the value contained within the product would be realized by the corporation.

The industrial processing of food continues to have significant consequences. The first is that processing eliminates the fibre that restricts the release of a food's sugars, making the food easier to digest. The second upshot of processing is a faster conversion of the refined carbohydrates found in starches into the glucose that the brain prefers as its source of energy. As Michael Pollan (2008) eloquently points out, food processing is engineered not only to make food more durable and portable but also to act as an exemplary rapid-fire energy delivery system.

There's more. The processed foods that Aramark sells are energy-dense, being high in sugars as well as fats. They are also, as a result of the processing, low in vitamins, minerals and other essential micronutrients; they are not nutritious, which is why so many processed foods have micronutrients chemically added to them after processing. Here then is how Jessica Carson's lack of choice in her food service provider affects her weight: the energy density of the processed foods that are needed to sustain corporate profits contributes to obesity because people "consume more calories per unit of food" (Pollan 2008: 112–113) even as they get fewer of the critical nutrients they need.

There's even more: being high in sugars means that the taste of processed foods is scientifically engineered to be sweet and, through the unleashing of a barrage of insulin production in the body, the eater is instigated to eat more (Pollan 2006, 2008). Of course, that's good for the corporate bottom line, which wants to sell more. But for Jessica Carson this means that when she goes into the Aramark cafeteria and orders her burger, fries and soda, she may be eating three-quarters of the calories that she needs in an entire day in one meal, a meal that, paradoxically, is clinically programmed to tell her body that she needs to eat more even as it fails to supply her with adequate amounts of the nutrition she needs.

Jessica Carson gets a meal that she can afford but is not good for her from a corporation that sells food cheaply but in such massive quantities that it is very profitable. This is the guilty secret of our food: that a historically-recent transition of epochal importance has culminated in a food regime based upon abdicating a responsibility to produce and distribute healthy, safe and nutritious food as part of the quest for corporate profitability. It is an absurd combination of potentially lethal intensity.

Food is that most elementary of life forces. It is essential for life, yet it can bring death. As such an existential force, it affects the way we see, enter into, arrange and understand our lives, our societies and our world. Consider this one example: North American society senses differences between sweet and sour. But how meaningful is that difference? Japanese society senses a taste that North American society does not: *umami* or "savoury delicious-ness" (Prescott 2001). Does that mean that North Americans are hard-wired differently? Of course not. It means that some of the critical core human software that shapes and is shaped by human cultures is exhibited in and refracted through our shared and differential perceptions of and relations to the production and consumption of food; by our singular and collective understanding of what is and what is not "good" food; and through that understanding, the rituals and symbols that we, in the homes and communi-ties that we inhabit, attach to and share in the food that we produce and eat (Levi-Strauss 1963, 1969).

So, understanding the creation and consumption of food in homes and in communities helps us recognize how the multi-faceted character of food can simultaneously synchronize and separate people when it is attached to a set of practices; for example, religious tenets accept or reject codes of behaviour dictating what can and what cannot be eaten, along with when permissible foods are consumed. Every human community is infiltrated by and implicated in a set of beliefs in which food occupies an important part; observed or not, every religion has its equivalent of Lent or Passover or Eid. Food is more than an existential necessity; it is a persistent condition of our consciousness and our common sense, and so our relationship to the production and consumption of food reflects and refracts the character of our society. Only the hard-edged, capitalistic, market-driven society of North America could create "fast food" (Schlosser 2005); only the romanticized, populist, market-averse societies of Mediterranean Europe could create "slow food" (Petrini 2006).

Human history can be powerfully — and critically — understood by the ways and mechanisms through which humanity has tried to meet its food needs. So, following a period of ecological upheaval that started 16,000 years ago and ended around 12,000 years ago, our ancestors, *Homo sapiens*, lived by hunting game, fishing and by gathering wild cereals and legumes in nomadic, small and quite possibly reasonably egalitarian social groupings. Then, probably around 10,000 years ago, in what today we would call "the Fertile Crescent of the Near East," and over a period of a thousand years or so, this changed; hunting-gathering gave way to the sowing, cultivating and breeding of plants and the management of animals kept in captivity (Mazoyer and Roudart 2006).

This was a neolithic agricultural revolution that alchemized and transformed human societies — and not immediately for the better. Dietary changes seen in the shift from a meat-based, protein-rich diet toward a cereal-based, protein-deficient diet and the shift to a more stationary, sedentary and settled mode of life led to widespread death by malnutrition or its accomplice, disease, and caloric intake collapsed for many societies. With the spectre of death haunting the neolithic period on a historically unparalleled scale, the control of food gradually became a dominant and determining social and economic fact in understanding the tempo and times of the late neolithic period (Kipple 2007). Cultivated grains, legumes, fruit and livestock and poultry conferred upon those who controlled enough of them not only better health but also enhanced standing in the community, as social and economic conditions within communities arranged and rearranged themselves around those who could and those who could not control enough of the food stocks needed by the inhabitants of a community.

Crucially, the capacity to control food stocks meant that those with such control were conferred with the material means to further increase their control of food stocks: those with control of food stocks could barter some of their food for more land to cultivate or use some of their food as animal feed and in so doing better their holdings of livestock and poultry. The control of food stocks became, in this way, a self-reinforcing process that recalibrated the configuration of social and economic conditions within communities around those who did and those who did not control adequate stocks of food. Here, then, in the dim light of a neolithic past, we can glimpse the burgeoning origins of the social inequalities in status and the economic inequalities in wealth that irresistibly order humanity to this day: those that, for whatever reason, came to command and control significantly greater stocks of a community's available food became, for better or worse, a dominant strata, an emerging class, with effective and authoritative hegemony over the community (Fraser and Rimas 2010).

The world may have changed over the tens of centuries, but this elemental fact has not. Haji Shahrukh Khan controls the land needed for the food in Noor Mohammed's unnamed hamlet to be produced. His control of the land makes him the local khan, which Pakhtun translate into English as "feudal lord." It is not a misleading description. The control of land and, through land, food gives Haji Shahrukh Khan the material cornerstone of social and economic power — at the very least, over his tenants but in many instances beyond, in wider tribal politics and society. Noor Mohammed is one of those tenants — for better or worse, wholly dependent on Haji Shahrukh Khan, and thus fundamentally and intently subordinate to him. Haji Shahrukh Khan's control of the land is the correlate of his cultural power and prestige, for land gives him autonomy, which, in Pakhtunwali, brings honour. It is the source of the wealth at his disposal, whether it be dressing in a white shalwar kameez or owning a tractor, a source that also brings honour in Pakhtunwali. It is continually self-reinforcing and self-expanding — the control of land today will bring more wealth, more power and more prestige tomorrow. The stark contrasts of a social system based upon the diverging paths that recreate the social and economic relations that confer power over others could not be clearer: the centrifugal forces that collide over land and food to construct and intensify class relationships and conditions are the brutal tectonics of village life to this day.

Jessica Carson stands in a remarkably similar position to Aramark. Behind the rhetoric of choice — that she could have chosen differently than she did — Jessica Carson faces, in substance, little; like a gatekeeper ensuring that less profitable, more nutritious foods are kept at bay, Aramark's contractual monopoly allows it to effectively and efficiently control access to food for the bulk of those living in the university's residences. This control over access to food gives Aramark effective power over their customers who, like Jessica Carson, lacking meaningful choices, provide the assured revenues that Aramark requires to meet the profitability requirements of its shareholders, the faceless and nameless pension, investment and equity funds that in reality own it. Control over Jessica Carson's access to food ultimately gives the owners of Aramark material wealth as well as significant social and political power over singularly anonymous people who, like Jessica Carson, are wholly dependent upon Aramark and are as a result wholly if unknowingly subordinate to the corporation and its dictates.

As with Noor Mohammed and Haji Shahrukh Khan, we can easily see the contours of a social system based upon divergent patterns of wealth and power that recreate the social and economic correlates of domination over others, domination that is a culmination of intensifying and inherently indiscriminate market forces that are extraordinarily successful in alienating individuals from the nasty realities of daily life. The difference between these two sets of circumstances are, however, of vital importance: in a transition of momentous significance, for the first time in human history the search for corporate profit has been mapped with uncanny accuracy onto the need for food, to stand four-square at the heart of the fundamental and divisive social conditions between the powerful and the powerless that define the current food regime.

We live in a world of unprecedented inequality, a world in which Bill Gates can have more wealth than 40 percent of the American population (Chernomas and Hudson 2007). Nowhere is this plutocratic inequality more profoundly illustrated than in food. True, there has been inequality in access to food for tens of centuries. However, what marks our world out from the world of 10,000 years ago is that unequal access to food takes place at the same time as the planet produces more than enough food to feed all; there is hunger amidst plenty. Although there are some problems in estimating global food production, it is reasonably safe to say that the world produces enough food to provide everyone 3,200 calories a day; there is enough food to feed probably 50 percent more people than are currently alive. Indeed, world food production is roughly equivalent to two kilograms of food per person per day — and by this, I am not talking about the heavily processed "empty calories" that Jessica Carson eats; rather, the world produces ample good, nutritious food (FoodFirst 1998, Weis 2007).

Yet even though the world produces enough food, according to the Food and Agriculture Organization of the United Nations more than 925 million people in developing capitalist countries are "chronically malnourished," living on less than US$1[4] a day (Food and Agriculture Organization 2011). Add in those that are malnourished in the developed capitalist countries and the number of hungry would probably top a billion. Many more do not know, like Noor Mohammed, where their next meal is coming from; the World Bank tells us that globally some two billion people live on less than $2 a day, and while this does not mean that they are chronically malnourished, it does mean that food insecurity is a clear and present danger in their everyday life (World Bank 2010a). With food insecurity comes another usual suspect: two billion people regularly suffer from micronutrient deficiencies (Canadian International Development Agency 2009). And food insecurity is not just a problem facing poor countries: in the United States, the richest country on earth, almost fifty million people were classified by the state as "hungry" in 2011 (Bread 2011).

Modern hunger is a historically unprecedented calamity of vicious intensity: as I have already said, every seven seconds or so a child around the world dies of hunger. That's 9 children a minute, 540 children an hour, 12,960 a day; and children are only one-third of those who die from hunger every day. Imagine the reaction of the world if the World Trade Center's Twin Towers fell thrice a day, relentlessly, 365 days a year. Yet that is what is happening amongst the hungry children of the world; and worse still, many people know of this calamity, this "silent tsunami," in the words of the World Food Programme, wring their hands and do nothing, as if nothing can be done.

Those who are more likely to be hungry lack secure and stable access to sufficient, nutritious and culturally acceptable food when they need it. They also tend to share certain common characteristics. For a start, as I have said, the majority of the food insecure live in the countryside: rural waged labourers without land; those who, like Noor Mohammed, are small-scale peasant farmers that rely on the rain but who have inadequate land or onerous tenancy terms that reduce their access to food; pastoralists and fisherfolk; female-headed households; indigenous people; and those displaced by conflict (International Fund for Agricultural Development 2001). These are the hungry of the planet: some 700 million people that live in the countryside (World Food Programme 2012). The rural labouring hungry can be found in Asia: in the countryside of India and Pakistan and Bangladesh but also in the vast countryside of rural China, amidst its apparent growing riches. They can be found in the rugged terrain of the Andes in South America or in the northeast of Brazil. And, of course, they can be found throughout sub-Saharan Africa, from Senegal to Sudan, from the fields outside Cairo to the fields outside Cape Town (World Bank 2007).

Noor Mohammed is not alone in his hunger, even though that is how he often feels, alienated in his misery from his neighbours. Neither though is Jessica Carson. Worldwide, some 1.5 billion people are overweight, and 500 million are obese. The health consequences of this epidemic are severe: the World Health Organization (2011) tells us that 2.5 million people a year die from obesity-related causes. Being overweight and obese increases the risk of cardiovascular disease, which is the number one killer in the world. As I have said, it increases the prevalence of type 2 diabetes, which is caused by the ineffective use of insulin in bodies that are now bombarded with sugars. Globally, some 180 million people suffer from type 2 diabetes, which is 90 percent of all cases of diabetes; some 1.1 million people a year die from it, and that number is expected to grow by some 50 percent in the next ten years. Being overweight and obese also results in people having increased susceptibility to musculoskeletal disorders and some cancers. The bulk of the deaths caused by being overweight and obese are not found in the world's relatively richer countries, though; they are found in the developing capitalist countries of Asia, Africa and Latin America, where health care systems, to the extent that they work, are not designed to deal with this kind of chronic, non-communicable, man-made and self-reproducing epidemic.

In a world of hunger amidst plenty, it is a unique obscenity that people like Noor Mohammed and his family try to go to sleep at night not having had enough to eat, while people like Jessica Carson eat too many calories that provide too little nutrition. There is, though, one other remarkably perverse aspect of modern food inequality: people in the same household can be undernourished and obese at the same time. When females are malnourished prior to birth or during the first two years of their life, their metabolism changes for good by storing spare calories as fat just in case. When, in later life, the woman's family has a diet that has ample calories but which lacks micronutrients, she will become overweight or even obese even as her children suffer the effects of nutritional deficiencies. Undernutrition and obesity can thus sit side by side in the household and, remarkably, in the woman, who is at the same time over- and underfed, receiving too many calories and not enough nutrition (Woodgate and Matthews 2010). Undernourished obesity is common in the countryside, where the bulk of the world's poor live and where small-scale peasant farmers and landless waged workers often have excruciatingly poor diets.

This was brought strongly and starkly home to me in a rural community in Embu district in eastern Kenya when, through a friend who had worked to promote development in the district, I met Grace Muchengi, a very poor woman who tilled a very small piece of land beside a minor road. It was 1993. Although the district produced cash crops like coffee and macadamia nuts, Grace Muchengi didn't have enough land to do this. Besides, she was more concerned with putting some food on her family's table, so she grew mostly beans and a small amount of corn on her plot. The land was all she had, but it was not enough, and she had to try as best she could to supplement what the land gave her by waged work if and when she could find a job, which was, she admitted, not often enough.

Grace Muchengi was a large, proud woman, with a smile as wide as her round face, who would do whatever she could for her family. Yet times had always been hard for her. She had not seen her husband in seven years — he had said he was going to Nairobi to find work and he had not been in touch since, leaving her solely responsible for making a living that could support her and her four children. Like parents around the world, Grace Muchengi wanted only one thing for her children: a better life. And to Grace Muchengi, the key to a better life was an education.

This meant making some pretty demanding sacrifices, which indiscriminately affected all the members of the family. I remember the effect on Grace Muchengi's youngest, her six-year-old, Paul, particularly well. Born just after her husband left, Grace Muchengi had been unable to eat well during her pregnancy: as part of Kenya's economic arrangements made with the World Bank under a structural adjustment program (Gibbon 1992), in the early 1990s parents had to make payments to schools in order to be able to send their children; thus any spare change that Grace Muchengi had went into paying the various fees and charges demanded by the school so that her oldest child, William, could attend. These "user fees" meant that Paul Muchengi was inadequately nourished before he was even born. After his birth, the shortage of money meant that Grace Muchengi continued to be unable to provide adequate nutrition for her children. The result was that Paul Muchengi, like other malnourished children, had a body that could not properly metabolize and store the micronutrients from food. I met Paul Muchengi when he was six, a short, chubby boy with a smile as bright as the sun, eating what the rest of the family was eating: a diet heavy in porridge and fat, with little in the way of fruit and vegetables.

I asked Grace Muchengi about this. Although she was smiling, as usual, she had not offered me a cup of tea, and we both knew, silently and respectfully, that this was because she did not have the money. Her inability to offer basic hospitality made her reticent when it came to the issue of food, but eventually she opened up. "Ah, you know," she said, somewhat hesitantly and quietly, in the way that many Kenyans can be, "I can't afford to buy vegetables. We will have some, though, when the garden is ready, and we will eat well." I asked her when she had last had some meat. "It was at a wedding in the next village; I think it was last year." Grace Muchengi was simply unable to pay for the fresh fruit and vegetables that, amongst other foods, both she and her family, including Paul, needed. The family therefore had an energy-dense diet high in fat and low in micronutrients; judging by his appearance, Paul Muchengi's caloric intake per day was not too bad, but his nutritional intake was visibly inadequate. This nutritional deficiency was then compounded by a lack of physical activity; the area around Grace Muchengi's rudimentary home was chock full of the detritus of abandoned construction work with lots of sharp, protruding objects littering the shared space, and Grace encouraged her son to stay indoors. At six, Paul Muchengi embodied the folly of the world in which he and I lived: a world of the thin and the fat, to be sure, but also a world where people can be what Raj Patel (2007) has so memorably described as being "stuffed and starved."

If the planet produces more than enough food to feed all and yet so many people are under- and malnourished, how is it possible to disinter the intricate arithmetic by which food that is produced is or is not made available to those who need it? Of course, we all need food; but how we get it and what we get differs profoundly by place, by class, by gender, by age, by ability, and by a host of other factors.

Enter Amartya Sen (1983), whose seemingly inexhaustible curiosity allowed him to exhume the rudimentary mechanics underpinning the provision of food. Food can be available to those who need it because they have grown it themselves, on the land they work, and make use of it themselves. Many people around the world rely on this direct provisioning of food needs, even if it does not meet all of their needs, as is too commonly the case. Food can also be available to those who need it because they have grown some food, sold it and used the money to buy the extra food they need. Many people around the world also rely, to a greater or lesser extent, on this market-based provisioning of food needs, even when they undertake some kind of direct provisioning. Food can also be available to those who need it because they have worked for someone else, been paid wages and used those wages to buy food. Market-based food provisioning that relies upon wages applies to both landless rural workers and many small-scale peasant farmers around the world, as well as, of course, those of us in the developed capitalist countries who rely upon someone earning a wage in order for us to obtain the food we need. Finally, food can be made available as a result of the direct transfer of food or cash to those in need: a transfer of food or cash from the state, from an international organization or a foreign state, from a non-governmental or community-based organization, or amongst those within a community or within a family so that those who need food can get it. Many people around the world rely on this social provisioning of food for at least part of their food requirements.

Within this multifaceted matrix of possibilities, Sen teaches us that it is apparent that food provisioning does not necessarily rely upon growing food but rather the minutia of food provisioning systems and structures, which Sen calls "entitlements." Certainly, that is visibly the case for market-based or social food provision, and it is unquestionably here, in the details of food provisioning systems, that we can uncover that which is so unique about the current food regime.

Clearly, in the contemporary globalized world one overdetermining factor in providing food to those who need it is money. Money is the irresistible means by which most people that do not have food become linked to what they need but have not produced. This is true of Noor Mohammed and Grace Muchengi who, like most other small-scale peasant farmers in the world, directly produce only a share of the variety of foods their families need; they must somehow come up with the money to buy the rest. This is also true of Haji Shahrukh Khan, who sells his receipts from sharecropping to get the cash that he needs to buy much of the food his family eats.

It is, finally, true of Jessica Carson who, like most urban consumers in the developed capitalist countries, has little, if any, idea of where her food comes from but knows that she needs money to be able to eat. Money is the critical correlate in determining how food is made available to us, and that this has happened has constituted a historic transition of immense importance to humanity, a transition that is, moreover, for most of the world, less than a century old.

There is, however, a second, critical, overdetermining factor in making food available to those who need it but do not produce enough of it: food markets. Only a few decades ago, the market for food in a community, if it even existed, would be essentially and incurably local, and transactions would very often not necessarily involve cash, especially in the poorer parts of the world, but instead involve complex modes and methods of social reciprocity. That has changed forever. In the early years of the twenty-first century, food markets have insinuated themselves into the most remote corners of the globe, and if you want to use food markets you have to have money; it is a rule that applies with even fiercer force to the poor when compared to the rich.

The deepening sway of money in food markets has had three impacts of consequence. The first is the expansion of choice. As food markets have globalized in the past quarter century, for us, sitting in the comparative affluence of the developed capitalist countries in which we live, our ability to buy out-of-season fresh fruit and vegetables, fresh fish and seafood products, cut flowers and fresh meat from obscure places has had an effect that has been nothing short of revolutionary. When we go to our supermarkets, we expect not only to be able to buy food from around the world, but also to be able to use our money to buy food from around the world that is fresh, whether it be Mediterranean tuna, Chilean sea bass or Vietnamese catfish. We expect to be able to always have a wide variety of fresh fruit and vegetables available for us to buy all through the year, even in the darkest nights of a Swedish winter. Indeed, not only do we expect to be able to buy fresh food year round; we also expect that that fresh food that we buy meets certain expectations of uniformity, colour and texture, and if it does not meet those expectations we do not buy it.

The second impact of the expansion of the accelerated use of money in globalized food markets has been a marked ratcheting-up of the hydrocarbon intensity of our food. When I was a child growing up in Scotland, the most common fresh fruit that we would see was bananas. Other fresh fruit and vegetables, dairy and meat would for the most part be produced within a comparatively short distance of where it was sold and, ultimately, eaten. So I grew up eating seasonal fresh food that was produced, in large part, in Scotland. This has changed irrevocably in the early years of the twenty-first century. In an oil-fuelled compression of time and space that has accelerated in order to expand choice as a means of capturing people's money, in the developed capitalist countries food usually travels an astonishingly long distance in order to arrive on a plate; the modern-day Scot sitting down to a meal of lamb, potatoes and green beans in the middle of winter may well find that none of the food being eaten has been grown in Europe. Similarly, year round, meals in southern Canada are just as likely to have spinach from California and tomatoes from Mexico as they are to have cucumbers or lettuce from Ontario. Even in the poorer parts of the planet, food now travels a very long way before it is bought: rice in the food markets of urban Ghana, for example, is most likely not locally-grown but grown in the southern United States, while soya used in China can come from Brazil and wheat used in Bangladesh can come from Australia. All this movement requires fuel, and the increasing oil dependence of our food regime has had profound and quite perverse ecological consequences: globalized agriculture has what Tony Weis (2007) calls an "ecological hoofprint" of the first order.

So the growing sway of choice in increasingly global food markets has been accompanied by an increase in distance. But this distance is more than mere geography. There has also been a spectacular increase in what might be called the "social distance" between the production and eating of food; as consumers we are buying food that, in many if not most cases, is produced by people whose lives and circumstances are completely alien to our own. This is the third impact of the deepening sway of money in the food regime. We may not understand the life of a Canadian farmer very well, if at all, but if we are Canadian we know the language they speak, the places where they shop and eat and drink, the sports they play and the television shows they are likely to watch. When we buy cut flowers grown in Colombia in the middle of a cold Canadian winter, we have no idea whatsoever who has grown those flowers. Is it a small-scale farmer or a commercially-oriented flower estate using waged labour? Is the farmer a man or a woman? What do the growers of the flowers eat? How much do they make? How many hours do they have to work? How do they relax? What television shows do they watch? Do they have televisions? Global food markets have, ironically, placed us, both geographically and experientially, further away from the farmer that has produced our food; our only connection to their world is the money that we anonymously hand over for the food that we buy. We have become, in a historically unparalleled way, alienated with a vengeance from the way our food is produced (Patel 2007, Atwood 2008).

In this disconnected world of money-driven global food markets, even the apparent diversification of choice may be illusory. In the relatively more affluent worlds of North America, Europe and Australia, a supermarket in Amsterdam will have the same core range of choices as a supermarket in Albany or Adelaide. There has been an expansion of choice, but this expansion has had the profoundly contradictory but not wholly unexpected effect of homogenizing a global food regime in which the dietary choices and lifestyle patterns promoted amongst a segment of the population in the developed capitalist countries of North America, Europe and Australasia increasingly dominate and indeed subordinate global dietary choices and lifestyle patterns. This ongoing, relentless and seemingly systemic homogenization of global choices begs the question: does the global food regime offer real choices?

Noor Mohammed does not have a real choice over whom he can rent his land from in order to produce some of the food that his family needs. There is only one landlord, and Haji Shahrukh Khan is the one who has the ability to provide Noor Mohammed with the land that he needs to try and make a living. Jessica Carson, living in the food desert that is the university, oligopolistically controlled as it is by a global food corporation, has little real say over where she buys her food. Her essentially enforced choice, living on campus, on a budget and with limited food knowledge, is to buy from Aramark: which is not really much of a choice at all. As with Noor Mohammed and Jessica Carson, the global food markets that we rely upon offer the appearance of choice, but the appearance is a mirage. The reality in global food markets is that along with the alienation engendered by a lack of connectivity with how our food is grown there is a lack of choice: there is one buyer for your crop, one landlord for your land, one retailer from whom you regularly buy. Effective, meaningful choice is not present in the practical nuts and bolts of daily life, and this is as true for Noor Mohammed as it is for Jessica Carson — and for us.

The deepening and accelerating monetization of access to food that is distributed in global markets in which consumers are increasingly alienated from the way food is produced and which results in a horrendous maldistribution of food between the thin and the fat: this is the reality of the food regime of the early twenty-first century. Linking these disparate forces and factors is a fundamental conflict between the quest for food and the quest for profit, a conflict that is the culmination of a historical process that has produced islands of extreme wealth set amidst seas of rampant poverty. But this conflict is not resolved. If anything, it is beginning to intensify in scale and scope as we enter what appears to be a new era in the social and economic conditions governing global food production and consumption.

For the past fifty years in the developed capitalist countries of the world food has been all but forgotten, a necessary but ultimately ephemeral aspect of our day-to-day lives. Even for those of us lucky enough to be able to go to top-end restaurants the food is only part of the reason we go to such places. But that world is changing with a vengeance; food is reasserting its extraordinary existential role in our lived experience. Instigated by the extreme growth in meat and processed food production in the developed capitalist countries, by the growth in heavily subsidized ethanol production in an era of declining oil stocks, by higher oil prices, by the perversity of financial speculators seeking to make a profit on hunger in a landscape dominated by credit crunches and global economic recesssion and by climatic and ecological changes leading to poor harvests in certain key grains, in the second decade of the twenty-first century world grain and meat prices continue to be higher than they have been in almost forty years. These higher prices come with a kick in the tail: the globalization of food markets has resulted in food production being increasingly destined for export around the world, and for food importers, which constitute a majority of the world's countries and peoples, the increased food dependence engendered by a reliance on imports has brought with it a heightened sense of precarious insecurity; across-the-board food price increases herald a new era of food scarcity amongst the poorest on the planet, dietary reconfigurations amongst those who thought they had made it into the global middle class and increasing anxiety amongst the world's rulers that the era of the cheap food on which they rely to keep the masses at bay is over (Akram-Lodhi 2012). We have created a world with an abundance of food in which the availability of food for many is actually, perversely, declining.

The World Bank conservatively estimates that 44 million people have slipped into poverty in the period between 2007 and 2011 as a consequence of rising food prices, wiping out more than a decade of poverty reduction (World Bank 2011). Another 34 million are at risk. Not surprisingly, in 2007 and 2008 over thirty-five cases of food price-induced rebellions were recorded around the world, in places like Dhaka, Jakarta, Shanghai, Rome and beyond (Holt-Giménez and Patel with Shattuck 2009). In Haiti, the government fell and four people were killed because of rising food prices. In the Philippines, the largest rice importer in the world, the state had difficulty securing reliable access to the food that it must buy on global food markets. Food is, in the here and now, becoming more important than it has been for a century, not only in terms of global economic processes and forces but also in terms of global politics, and the result has been, since 2008, a series of "land grabs" by corporations seeking to acquire land for the production of food and non-food agricultural crops (Akram-Lodhi 2012). The production and consumption of food, and the ability to control the production and consumption of food, is reasserting its primacy as that most essential of subjects.

The worlds of Noor Mohammed and Jessica Carson have collided through a set of historical processes and social and political forces whose main contours can be discerned and that underpin the contradictory and hybrid dynamics of a lurid contemporary food regime that brings instability and insecurity to many even as, for a few, it brings the illusory promise of choice. How this collision will unfold is, I think, the great agrarian question of our time, a time that is hungry for change and out of which a future will be built largely as a result of how we collectively answer this agrarian question.

There are now on offer two clear alternative answers to this agrarian question: one that offers up what can only be described as more of the same, by promoting yet even deeper food globalization and the gradual transformation of the small-scale peasant farmers in the poorer parts of the world into agricultures that more closely resemble the capitalist agricultures found in our own developed capitalist countries; and one that fundamentally challenges current trends and prospects by promoting a reconstruction of local food economies, land justice, sustainable biotechnological change and food sovereignty. These two visions offer an answer to the great agrarian question of our time, but is either the right answer?

To answer this the social and economic dynamics sustaining the hybrid forms that constitute the contemporary food regime must be located within processes of historical rural change around the world in order to tease out and focus upon the place of farmers and particularly the small-scale peasant farmers that make up the mass of the rural poor. I'm going to do that later in the book. First, though, I need to unpack and disinter the meaning of the agrarian question, delving deeper into the intimate connections between money, markets and the emergence of rural capitalism. This unpacking starts with the introduction of Sam Naimisi and Qing Youzi in the next chapter.

2

QING YOUZI UNDERSTANDS CAPITALISM

MONEY, MARKETS AND THE AGRARIAN QUESTION

To fathom the meaning of the agrarian question it is necessary to probe the intimate and intricate connections between money, markets and the emergence of rural capitalism. And, as I have shown, money shapes and structures our contradictory and complex relationship to food in the modern age: most of us don't farm, but we need food, and money is the machinery that allows us to get the food we need. Money means we are enmeshed within and engaged with food markets: ultimately, for all of us there is a physical exchange where those who have food to sell are able to connect and interact with those who want to buy it. But that exchange is not with the grower, who, barring the relatively small numbers of farmers' markets, is alien to us. It is with someone or something that stands between the grower and us as the final buyers in a chain of events that serve to get the food from the field to the plate. For most of us in the developed capitalist countries the intermediary that we see between us and the grower is the supermarket or caterer or fast food company that lies at the end of a sequential yet paradoxical food supply chain that places food before us. For small-scale peasants using food markets, the intermediary is a petty trader of food.

To begin to dig into the meaning of the agrarian question I want to first open up this alienated food supply chain, taking it apart to see how it works. So consider if you will the cup of coffee that Jessica Carson gets from Aramark in the morning. Aramark's coffee is a blend designed — and designed is the word — by a coffee supplier to have a specific flavour, body and aroma. One of the coffee robustas in the blend supplied to Aramark originates in Uganda, so between Jessica Carson's cup of coffee and a small-scale Ugandan coffee farmer called Sam Naimisi who grows some of the beans that go into the blend that she drinks, are a series of steps in a food supply chain that serve to get Sam's coffee to Jessica's cup.

One of 25 million small-scale coffee farmers worldwide (Oxfam 2002),

Sam Naimisi, a man who frequently flashes a vibrant smile, operates a small coffee farm of 250 trees in a flatter part of the gently rolling, vibrantly green Sironko District east of Kampala, Uganda's capital. It is 2002. Sam Naimisi's family has been farming coffee in this area for decades, and some years ago he planted new seedlings in his small shaded orchard. Sam Naimisi weeds the soil, fertilizes it, manages the water it needs and prunes the trees as and when necessary; the coffee trees take ten months to produce coffee cherries, which Sam Naimisi harvests along with members of his family.

Like most small-scale coffee farmers in the world, Sam Naimisi doesn't drink coffee himself; he doesn't like the way it tastes, preferring tea. For Sam, coffee is a cash crop, a way to make the money he needs to buy the food and other things that he and his family need. So Sam Naimisi sells his coffee cherries to a middleman he knows as John, for the equivalent of fourteen cents a kilo.[1] He can remember a time when he made sixty-nine cents a kilo and says that he needs a price of thirty-four cents a kilo just to break even. For Sam Naimisi and his family, life as a coffee farmer is hard: it is back-breaking work, to be sure, but to make difficult matters even worse, world coffee production has exploded as Vietnam has transformed itself from being a non-producer into being the second biggest exporter in the world over the course of the last decade (Hallam 2003). The incomes of small-scale coffee farmers around the globe have as a consequence plunged disastrously; world coffee supplies have swollen even as world coffee demand has failed to keep pace. Sam Naimisi is directly affected by the international coffee crisis: the range of his family's diet has compressed into a much narrower spectrum of foods, and he particularly regrets the fact that fifteen years ago he was able to eat meat once a month, which he cannot do any more because he cannot afford it. Sam Naimisi could make a little more if he separated the coffee bean from the skin and pulp of the cherries himself, but the mill that could hull the cherries is too far away for him to be able to afford the cost of getting them to the mill.

So Sam Naimisi sells to John, the middleman, and it is John who takes Sam Naimisi's coffee cherries to a miller so the outer layer of the cherry can be removed, leaving the green coffee bean. John sells the green coffee to an exporter in Kampala for twenty-six cents a kilo; in addition to the fourteen cents paid to Sam Naimisi, there have been milling costs of five cents a kilo, transport costs of two cents a kilo to get the beans to Kampala, and John has marked up the price in order to pay himself five cents a kilo. It's not a lot, but it is a livelihood for John.

The exporter in Kampala runs a small company with ten employees. The exporter has to clean, sort and grade the coffee they buy so as to determine its quality. Green robusta coffee beans like those grown by Sam Naimisi are what is called a bulk commodity, basically being used not so much for flavour as for volume, so usually the grade of the bean is determined by its size and the number of defects. The exporter transports the bagged green coffee beans from Kampala to Mombassa on the Indian Ocean, getting a price of forty-five cents per kilo for standard quality green robusta beans. John the middleman was paid twenty-six cents a kilo: on top of this, the exporter has paid ten cents a kilo to bag and transport the coffee to Mombassa; the remaining nine cents has had to cover the exporter's costs and provide the exporter with a livelihood. Like Sam Naimisi and John, earnings for the exporters are often very low: some only earn one cent a kilo for themselves, which is not even enough profit to run the business.

Some of Sam Naimisi's coffee is destined for North America and perhaps the cup of Jessica Carson, whom of course he does not know, and some of it is destined for the United Kingdom and other anonymous drinkers. When Sam Naimisi's coffee arrives in North America, the importer has to buy it at fifty-two cents a kilo — the extra charges meeting the cost of shipping and insurance. The importer will sell the bagged green coffee on to a coffee roaster for a price of sixty-three cents a kilo, which meets their costs and provides a small profit.

Coffee roasting is an activity that can be quite simple or quite demanding, depending on the quality requirements facing the roaster. Once the green coffee beans have been blended in order to standardize the final product, the colour, taste and aroma of the roasted coffee is engineered by controlling the amount of time spent in a heated rotating drum, the conditions under which the roasting drum is heated and the cooling period. Kraft, Nestlé, Procter & Gamble and Sara Lee are the big coffee roasters in North America, and they are, like Aramark, global food corporations (Green America 2009).

Adjusting for the loss of weight that occurs in roasting, the global roasters pay about seventy-five cents a kilo before blending and roasting. The roasted coffee is then ground, packed and transported to the next step in the food supply chain, which could be a supermarket company, a fast food company, or a catering company like Aramark, who sells the coffee to the customer. A supermarket retailer charging a price of around $6.50 a kilo for the packaged coffee is charging a price that is 4,000 percent more than the price paid to Sam Naimisi at his farm gate. Aramark, selling a large cup of coffee for more than $1.50, is getting more. The largest price markup has occurred at the end of the food supply chain, by the roaster and by the retailer, both of which are global food corporations.

Incredibly, instant coffee is an even worse proposition, from the standpoint of both the coffee farmer and the coffee drinker. Blended green beans can release a liquid coffee extract that can be dried, packaged and transported for sale as instant coffee. If the sixty-three cents a kilo for which the importer sells the green beans is adjusted to account for the weight loss involved in producing instant coffee, the equivalent price at which the importer sells is $1.64 a kilo. The instant coffee that is then packaged by the global food corporation and that is found on the shelves of supermarkets retails for about $26.40 a kilo, which, accounting for the loss of weight, is 7,000 percent more than the price received by Sam Naimisi for his green beans. The markup of final sales price over cost of production is for the most part captured as profit by the coffee manufacturer and by the retailer.

Coffee is a starkly striking symbol of the global food crisis. The farmer gets a little, the consumer pays a lot, and most of the money ends up in between, in the hands of global food corporations. But while this seems to show how food inequality emerges from the ways money is made in the food supply chains that constitute global food markets, such an appearance is deceptively misleading. Money has been used in food markets for thousands of years and has not produced the depth and breadth of the inequality that we see today, which implies that we need to look beyond the interaction of money and markets if we are to understand how the inequities of the contemporary food regime have become established.

This was brought vividly and dramatically home to me by Qing Youzi, a small-scale peasant farmer outside Guilin, in Guangxi province of China. It was 1993. I had been working in Guanghzhou, and was taking a short break in Guangxi, where I had rented a bicycle and was happily cycling through the farming countryside around Guilin, a landscape that is remarkably powerful: small, steep, craggy black and green hills that sharply spike out of the earth and then just as rapidly disappear back into it, like sculpted mounds of clay plopped down upon a flat blank sheet. In the vastness between the hills, the land belongs to the Chinese peasant: not literally, for all land in China is ultimately owned by the state, but figuratively, for this is a land in which rice and fish, two of the most important parts of Chinese food culture, are found in abundance.

I was fortunate that I when I met Qing Youzi by the side of the road she was with someone who spoke a little English. Qing Youzi was a woman in her early twenties, but looked older. She was dressed in a simple cream-coloured tunic-like blouse and dark loose-fitting trousers and her black hair was cropped at the neck. We eventually ended up sitting in the small courtyard of her home under an overcast sky; it felt like rain was coming. Out of our view but directly behind the brick home were rice paddies wet with muddy water; green paddy shoots were reaching for the sky. If I had put my hand into the paddy, as I had the day before, the mud would swallow it up, and I would not feel the bottom. With scrawny chickens clucking in the background, it certainly sounded like I was on a farm as Qing Youzi explained to me through her friend how her family made a living.

"Before I was born everyone worked for the commune, growing paddy on the commune's land. When my father was a little bit younger than me this changed; peasants were given commune land to farm and were allowed to grow and sell what they wanted, so the more we produced the more we earned. That's the way it should be.

"We don't own the land, the state does. Every little while the People's Committee can alter the land families have, to take account of changes in the village — peasants get land to farm based on the size of the family. The last time the land in the village was altered there were six of us, so we were given three mu [about a quarter hectare], because half a mu will produce enough rice to feed an adult for a year. So our farm produces enough rice to feed us well, but it doesn't give us much more.

"Five years ago my older brother got a job in a factory in town and moved to its dormitory because he had to work six days a week, fourteen hours a day. This meant that we had some extra paddy rice that we could sell. My brother also started to send my father some money. We were lucky: we had a little bit of money to spare, for the first time. One of the things we did with the money was to rent some more land from a neighbour who didn't want to spend as much time farming. We can do that under the two-land system. At first we grew more rice; that was what we knew how to grow. Then my mother heard about a family in a nearby village who had a fish pond, who took their fish into town to sell to the hotels where the tourists stay. My father didn't know anything about raising fish, but got some help from a friend. He turned some of our paddy fields into fish ponds and used some of our land and the land we rented to keep growing paddy rice. Not only were we producing enough rice to meet our needs, we were able to sell some of the rice we produced and, of course, the fish that we were raising. The fish pond was so profitable that we were able to rent in some more land, and convert more of our own land into another fish pond. Before long, we were making far, far more from fish than it ever did from rice. We still keep growing rice, though; you never know what might happen."

I asked Qing Youzi whether her father thought his life was more secure under the old system of collective farming or under the new system — no longer so new —which the state called a "socialist market economy."

"Of course, the more we rely on fish to make a living, the more we must sell the fish that we farm. So we have to make sure we sell our fish! This means our fish has to be at least the same price as our neighbour's fish. After our success many of our neighbours farm fish; why would the tourist hotels buy from us if our fish costs more? Even better, our fish should be cheaper. To try and make our fish cheaper we take some of the money that we make and put it back into our business, improving the way we farm fish: new types of fish food, better ways of keeping the ponds clean, watching out for disease, things like that. Also, as we increase the area of our fish pond and are able to produce more fish, our improvements go to what are bigger ponds, which is more cost-effective. And we also try to make sure that our fish taste better. That's important in getting the hotels to buy our fish.

"The other thing we have done is entered into contracts with the hotels. That's getting quite popular around here. Rather than taking our fish to markets and selling them, we go directly to the hotels and negotiate with them. They agree to buy a certain amount of our fish over a period of time. We agree in turn to provide them with fish over that period of time. We agree the price at the time that they will pay for the fish later on. We also agree that we have to make sure the fish is high quality. So the contract gives us guaranteed sales at prices that we know, so that we can properly plan for our farm needs while cutting out the middleman.

"Our farm has to get bigger to meet the needs of our customers. There is a lot of demand for our fish, because it tastes so good. And that is one of the big problems farmers face now. China has 200 million peasants producing the rice they need and raising four or five pigs for the market. How can we manage such a system? It's too fractured. The gap between the modern economy and the peasant economy is getting bigger and bigger. We need to modernize farming, and that means increasing the use of technology, increasing the size of farms, increasing the scale of farms. It means expanding successful farms like ours and continuing to encourage young and middle-aged men to think about leaving the countryside, like my brother, for a better job in the city. Here in Guanxi, most people know this.

"It's a very different life now than the one my father had when he was young. We talk about it, but only once in a while. We are both sure that life is better now than it was when my father was my age, under the old system. That's what he thinks, and that's what I think."

I will never forget Qing Youzi because she gave me a remarkably literate and sophisticated understanding of the economic system under which she and her family lived. It was not just that money and markets mattered, as they always have; it was that for an entrepreneurial small-scale peasant family like Qing Youzi's to succeed — if you like, for the awkward balancing act between capital and labour on the farm that is inherent in small-scale peasant farming to start to shift in favour of capital and for the farm to become more of a business — some of their choices were not really choices at all. The family had, for a long time, grown the rice that they needed and used most of what they grew, occasionally making a choice to sell some rice rather than store it for the future, in order to get some cash. When they started to rely upon selling fish, selling was no longer a choice, it was a compulsion, because a failure to sell would spell ruin. Sam Naimisi faced the same false choice — one that is better called compulsion. Being compelled to sell, Qing Youzi's family was obliged to pay close and exacting attention to what they charged for their fish; if something could bring down their price without compromising the quality of their fish, they might be able to sell more.

Some 250 years ago Adam Smith identified the compulsion faced by Qing Youzi's family: what Ellen Meiskins Wood has called the "market imperative" to specialize, to invest and to innovate, so that costs can be reduced and sales revenues maintained and, if possible, improved (Wood 2009). Better than any textbook, Qing Youzi understood capitalism, a system in which the profitability of Qing Youzi's farm is a necessary condition of its continued survival and is a consequence of responding appropriately to highly contingent market imperatives. It is a Darwinian metric, and so it was hugely ironic that here, in a rural China that was becoming capitalist, a small-scale peasant farmer named Qing Youzi reminded me of a phrase that Karl Marx had written in the first volume of *Das Kapital* when discussing Adam Smith and others: "Accumulate! Accumulate! That is Moses and the prophets!" Deng Xiaoping had said something similar to China's small-scale peasant farmers: "To get rich is glorious."

On a golden yellow, seemingly endlessly flat prairie outside Carman, in southern Manitoba, Canada, John Hrudy also understood capitalism. It was 1991. Here, mirrored against a cloudless blue sky that seemed to stretch to the end of the world, was endless wheat, wafting in the breeze as far as the eye could see, for there were no hills. To the farthest frontier, wheat was what was grown here. John Hrudy, a man in his early fifties, of modest height, short, slicked-back black hair streaked through with grey, with hands that reflected a lifetime of work, was standing beside an older battered blue Ford pickup truck. His red shirt, jeans and workboots were all dusty, the dust of a land whose wheat could, literally, feed the world. I knew John Hrudy because he was a friend of my mother's, and we had come here from John Hrudy's unassuming kitchen in his home in Carman, in his truck, because he wanted to show me something. "This used to be mine," he said, pointing to an expanse of wheat, the boundaries of which could not be seen.

"I've been a farmer all my life. My father was a farmer, and it was what I always wanted to do; I never thought about doing anything else. I worked a section and a half; just under 400 hectares. But for a long time it was near to impossible to make a living from farming."

I asked John Hrudy why.[2] "Wheat is what people grow around Carman. We don't grow much else. We sell our wheat to the Manitoba Wheat Pool, which then sells on. But the world's had too much wheat for most of the time that I've been farming. You see, the Americans subsidize their farmers — they pay their farmers to farm — which means the American farmer doesn't have to get as much money for a bushel of wheat as a Carman farmer to make a reasonable living. That hurts Manitoba's farmers, because so much American wheat is sold internationally that American farm subsidies affect the price that the Pool can get for our wheat. For a long time the price we got for a bushel didn't give the farmer enough to make a living."

John Hrudy continued. "For years the government kept telling us we had to become more 'efficient.' Efficient — there's a word for you. What they meant was that we had to get our costs down if we wanted to make a living growing wheat, because the Pool had too little influence over the price. For farmers on the prairies, this meant you got caught in a bind. To cut your expenses meant going out and buying better and bigger farm equipment and machinery, but without the money the only way of buying the machinery was to get a loan. So you take out a loan in order to sell your wheat more cheaply, but cheap wheat means you don't make enough to pay off the loan unless your crop yields go up a lot. Most of the time, the yields don't go up as much as the price drops. Farmers end up sitting on a mountain of debts that they can't repay. Debts for machines that cost a fortune but are only used a few days or weeks a year. And the price they're getting for their wheat at times doesn't even cover the interest they have to pay.

"Of course, farmers being farmers, when they get behind on their loan repayments, they go out and get a paying job, on top of their farm work. Or the wife goes out and gets a job. Or both do. But there ain't a lot of jobs that pay well 'round here, so you're working hard, but not making a lot. Me, I knew a thing or two about explosives, so I started getting some work. Pretty soon, I realized that I was working two jobs, one of which, the explosives work, allowed me to stay in farming, but the other, farming, had no prospects — it just sucked the money away from us. I said to myself, for years, 'Why am I doing this?' Eventually, I realized I shouldn't be. So I sold everything and got out. Lots of farmers around here have done that. Sold out to a farmer from Morden who hires guys to do the farmwork; he's more of a manager than a farmer. I'm still a farmer; I just don't farm any more."

Like Qing Youzi and Sam Naimisi, John Hrudy understood the Darwinian metrics of market imperatives: that when you earn your living by selling what you produce and have no other way of making a living, you have to be able to sell at a price that buyers are willing to pay. The market imperative propels farm specialization, farm investment and farm innovation, all to cut costs and survive the compelling cutthroat logic of the marketplace. But John Hrudy had specialized; because everyone else specialized in the same thing the price was driven down. John Hrudy had invested, but the investment had not cut his costs enough to make his earnings per bushel profitable. He had done what he was supposed to do but had not been able to produce the profits necessary to compete successfully, so in the end he had to sell his farm and work for somebody else.

Sam Naimisi, Qing Youzi and John Hrudy might, at first glance, appear to be distant and disconnected. They live thousands of miles apart and have lives and lifestyles that are totally alien to each other. But behind difference lies uniformity: the reasons for the choices that they were inescapably compelled to make were identical. Trying to make a living as farmers under an economic system in which you have to sell in order to be able to survive as farmers means that the need to make money impelled them to make certain choices — about what to produce, about how to produce it, about whom to sell it to, and indeed, about whether to remain in farming. The compulsive character of these false, illusory choices sets Sam Naimisi, Qing Youzi and John Hrudy apart from other farmers who have lived and worked for most of the previous 10,000 years.

For thousands of years small-scale peasant farmers produced to meet their own needs and for their own use — as Noor Mohammed tries to do. Unlike Noor Mohammed, if they didn't produce enough, they would still manage; for most of the history of settled agriculture within farming communities there have been complex mechanisms of redistribution between those who produced relatively more food and those who produced relatively less food, so that those who produced relatively less could manage to survive. These mechanisms were part of the basic fabric of social life in rural communities, with elaborate rituals and rites often attached to the redistribution of food. When peasants used markets, it was to buy the things they needed that they did not produce themselves: salt, cloth, farm and food preparation equipment, tools and utensils. It was very common that these transactions would be part and parcel of the mechanisms used by a community to redistribute food from those who had some to those who did not have enough. So, often payment was not in cash but in-kind, with small-scale peasant farmers bartering the food they produced or their ability to work in the future in order to pay for something. Money was found, but was rare and was not an important part of the way in which life and its basic necessities were organized. Peasant farmers had little need for it in their world.

The world of Sam Naimisi, Qing Youzi and John Hrudy is very different. The three of them live under an economic system that is, historically, quite singular and unique, having developed in one part of Western Europe so recently in human history — less than 300 years ago — that it should be seen as being a rare way to organize communities, societies and social relationships. So rare that it might even be an accident of history.

Capitalism is the system in which we all live but which surprisingly few of us understand. But as I have said, Qing Youzi understands it; John Hrudy also understands it. Indeed, most of the world's farmers intuitively understand it. Capitalism is a system in which most goods and services, including food, are produced so that they can be sold. The one complex exception to this, which sometimes is not an exception, is the unpaid work and care carried out in the household, and in any case, the way in which unpaid work and care is performed is affected by the character of capitalism. So, in the jargon of capitalism, most goods and services are "commodities": made to be sold.

Sellers must also have buyers. This means that capitalism is a system in which the majority of the people must not be able to meet their needs by making goods and services for themselves; if they could do this, they would not need to buy, and sellers could not sell. So, most people rely on meeting most of their immediate needs by buying. Capitalism is not a system of autonomous self-sufficient small-scale peasant farmers producing their own food for themselves, as Qing Youzi or Grace Muchengi or Sam Naimisi or Noor Mohammad shows. It is a system in which an incessant and ongoing reliance on others is a condition of survival; when you depend on markets to meet your food needs, you rely on others to survive. But just because you rely upon others does not mean you rely upon them as your equal; you may rely upon them, but from a position of superiority, like Haji Shahrukh Khan, or a position of subordination, like Noor Mohammed or indeed Sam Naimisi, reliant as he is on John the middleman.

In the capitalist societies in which we live, workers like ex-farmer John Hrudy meet their needs, including food, only by selling their labour-power for a wage. Their labour-power is sold to the capitalist corporations that own and control the vast bulk of the natural, physical and financial resources found in a community and in a country, resources that are needed to make goods and services that can be sold. Capitalist corporations create value from resources through the process of production and exchange under the market imperative. The value thus created — and the corporations responsible for creating it — are what I refer to henceforth, collectively, as "capital."

But goods and services don't make themselves; people are hired by capital to work with and act on those resources, transforming them through work into goods and services that people can be compelled or convinced to buy. And it is here, in this, that the hidden secret of capitalism can be found: in buying labour-power, capital not only buys a person's ability to work but also their capacity to make goods and services with a value that is greater than the cost of the wages that go into making the goods and services that they make (Mandel 1976). Capitalism is a system in which capital is able, because it owns the resources, to "appropriate" this additional "surplus value" created by the workers who actually produce commodities. This surplus value is realized by capital as profit when the commodity is sold.

Workers depend on markets for the goods and services, including food, necessary for them to survive and to prosper, but are subordinate to capital precisely because workers rely upon selling their ability to create surplus value in labour markets for a wage in order to survive. Capital depends on workers to be able to create the surplus value that can be realized as the profit necessary to cope with the complex Darwinian metrics of the system.

It is an inherently contradictory and unstable articulation of interests, as the global economic meltdown of 2008 revealed in all its glory.

In that commodities are made to be sold, it is imperative that capital sells the goods and services that it produces if it is to survive. So too, though, must other capitals: competition between capitals is a necessary outcome of the market imperatives facing individual capitals. In order to compete, capital must seek out profits: selling goods and services at a price that is greater than the cost of producing those goods and services. But with competition, capital cannot dictate the prices or the conditions under which the sale of a good or service might take place — which is one reason why capital tries to restrict competition, through oligopolies of the sort faced by Jessica Carson.

If capital seeks profits, but cannot dictate prices, then profit is uncertain. What capital must control, in order to be competitive, are costs; and the most effective means of controlling costs and being competitive is, as Qing Youzi and John Hrudy know, to continually try and cut costs. As labour-power has the capacity to produce goods and services of greater value than the wages that are paid, cutting costs means, above all else, increasing the value of the goods and services produced by labour-power relative to the wages paid to labour. In other words, capital requires organizational and technical forms and features that increase the surplus value that can be appropriated from labour in a given period of time. This is known as increasing labour produc-tivity, and it is something that Qing Youzi is continually trying to do.

But increasing labour productivity requires profits. Without adequate profit, capital cannot invest in new technical or organizational forms and features to try and lower costs of production. Without adequate profit, capital cannot expand production, to try and capture more of the market. Without adequate profit, capital cannot innovate in the production of new products that may, by virtue of their uniqueness, allow surplus value to be realized as profit. Qing Youzi has tried all three and, like that capital whose success brings with it higher profits, is in a far stronger position to lower her farm's costs of production, expand and innovate, in terms of technical or organi-zational forms, factors and products. By way of contrast, those investments that produce inadequate profits, because costs rise faster than productivity, prices or both, diminish the capacity and incentive to invest. By his very failure, John Hrudy understands that it is profit that gives capital the ability to invest as well as the reason to invest; profit that is realized as reinvestment can fund the self-expansion of capital, or what is called accumulation.

These requirements are imposed on the owners of capital without regard to their own personal desires or preferences; it is not that they are good, bad or indifferent — which they can be — but that these requirements are a condition of survival. Like Qing Youzi and John Hrudy, all capital must adopt behaviour that is consistent with the continued, essentially coercive, compulsions of this imperative: dependence on the market to sell requires that capital continually strive to be competitive, which in turn requires continually maximizing profit and continually reinvesting in order to improve labour productivity. The world of capitalism witnesses a need for incessant capital accumulation, as a result of which capitalism has created a historically unparalleled period of economic growth. But in so doing it has also given rise to the social inequalities we see on a historically unparalleled scale.

What does this have to do with the global food system? And how do the lives of Noor Mohammed, Haji Shahrukh Khan, Jessica Carson, Grace Muchengi, Sam Naimisi, Qing Youzi and John Hrudy fit into the picture? I'm not suggesting that they are all capitalists — even though Qing Youzi may be on her way to becoming one. They fit because the market imperative of capitalism has imposed behaviour and needs on them without any regard to their own personal desires, preferences or wishes. They fit because of something that I have so far only alluded to: the "agrarian question."

The origins of the idea of the agrarian question lie, paradoxically, in London in the 1890s, in a sprawling home at 122 Regents Park Road of a man who was about to die. There, in the largest, wealthiest, most unequal and most corrupt city in the world, lived Friedrich Engels, a man born in Westphalia, whose deep-set eyes appeared distant, the result of having a high forehead and a lengthy grey-white beard, which together made his head look somewhat large for his body.[3]

Despite being revered in the socialist world for most of the twentieth century, Friedrich Engels is pretty well forgotten today and when he is remembered is recalled for being the financier and sidekick of Karl Marx. Yet Friedrich Engels was a far more interesting man than this. For much of his life Friedrich Engels had lived a double life in Manchester, the dark, coal-fired, smokestack-dominated city that deserved the sobriquet "the workshop of the world" because it was where many of the world's manufacturers originated. Engels worked for nineteen years in the family business, in which eight hundred people were employed in the manufacture of sewing thread; ostensibly, Engels was a senior clerk, but in reality he was the manager of his distant father's capital and, upon the death of his father in 1860, the manager of his German family's capital. Although he was by all accounts quite bored by it, Friedrich Engels was very successful in business, and he enjoyed the trappings of being a successful capitalist: orchestral concerts, hunting with horses and memberships in private gentlemen's clubs, where he could entertain himself by drinking copious amounts of imported claret.

But Engels had another life. In late 1841 he did his military service in Berlin and became attracted to a group known as the "Young Hegelians," who combined their criticisms of religion and politics with a humanistic and emancipatory materialism that was, particularly for the time, very radical. By the time Engels finished his military service in late 1842 he was a revolutionary, and as a result on his way to England he stopped in Cologne to meet the editors of a radical newspaper, the *Rheinische Zeitung*. There he met, for the first time, a youngish Karl Marx. Although the meeting did not go particularly well, Engels started to write for the newspaper and, following its suppression by the state, for other newspapers, developing his materialist ideas about history and the role played by social classes and forces in the shaping of history. When Engels met Marx again just two years later, they found themselves speaking the same language, and thus began a deep friendship that lasted the rest of their lives.

In the 1850s and 1860s Engels was a successful capitalist by day and, in the evenings and on weekends, a revolutionary journalist. When he retired in 1869, a prosperous fifty-year-old gentleman of independent means, he moved to London to focus on a life of revolutionary scholarship, journalism and politics, infused with more than a little debauchery, choosing his home on Regents Park Road so that he could walk to Marx's house. By the time of Marx's death in 1883, the bad health from which Engels had suffered for a quarter century had started to lessen his ability to work: weak eyesight, at first, followed by rheumatism and bronchitis led to a series of episodes of ill health over the next decade. But just before his death from throat cancer in 1895, Engels completed work on *The Peasant Question in France and Germany*, from which part of the meaning of the agrarian question would emerge, building on the ideas of his lifelong friend Karl Marx.

Karl Marx. Everyone knows the name, everyone has an impression and yet few know anything about the man. Marx was, at the very least, an ideological enemy in the hallowed halls of the developed capitalist countries during the Cold War, standing accused of crimes committed decades and more after his death. It was only with the onset of the world economic crisis in 2008 that a broader swathe of people started looking more widely at the thrust of Marx's ideas for the first time in decades; it is funny how economic crises seem always to lead to a revival of interest in the ideas of the person Chinese friends of mine called "old grey beard."

In *Das Kapital* Karl Marx had produced an account of the complex and contradictory "laws of motion" sustaining and supporting capitalist society, which in part suggested that capitalism had to overwhelm and destroy non-capitalist modes of production (Marx 1976). In Part Eight of that book, he wrote at length about that: how capitalism came to exist in the first capitalist country, England, through a process of "so-called primitive accumulation," in which the small-scale peasants that, in sheer weight of numbers, dominated the English countryside, were forcefully displaced from the land they needed for the production of their own means of survival. Through a series of enclosures of common land, which peasants needed to use in order to complement the production of often meagre farms, peasants found they could no longer cope by relying on farming. This displacement from the land meant that ever greater numbers of peasants became dispossessed and compelled to move out of farming; they became waged workers who had to sell their labour-power in order to survive. At the same time competition between emerging corporate interests in agriculture led to the expropriation of weaker interests by stronger ones, and concentration into ever-larger agricultural units. The capitalist farmer emerged, sitting side-by-side with rural wage labour, a classic dichotomy that is central to the revelatory logic of *Das Kapital*.[4]

Engels had been a journalist for Marx during the European revolutions of 1848 and had observed first-hand the small-scale peasantry in southwestern Germany and France. Like Marx, Engels believed that the material difficulties of peasant life generated at best political apathy and at worst political reaction. However, he had also seen peasant militancy. Later in life, in his revolutionary politics, he helped to draft the German Social Democratic Party's (SPD) Erfurt Program, which committed the SPD, one of the largest political parties in Germany and one of the largest working class parties in Europe, to an explicitly Marxist political agenda. Proclaiming that the end of capitalism was imminent and that a socialist revolution was inevitable, the Erfurt Program renounced the violent overthrow of the existing capitalist order in favour of peaceful parliamentary and extra-parliamentary struggles that would use existing legal conditions to improve the living standards of workers and build a mass membership party that could await the moment that a revolutionary rupture occurred as capitalism collapsed.

Although separated by three decades from the writing of *Das Kapital*, the concern with peasant apathy and the need to build a mass political party capable of capturing power are central to the argument of *The Peasant Question in France and Germany*. Despite the logic developed by Marx in *Das Kapital*, across the Europe of the 1890s peasants remained key parts of "the population, production and political power," according to Engels (1950: 381). They were not disappearing, even though, clearly, in some places and spaces displacement of the type described by Marx could be seen. But, just as Sam Naimisi has trouble coping with competition from Vietnam, small-scale peasants were "irretrievably going to rack and ruin" as cheap grain flooded into Europe from outside it and, unable to compete with market imperatives, peasants were becoming gradually but inevitably, legally and illegally, dispossessed from the land they worked (Engels 1950: 382). Dispossession as a consequence of an inability to compete is a circumstance that John Hrudy would understand.

Engels also saw that as this process of dispossession took place, subdivisions emerged within the peasantry, as a continuum of strata with different quantities of and relations to land, tools, equipment and labour-power slowly and unevenly became evident. Distinct social classes were created, which is why this process is now called peasant class differentiation. With peasant class differentiation taking place amidst episodes of displacement, Engels argued that too many peasants put their fate in the hands of "false protectors" — big landowners that, like Haji Shahrukh Khan, did not share their interests and indeed stood to benefit from their plight (Engels 1950: 382). Engels' "question" was, in this vein, intensely political in character: the development of capitalism was creating an agrarian crisis in which the apathy of some within the peasantry might be transformed into political activism if an appropriate agrarian program was formulated by socialist parties. Marx himself, in *The Eighteenth Brumaire of Louis Bonaparte*, had more than four decades earlier noted that the emergence of subdivisions within the peasantry could create differential political interests amongst sections of the peasantry, with the conservative peasant wanting "to consolidate the condition of his social existence, the smallholding" while the revolutionary peasant "strikes out beyond" the smallholding (Marx 1967).

For Engels, the power of the socialist parties awaiting the collapse of capitalism could be substantially strengthened by bringing in those subdivisions of the peasantry that could be convinced to take up the cause of socialism. There was a need for socialist parties such as the SPD to "become a power in the countryside" by formulating a political program for rural society that would represent the needs of emerging classes within the peasantry and in so doing build a political alliance between segments of the peasantry and the socialist party (Engels 1950: 382). It was a complex and difficult task, but for Engels, it was an urgent and crucial one.

In 1898, in the small Russian village of Shushenskoye in southern Siberia, Vladimir Ulyanov was living in exile with his recent bride, Nadazhda Krupskaya. It was a remote and isolating existence, hundreds of miles from the nearest railroad and life's minor luxuries, but it was not an especially difficult life: even as an internal exile Ulyanov received a small allowance from the Russian imperial state, which he used to rent sleeping quarters and an office from the local peasantry. Indeed, in his exile Ulyanov undoubtedly learned more about the Russian peasantry than he would at any other time of his life, and the experience shaped his views of social change. Exile was certainly better than the fifteen months he had spent in prison in St. Petersburg for being part of a Marxist organization called the Union for the Struggle for the Emancipation of the Working Class. It was that involvement that had led to his exile.

Today the world still knows Vladimir Ulyanov, but under his pseudonym: Lenin.[5] For better or worse Lenin is intricately and intimately bound up in the history of what Eric Hobsbawm (1994) called "the short twentieth century."

For many, Lenin remains a figure of intolerable and incalculable evil; for a few, a complex yet inspiring man. The world knows him from numerous photographs as a slightly balding, goateed, oval-faced man with strongly penetrating eyes, a man who seemingly always wore a dark three-piece suit, which was the norm for a man from his moderately well-to-do background. But in 1898 almost no one outside the hallways of the Russian state knew who Lenin was; he was a bit player in the drama of Russian history and, but for a peculiar and entirely unpredictable chain of events, would have undoubtedly remained that way. Physically, in Shushenskoye he was the same man; just slightly younger, with more hair and, as pictures from the mid 1890s attest, a less-sharpened, less-hardened, softer face, lacking the piercing eyes of the later years. The suit remained, though.

In 1898 Lenin, despite being in exile, was spending a lot of his time writing a book: *The Development of Capitalism in Russia*. Lenin was deeply immersed in what had been a rather long-standing debate amongst Russian socialists: in a predominantly agrarian country such as Russia, where small-scale peasants had only recently been released from centuries of bitingly cruel, slave-like servitude, and where capitalism was wholly underdeveloped, would capitalism emerge? That this question was even entertained shows how different Lenin's world was from ours; to us, capitalism can come across as all-encompassing and inevitable. Not so to most of the world a century ago. For Russian socialists, concerned as they were with transforming the character of their society and the state that managed it, a critical and timely question was if capitalism were to emerge, how would capital root out and expunge non-capitalist modes of production and establish itself as dominant? This question had concerned Vladimir Lenin long before prison and exile, and it was this question that he wanted to answer in *The Development of Capitalism in Russia* in a way that was accurate to the process of "so-called primitive accumulation" explained in *Das Kapital* and *The Peasant Question in France and Germany*.

In order to describe primitive accumulation in Russia, Lenin had been amassing, for years, often by hand-copying, volumes of data compiled by the statistical agencies of Russia's tsarist state. While in prison in 1895 and 1896 he had copious amounts of source material copied for him from within the libraries of St. Petersburg, the best in the Empire, and later, in exile, he had relatives send him yet more books and materials. When finally published in Russian in 1899, *The Development of Capitalism in Russia* would contain forty-six pages of notes and sources, including such riveting reading as D.N. Zhbankov's *Sanitary Investigation of Factories and Works of Smolensk Gubernia*.

In the mid 1890s Lenin was the leader of St. Petersburg's Marxists and a well-known figure in Russian socialist circles, if nowhere else — across Europe almost no one had heard of him, although that would, of course, be rectified later. One could not say that of Karl Kautsky: totally forgotten today, Kautsky, a balding, bearded man who wore round glasses, was a key leader of the inner sanctum of the German SPD and had been, along with his very close friend Friedrich Engels, extremely influential in drafting the Erfurt Program. Kautsky was the editor of one of Europe's most influential Marxist newspapers, *Die Neue Zeit*, and would write a series of books that popularized Marxism for the masses. So close were Engels and Kautsky that while he was dying of throat cancer Engels gave Kautsky the mammoth task of assembling and editing *Theories of Surplus Value*, the "lost" fourth volume of Marx's *Das Kapital*; at one time Kautsky's ex-wife was even Engels' house-keeper in London. With the death of Engels in 1895 Kautsky became the best known Marxist scholar, journalist and revolutionary in the world; he was far more famous than Lenin right up to the Russian Revolution.[6]

In the late 1890s what Kautsky did not know was that the attention of much of his intellectual energies was covering the same terrain as Vladimir Lenin's. Kautsky was, in his journalism and scholarly work, defending the mantle of Marxist "orthodoxy" that he had inherited from Engels against the "revisionism" found within some of the leaders of the SPD, most notably Eduard Bernstein. Initially that defence focused on what was considered in western European Marxist social democracy a critical specific issue: the question of the development of capitalism in the countryside. Kautsky addressed the issue in the form of a mammoth two-volume work, *Die Agrarfrage* (The Agrarian Question), published in 1899, the same year that Lenin published *The Development of Capitalism in Russia*.

Unlike Lenin's book, which looked at whether capitalism might develop in a predominantly rural, economically less-developed country, and if so how, Kautsky's book explored the core distinctions between agriculture and manufacturing under capitalism in Germany, France, England and the U.S. The differences between the two books are fairly minor though; both *Die Agrarfrage* and *The Development of Capitalism in Russia* are magisterial works of thoroughly detailed archival research, penetrating empirical analysis and tenaciously trenchant political economy that are meticulous in their attention to every facet under consideration. More to the point, both books have a cohesive and unified understanding of change. This is, frankly, remarkable: neither man knew the other at the time, showing that a shared analytical framework can produce a consistent understanding of underlying procedures, processes and practices in a diverse plurality of settings. Both Lenin's and Kautsky's books are critical to our knowledge of what is meant by the agrarian question today, but in a way that is different to that of Engels.

What both Kautsky and Lenin wanted to do was what Marx had done in "so-called primitive accumulation," but in other settings: understand both the processes by which capital emerged in non-capitalist settings and the specific differences between capital in agriculture and in industry. Of course, given that the world was, outside the industrial core of Western Europe and parts of North America, principally agrarian, the emergence of capital self-evidently had, in the first instance, to occur in the countryside. According to Lenin and Kautsky, the emergence of agrarian capital started with the introduction into rural societies of simple manufactured products that were not made in the countryside but produced in factories by workers working for incipient capitalists already under the thrall of the market imperative. Basic farm and households tools, building materials, sheet metal that peasants themselves could work on: these were the sort of simple manufactures that they meant. Of course, historically some simple manufactures had been made in the countryside; and it had always been the case that the countryside had relied upon some small amount of urban manufactures. What changed with the purchase of urban manufactures produced by incipient capitalists was that these were cheaper than the manufactures produced under non-capitalist conditions, because capitalist manufactures had to be competitive: competition was a market-induced coercive force borne by emerging capitalist manufacturers.

Kautsky and Lenin believed that as the expanded use of manufactures produced by incipient capitalists occurred, the need for money amongst the small-scale peasantry would be created. To get the money they needed the peasantry would start to sell some of their farm products; often a food staple, like Qing Youzi's paddy rice, would be sold, as there would be a market for it beyond the farming community. As small-scale peasants expanded their production for sale, the coercive disciplines of market competition kicked in: as more was produced to be sold, the need of small-scale peasants to sell to survive increased. Just as Qing Youzi could not control the sale price of her fish, so too were small-scale peasants, starting to compete in food markets for the first time, forced to try and control their costs.

As Sam Naimisi and Qing Youzi know, one way of controlling costs is to specialize in producing only certain crops that the land or the peasant was particularly suited to growing. Specialization though only served to increase market dependence, as small-scale peasants would be producing even less of their own needs. Sam Naimisi is heavily specialized in growing a cash crop, and this dramatically exacerbates his market dependence. Another way of controlling costs was to reinvest earnings from crops in extending the culti-vated area, and thus spread certain fixed costs over a greater physical space, as Qing Youzi's father had done when he had rented land in a neighbour's fields. Yet another way of controlling costs was to innovate, by reinvesting earnings in farm technologies that had previously not been used: chemical fertilizers, more "modern" farm equipment and machinery, more effective ways of getting crops to buyers, switching to more profitable crops — or fish

— that competitors were not producing, or, in all likelihood, a combination of these. Controlling costs to sustain their market competitiveness, small-scale peasants would be increasingly following the core principles of capitalism, seeking to incessantly get more out of every piece of land that they had, and as Qing Youzi has experienced, this required, at its heart, reinvesting earnings to improve market competitiveness.

Investment meant that small-scale peasants had to produce, keep and indeed increase a "surplus." All successful farmers, peasants or otherwise, produce more than they need. This can be used to increase what the family eats, either immediately or stored for later use. It can be used as seed and farm inputs in the following growing season. It can be used to pay for land, labour and tools and equipment that the peasant does not have but that are needed for farming. It can be sold in food markets, in order to get money, which can be saved until needed. This difference between what the farm produces and what the peasant needs, for both survival and continued farming, is the surplus: the farm produces crops and farm products over and above that which the farming household needs.

So for thousands of years successful farmers have, like Qing Youzi, always produced surpluses (Fraser and Rimas 2010). What differs with the entry of capitalism into agriculture is that the market imperative requires that the surplus be invested to try and cut costs per unit of land and labour, improving the ability of the farm to sell its crops and farm products. But there's more: this compulsion maintains growth in the surplus, the capacity to continually reinvest and the capacity to become ever more market competitive per unit of land and labour. The surplus becomes how some small-scale peasants, calibrating the complex dimensions of a fulcrum of possibilities between capital and labour, are slowly converted into profit-seeking capitalists trying to accumulate. Accumulation becomes embedded in the countryside, as emerging capital in farming uses it to self-expand.

Of course, many peasants are not able or willing to see their lives changed beyond recognition like this. Those peasants not able to compete are less able to sell their crops and farm products at a price that covers their expenses, even though their growing market dependence means that they need money to buy goods that they do not produce. The flip side of surplus-producing peasants is deficit-producing peasants: those peasants that, like Noor Mohammed and Grace Muchengi, produce less than they need. Most peasants in deficit, in the first instance, try and make what are called "distress sales": they sell their crop at an unfavourable price before it is ready to be harvested, in order to get money that is needed immediately. The peasant's equivalent of a payday loan, it is something that Noor Mohammed has tried. Like payday loans, however, distress sales, in most instances, do not solve problems but compound them. A second option for peasants in deficit is to try and borrow to make up for the shortfall they face, which is what John Hrudy tried to do. Sometimes going into debt solves problems if it is properly used and repaid. Often, though, people that borrow have problems repaying their debt: think of credit cards. If debt does not solve the problems small-scale peasants face, it can become a vicious, self-perpetuating vortex, just as credit cards can be.

There is a third option for market dependent deficit peasants: go out and get a paying job. Waged labour can be done for the more dynamic surplus producers, who, as they come to expand their operated area, may start to rely upon hired labour. Waged labour can be done for the merchants, traders and other petty intermediaries that stand between the surplus-producing peasant and the market. Waged labour can be done for manufacturers, most of whom live in urban areas, which requires migration from the countryside to the town by some or all of the farm family.

Kautsky and Lenin both thought that as farm production became geared toward selling crops, farm products and labour-power would become subordinated to markets, which, because of market dependence, would increasingly dictate the behaviour of small-scale peasants. As differences developed between peasants in the type of market dependence they faced, changes amongst peasants in their use of land, tools, equipment and technology and labour-power would take place. Accumulating peasants like Qing Youzi would come to rely on labour markets to buy labour-power and product markets to sell crops and farm products profitability and to buy the land, tools, equipment and technology needed to further agrarian accumulation; hence market dependence would deepen. Deficit peasants like Noor Mohammed and Grace Muchengi came to rely on labour markets to sell their labour-power and product markets to buy the food and other goods and services they needed to survive and to lease out or sell any land or tools and equipment that they had less use for: market dependence deepened.

Over time, then, changes in the distribution of wealth — of land, of equipment, of technology and of labour-power — take place. A majority, deficit peasants became part of the labour force and of the market needed by surplus-producing peasants who were increasing farm production and extending farm holdings. A minority, surplus-producing peasants had relatively higher incomes, and by producing commodities, they contributed to the creation of the market and spurred accumulation. The result was the slow emergence of types of rural farms that differed in purpose. One strata comes to produce surplus value for accumulation, while the other strata tries to maintain subsistence with increasing difficulty. This was the dispossession by peasant class differentiation identified by Engels and, earlier, Marx.

Peasant class differentiation, which separates Qing Youzi from Sam Naimisi, Grace Muchengi and Noor Mohammed, is the key to understanding change in the countryside and the development of capitalism in agriculture. For Kautsky and Lenin the development of capital in agriculture was not about market dependence, which was a symptom but not a cause of deeper change. Market dependence was a consequence of the necessity to sell, which was in turn a result of both producing to sell — as capital does —and not having the means to survive independently other than by selling the ability to work — as labour does. In other words, the development of capitalism in agriculture was about the transformation of the majority of the peasantry into waged labour as they became divorced from the land, in much the same way as John Hrudy had become, even as agrarian capital emerged to dominate the rural landscape. It is, as Hall, Hirsch and Murray Li (2011) argue, a process of intimate exclusion, because it occurs within communities, amongst neighbours that are finding their social relationships to each other changing.

At the same time, Qing Youzi, Sam Naimisi, Grace Muchengi and Noor Mohammed show that we have not reached the end of these dispossessive and repossessive exclusionary transformations, and, because of that, we cannot be completely sure how these transformations will end. Lived life cannot be foreseen with the degree of certainty outlined by Kautsky and Lenin; it is more contradictorily complex than that, and although they wrote massive tomes, Kautsky and Lenin understood that what they were describing was, at best, the bare bones of the contours of capitalist transformation. They did not predict that it would happen everywhere at the same time and at the same speed: it would take multiple forms and paths, just as the path of change witnessed by Qing Youzi, Sam Naimisi, Grace Muchengi and Noor Mohammed cannot be identical, because they live under very different circumstances.

Lenin himself studied two broad paths in the development of capitalism in agriculture: capitalism from below, where the class of capitalist farmers emerges out of the intimate exclusionary dispossession created by peasant class differentiation; and capitalism from above, where the class of capitalist farmers emerges out of the transformation of the pre-capitalist feudal landlord class that dispossesses through displacement the small-scale peasants that had worked their land. Kautsky too was able to envisage circumstances where emergent and mature agrarian capital might restrict itself to certain activities and not transform small-scale peasants, because some of their unique characteristics might be more appropriate to certain conditions facing capitalism. So, it might be worthwhile to have Sam Naimisi producing coffee that he sells and some of the food his family needs, so that the coffee price does not have to entirely meet the family's survival needs.

Indeed, the transformation of small-scale peasants into waged labour might be incomplete, as with Grace Muchengi; as agrarian capital develops, small-scale peasants might make part of their living selling their labour-power and part of their living from farming. Lenin called this state of affairs "semi-proletarian;" Kautsky called it "the proletarianization of the peasant." As Michael Watts (1998) has acutely put it, agrarian capital is "recombinant," emerging out of, as Marx put it, "the 'swamp' of pre-capitalist labour relations," creating a diverse plethora of forms of capitalism that reflect past histories, propel current trajectories and create future realities .

In Kautsky's and Lenin's sense then, the agrarian question explores the reorganization and reconfiguration of small-scale peasant production in ways that may or may not create capital and labour. It is a shifting world where "all that is solid melts into air" (Marx and Engels 2012), a world of change that Qing Youzi, Sam Naimisi and Grace Muchengi would understand. It examines the implications of change, a lack of change or a hybrid change for self-expanding accumulation, both inside and beyond agriculture. It also explores, in Engel's sense, what these changes suggest for rural politics, for rural politics is very often about the character of agrarian production and accumulation. The agrarian question uses these to ask, as Kautsky (1988: 12) did, "whether, and how, capital is seizing hold of agriculture, revolutionizing it, making old forms of production and property untenable and creating the necessity for new ones."

In the sense employed by both Kautsky and Lenin, on a global scale capitalism obviously has not fully transformed small-scale peasant farming into capitalist agriculture. It has in many places, but there are many other places and spaces where small-scale peasant farming, in one form or other, stubbornly and persistently lives on as peasants produce partly or principally for their own use. There are also many places and spaces where poor rural people have to combine farming small plots of land with waged labour in order to have the most basic life; Lenin's semi-proletarians are everywhere in the world today. And even where production is squarely and only for sale, large-scale family farmers, who still combine their capital with their labour to try and eke out a living, have a hard time surviving under capitalism. Just ask John Hrudy.

Is the problem of the global food crisis that capitalism has not yet developed agriculture sufficiently? Would this solve the crisis? Or is the problem that capitalism has developed agriculture in a way that contributes to the global food crisis, and it is necessary to put need before profit? Does the agrarian question need an answer, or are attempts to answer the question contributing to the crisis? With a billion hungry people on the planet, and another two billion overweight and obese, these are critically important questions. To answer them, and have a better view of the relationship between the agrarian question and the global food crisis, we must dig deeper and uncover the roots of the global food regime in order to see how it shaped and was shaped by attempts to answer the agrarian question. I begin first by going back to my own roots and the way in which the reconfiguration of the lives of my family and many, many others like them refashioned their dependence on the powerful and laid the groundwork of the crisis that threatens to engulf us all.

3

WHY PERVAIZ QAZI WENT HUNGRY

CAPITALISM AND THE ORIGINS OF A GLOBAL FOOD REGIME

The northern Punjab lies at the foot of the extremities of the Himalayas, and on a clear day you can see snow-capped peaks in the distance. It is quite stunning. As the mountains give way, undulating hillocks and hollows emerge, forming eventually into what can only be described as rough moorlands, where ground vegetation can be thin and tree cover is often scarce. Set against a luminously glowing blue cloudless sky, the scorched, dehydrated soil, fawn-russet in colour, provides a stark contrast: other than low-lying streams, it is rain that provides the water here, so blue and fawn-russet dominate what the eye sees. Walking across the moorland over the coarse, gravelly soil in 1992, I instinctively knew that drawing life from this stern land must be hard.

In 1526 the armies of Ibrahim Lodi met those of the Mughal adventurer Babur at Panipat, sixty-five kilometres north of Delhi, which was under six hundred kilometers from where I was walking (Davis 1999). Babur had ruled Kabul for over twenty years, but Ibrahim Lodi, as sultan of Delhi, was heir to a throne that had imperiously ruled north India for 320 years; it was in 1206 that Qutubuddin Aybak, a lieutenant of Muhammad of Ghur, the Afghan Muslim conqueror of north India, established the Lodi Dynasty. The Lodi Dynasty was responsible for a history of violence; for three hundred years the sultans had invaded, conquered and looted neighbouring kingdoms, while brutally suppressing a series of rebellions on its frontiers.

To fight these wars, the dynasty had established a centralized and hierarchical bureaucratic administration over its territory, using harsh systems of tributary taxation to pay for both the administration and the army (Richards 1965). It was an oppressed, servile and impoverished small-scale peasantry that paid the taxes that financed the nobility, the army and, as a consequence, their own bondage; but by the time of Ibrahim Lodi the state was in disarray. Ibrahim Lodi had centralized complete authority in himself, and his infamously absolute rule and vainglorious humbling of the nobility had produced widespread discontent.

Ibrahim Lodi's army vastly outnumbered that of Babur that day at Panipat. Yet his military tactics were inferior, and the day was lost. Babur marched into Delhi, and the Mughal Empire was established, while the scattered remnants of the Lodi Dynasty fled in fear of their lives. Some fled to the northern Punjab, and in the village of Qazian, outside of which I was walking on that day in 1992, a few kilometres from the market town of Gujar Khan, on the section of the Grand Trunk Road that was built by the British Raj between Rawalpindi and Lahore, there is a grave. Local legend has it that buried in this grave is a noble from Ibrahim Lodi's court; a noble who is, supposedly, my distant ancestor.

Qazian is now a village of several thousand, but five hundred years ago it would have been a small community of several hundred, with mostly Muslim and Sikh small-scale peasant families living in flat-roofed, mud-plastered single-storey hovel-like buildings containing dark, dungeon-like rooms that were mostly unfurnished. These buildings can still be found in the area; I have visited the people who, by force of circumstance, have to live under such impoverished conditions. Alongside the Muslim and Sikh peasant farmers would have been a few petty shopkeepers and moneylend-ers of the Hindu faith, who were probably marginally better off than their peasant neighbours. Life would have been hard, and all of them would have been poor by our standards, with people having only a few clothes and not having enough to be able to pay for the horse-carts that could take them into Gujar Khan, having instead to walk; but they would not have been destitute by any means. In many ways, the lives of the small-scale peasants of Qazian then were probably better than that of Noor Mohammed and his family now; Noor Mohammed knows that he is excluded from the opportunities of the world around him by his poverty and his servitude, but the peasants of Qazian quite likely did not feel that five centuries ago. They were simply part of the world in which they lived.

Small-scale peasants, like those living in Qazian, rely upon using their own labour and the labour of other family members to work their arable land and, as Noor Mohammad shows, either do well or go hungry on the basis of whether the land produces a surplus. Compared to Noor Mohammad, the peasants of Qazian were lucky; they did not have to deal with powerful landlords. But when they wanted to sell their surplus food, the peasantry of Qazian, like Sam Naimisi and many others then and now, might well have had to deal with somewhat more powerful petty food traders; and when try-ing, if necessary, to work for others because they had not produced a surplus, the peasants of Qazian, like Grace Muchengi and so many others, might have had to simply accept what was offered. The peasants of Qazian were, like all small-scale peasants, subordinate to wider social and economic forces because of their need to get things that they did not themselves produce: salt, spices, cloth, tools and more.

Qazian and the northern Punjab had a developed state for centuries, as the Lodi Dynasty was succeeded by the Mughal Empire (Richards 1993). With government came demands for tax payments from the subordinate peasantry and, to meet such demands, the establishment of customary usufruct rights in land: Qazi peasants had the right to occupy land and to control the crops that such land produced provided that the land was used and so capable of supporting tax payments (Maddison 2005). Taxation had led to the development of some commercialized agriculture and petty craft and artisanal production around Qazian, which was mostly sold in Gujar Khan.

But while some had access to land, others did not, and there were landless rural workers as well as dispossessed peasants lacking any kind of customary rights to the use of land. Some of these workers were not free in most areas of their life, being servants of their villages; some resembled serfs and some resembled slaves, although this was rare, while many were free wage labourers, working in various jobs. There was, in other words, social hierarchy and differentiation even within the peasant community.[1]

For the peasantry of Qazian, when they needed to get products that they did not themselves produce, who they were, in terms of social status and hierarchy, would affect the conditions by which such things were obtained. Social status bore down immediately on everyday life, as it always does: the relationships of Qazi peasants to their social superiors and inferiors; to each other, in their families and in their communities, on the basis of gender, age and kinship; to the state; and to the operation of the product and labour markets that they might use. Social status reflected and affected material relations and interactions over land and livelihoods, but would also affect and be affected by culture, custom and the rudimentary politics of everyday life. As the agrarian question reminds us, the messy ensemble of these intimate, complex and contradictory relationships would have had a direct bearing on the conditions by which Qazi peasants may or may not have produced the surplus that could have allowed them to prosper.

In trying to produce that surplus of food, using bullock and plow, picking their way between boulder and stone, the peasants of Qazian did not furrow deeply, for the soil was coarse. After several rounds of plowing, bullocks and flat planks would break the clods of earth brought to the surface and — following broadcast sowing, in which the peasants literally threw the seed that they had stored from the previous harvest over the fields — level the fields so that precious moisture gathered from the earlier monsoon could be retained by the soil, rendering it fertile, a fertility that was sustained by using compost and farmyard manure as fertilizer.

Retained moisture allowed wheat "as green as the emerald" (Darling 1947) to grow in the dry *rabi* (winter) season from October to March, along with lesser amounts of barley, pulses such as gram (chickpeas), peas, lentils and mustard. In the wet *kharif* (summer) season from April to September, millet and some hearty pulses were grown. These crops, all of which originated in the Fertile Crescent (Kipple 2007) that runs from the Persian Gulf to the eastern Mediterranean then south to the Nile Valley, and which may have travelled east with the armies of Alexander the Great, provided the basic diet of the Qazi peasantry for centuries. Supplementing this diet were the byproducts of livestock: eggs, milk, butter, and, very occasionally during religious festivals, goat meat. The peasants owned very small amounts of livestock: cattle, such as cows, buffalo and bullock for draft power, hens and goats. These were the farm products that together formed the surplus — when the small-scale peasant farmers of Qazian produced a surplus.

Harvesting the *rabi* crop took place in April and May. Wheat and other crops would be cut with a sickle by the male members of a peasant family, by friends and by other members of the village who would expect similar help in return. Once harvested, the grain would be threshed by draft power, while the winnowing and cleaning of the grain would be done by hand.

For the Qazi peasantry, everything flowed from the land. They said — and still do — that the land was like a mother and was just as precious. So, social hierarchies were reflected in the differences in the land worked by the peasants of Qazian: there was very elementary peasant class differentiation. But it was elementary, as the farms of the Qazi peasantry were mostly small: two hectares was a good-sized holding, and holdings were subdivided amongst multiple plots, some of which might be near to Qazian, and some of which might be a long walk away from the village. If a plot was around a sixth of a hectare, as many were, the Qazi peasantry spent a lot of time simply getting to the fields to work, which reduced the time that they could spend farming, and so reduced the productivity of their labour and the yields from their land.

For Qazi peasants the purpose of what they did was deceptively simple: to improve their ability to produce a surplus from their mother, the land, and so better meet their needs. They were inherently creative and fundamentally emulative in trying to do this. Yet for many this goal was elusive; while some peasants did produce surpluses, others only produced enough food to meet their household's needs for eight months or so, while still others only produced enough food to meet their family's needs for four months. Many families faced hungry months.

The outcome of farming was and is always uncertain, as well as being uneven, across and between the peasants of Qazian. So the community had customs that allowed redistribution from food surplus to food deficit families.

Elaborate ritual exchanges took place between close kin with a common male ancestor. Religious festivals such as Eid-al-Fitr were always important in redistributing food to those that did not have enough, but so too were weddings, births and deaths; all redistributed food through communal community feasting. Of course, this did not demonstrate the egalitarian character of Qazian, for such was not the case; who you were affected what you received, how you received it and what was expected from you in return. There were those who did consistently better, year in and year out, and those who did reliably worse, year in and year out. The latter relied upon the former, and the former's dispensation of food to the latter was a traditional source of clientalistic prestige and status within the community of Qazian.

It was more, though. Behind the social status that came with the capacity to redistribute food was the material fact of consistent surplus food production and the facility to enhance social standing. Yet these redistributive mechanisms tended to tightly temper the effects of social differentiation, which was, in any event, also weakened by relatively small land holdings: inequality existed, but was not luridly pronounced because everyone in Qazian had the implicit right to claim their survival from their neighbours. Such mechanisms of, in a sense, "forced generosity," have been very common in the history of peasantries (Scott 1976).

The lives of the peasants of Qazian changed dramatically in 1849 when the Punjab, and Qazian, was forcibly incorporated into the British Empire. Six years later the Permanent Settlement brought the imperial state directly to Qazian: homes and farmlands were, over time, measured, and land records began to be registered, so that land taxes could be levied (Smith 1996). The village land registrar, called the *patwari*, the local revenue officer, the *gardawar*, and the village revenue collector, the *lambardar*, became agents of the imperial state, reducing the independence of Qazian. So too did pre-incorporation village officials; revenue collectors, called *tehsildars*, continued in their judicial and policing roles, and the village watchman, the *chowkidar*, maintained village birth and death records.

In 1868 these intercessions and their instruments were regularized under the *Tenancy Act*, which determined the terms and conditions of tenancy in the Punjab (Rothermund 1969). This had the effect of making land, which had been used customarily by peasants as long as it was cultivated, the formal private property of some of those peasants: Qazian forcibly succumbed to the commodification of land even if, as Polanyi (1957) reminds us, land cannot be produced, so cannot be produced exclusively for sale, and is as a consequence a "fictitious commodity" created in the course of capitalist development. Peasants that had cultivated the same plots for twelve years or more were given ownership of them as long as taxes were promptly paid; peasants that had cultivated the same plots for less than twelve years became tenants, contractually obliged to sow seeds, cut crops and pay rent to the landowner, in the form of a share of the crop, who in turn paid the land tax (Darling 1947). The British began a process of imperial enclosure like that described by Marx in *Das Kapital*, creating landlords and tenants on the back of a fictitious commodity.

Needless to say, this had a profound effect on the small-scale peasants of Qazian because it reorganized social and economic relationships within the village. The strata of peasant landowners created through enclosure were called *zamindars*. Being a zamindar brought status in the village, as land was a mother that was now owned by the few. Alongside zamindars, enclosure created sharecroppers who became, literally, motherless, the clients of their zamindari patrons. Land taxes were high. Prior to incorporation, around a third of the peasant's crop was taxed away; following incorporation, this level was maintained but converted into cash — a second of Polyani's fictitious commodities, created not to be sold but to be used as a medium of exchange. Cash began to occupy a place in the life of the peasantry that it had not held before, because as land taxes had to be paid in cash, both zamindars and sharecroppers were forced to market at least a portion of their crops in order to get money. Taxation was also stringently enforced, because both the patwari and the lambardar were paid out of tax revenues, being, in effect, "tax farmers" (Smith 2004).

Qazian had existed before the British, but the effect of the imperial state was to formalize and regularize social positions and space, constructing a village where previously there had been a community, in order to tax so that those who had been conquered became responsible for paying for their conquest. But the construction of Qazian did more. Enclosure and taxation irresistibly subordinated land and labour — Polyani's final fictitious commodity, which, barring slavery, has never been produced simply to be sold — so that Qazian, like much of northern South Asia, could export its wheat.

The need for cash meant that the small-scale peasants of Qazian had to sell part of their crop in food markets. These markets were not the pure free markets of romantic liberal mythology: resembling the circumstances faced by Sam Naimisi, Qazi peasants faced a few tight-fisted merchants to whom to sell; British capital was extraordinarily successfully in manipulating urban grain markets; and fed by the expansion of the telegraph, speculation was vigorously and extensively rampant in the quest for quick profits, forcing up export prices but not prices at the farm gate (Davis 2001). The theoretically-elegant balance between supply and demand eulogized by liberal economists never existed; what did exist was a notoriously lopsided, egregiously unequal transaction in which the invisible and the powerless became the source of profit for the visible and the powerful.

The peasants of Qazian were grudgingly paid absurdly depressed prices for their wheat and moreover received a tiny fraction of the price paid by the person who actually ate the wheat, in the form of bread, in England. At the same time, when they were paid they had to then pay the land tax, which was steep. The land tax paid for the administration of the enforced subjugation of the peasants of Qazian, as well as for the construction and operation of the railways and ports — in this case, Karachi — that took the wheat out of Qazian and to England, as well the irrigation works that were constructed to increase agricultural production for export in the Punjab and elsewhere.

The British saw to it that local manufacturing in the Punjab was decisively destroyed. Cheap imports from England — was Engel's sewing thread amongst them? — flooded into the markets of Gujar Khan, undercutting and thus undermining local artisans and craftsmen, forcing them to seek other occupations. Once local crafts had been swept away, the adoption of the Gold Standard in the restricted and constricted markets that passed for international trade in the Empire led to a sharp fall in the value of the rupee against sterling, and the price of imported manufactures soared beyond the reach of most (Cain and Hopkins 1993). The betrayal of local crafts at the hands of the Raj whittled away at the livelihoods of many, regressively resulting in many being compelled to try to get work in agriculture. With increasing numbers of people becoming dependent on a farm economy that was ultimately not able to support its existing labour force, even the parasitical tax farmers became impoverished.

The small-scale peasants of Qazian paid brutally for the travesties of British rule. The imperial state rigged farming against the peasant in favour of imperial capital so that surplus could be appropriated and extracted, through depressed prices and taxes, literally, from the peasants of Qazian to the shores of England. Amiya Bagchi (2009) calls this, appropriately enough, "export-led exploitation." Unsurprisingly, the effect of export-led exploitation for the peasants of Qazian was systematically disastrous: forced to sell what they needed to live, mind-numbing poverty was created, which quickly turned to distress as catastrophic malnutrition collided with the particular horror of the market. No longer able to use wheat to make chapatti, the flat bread that was a staple, the peasants of Qazian turned to eating mustard leaves and gram with a little salt if they were fortunate. When the monsoon failed, as it did in 1876, the pauperization of the peasantry turned into a vicious famine (Davis 2001), which recurred over the next several years and which would continue to haunt Qazian until the eve of the departure of the British in 1947. Such famine was, of course, created by the imperial masters seeking profits on the backs of peasants; Engels would memorably call such acts "social murder" (Chernomas and Hudson 2007).

I have an old photograph of my great-great-great-grandfather. His name was Pervaiz Qazi, and while he does not look like me, he does look like some of my now-dead uncles. Pervaiz Qazi had a round face, a nearly triangular nose and, under his arched brows, eyes that seem friendly. He had a full beard, but in my photograph it is in need of a trim. He is sitting on a chair and wearing a white shalwar; I cannot see if he is also wearing a kameez, for he is wearing a white jacket; it doesn't look as if the shirt under the jacket, which is tight around his neck, is a kameez. I can't see his footwear, but draped over his shoulder is a shawl, and in both hands he is lightly grasping a cane. Most dramatically, from a twenty-first century perspective, he is wearing a full white turban that completely covers his hair and possibly part of his forehead: while such was the normal attire of the day, few Muslims in the Pakistani Punjab, if anywhere, would now wear a piece of dress that is indelibly linked to Sikhism.

In the photograph Pervaiz Qazi looks prosperous, and he was; but this was later in life. He was born a peasant and worked a small farm in the village of Qazian and knew, no doubt, the family myth of origin, as I do. He would have lived through the famines of the 1870s, but would probably have believed that they were caused by the drought that the peasants were experiencing, even though the drought had not emptied the granaries of many in the region around Gujar Khan. He would probably have castigated the elements rather than the social murder caused by the Empire's export-led exploitation, which, couched in the incorrigible rhetoric of laissez-faire and free markets, refused to intervene in the export of grain in markets that were controlled by a few imperial trading houses, enabling prices to soar out of his reach while hundreds of thousands went to their death, long before their time, in a perfect storm of irresistibly decaying entitlements to food coldly aligned with profit-taking that crushed the poor and the weak. As eating wheat gave way to eating corn, and then millet, and then mustard leaves and then whatever could be found, Pervaiz Qazi would not have known that even as he and his family went hungry (no one knows if any died), English grain merchants were exporting record amounts of the wheat surplus to England to feed the growing working class of Manchester, Birmingham, Sheffield and Leeds. As Mike Davis (2001) memorably reminds us, "Londoners were in effect eating India's bread" as "markets accelerated rather than relieved the famine."

No doubt, Pervaiz Qazi tried to get more from his land and his labour; one way might have been to creatively improvise some kind of specialization, something that, with the failed monsoon, would not have worked. No doubt he would then have sold whatever he could to try to stave off collapse. No doubt he would have gone to the local Hindu Brahman moneylender, who, if the debt was not repaid at the time of harvest, because there was no harvest, would have been perfectly within his customary and legal rights to take Pervaiz Qazi's entire crop, if there was one, as interest, with the debt still being owed. In such ways was bondage ruefully replicated. How he held onto his land is not known to me, and perhaps he did not; perhaps he sold it or used it to pay off his debt and then bought other land later, for he did have land later in life.

What I do know is that when faced with the immiserizing havoc of starvation or near starvation, Pervaiz Qazi, like tens of thousands of others, was able to find a way out: in the late 1880s he joined the Indian Army. The districts around Rawalpindi had, for a long time, been a prime recruiting ground; the English believed that the inhabitants of the district were more "martial" in outlook and inclination, natural-born warriors that could be used to maintain the tight grip of the British on their Empire (Roy 1997). From the army came a steady income, which was good, for Qazian's farm economy continued to deteriorate in the aftermath of the famine. The number of landowners was reduced over time, while the number of tenants increased, a clear indication of the growing social and economic inequality that was coming to define village life and that was leading many, like Pervaiz Qazi, to join the army or migrate in search of waged labour. Imperial enclosure and market imperatives had fostered a time of transition in Qazian: the dispossession through differentiation or outright displacement of many.

Fortunately for me, Pervaiz Qazi prospered. He made sure that one of his sons got into the police force — my great-great-grandfather, who does look like me — and in his later years he returned to farming part-time. This is the Pervaiz Qazi of my photograph; perhaps, even as he was staring into the camera, he was thinking about the famine, trying to forget it.

Pervaiz Qazi went hungry because his wheat-producing village was being forcibly integrated by imperial diktat into the peripheries of the world's first global food regime. The enclosure of the lands of the Punjab; the tribute that was exacted from him and his neighbours in the form of depressed prices and high taxes; the forced specialization in export markets controlled by imperial trading companies; the destruction of local crafts and industries and their replacement by imports from England; the starkness of the social murder of between fifteen and seventeen million people between 1866 and 1906; the dispossession and outmigration of peasants from the land: the structural subsumption of the Punjab to European industrial and commercial capital was a necessary condition for the establishment of capitalism in Europe in the nineteenth century — necessary because European capital required cheap food to feed its workers (Watts 2009).

Throughout the world of tropical and semi-tropical agriculture, for centuries Europeans had with equal fury invaded landscapes occupied by indigenous peoples, massacred those peoples, plundered their mineral wealth and established plantations, often worked with brutalized slave labour, to grow sugar, cotton, coffee, tea, cocoa, palm oil, copra, jute and indigo for export from Latin America, Asia and Africa to Europe (Blackburn 1997). What happened in the late nineteenth century, to people like Pervaiz Qazi, was different though. The establishment of export-oriented agriculture in the tropical and semi-tropical regions of the world before the late nineteenth century had been to cater to the tastes of Europe's ruling aristocratic and proto-capitalist classes. It had not been about producing food for the masses, and it had not led to the mass movement of people from Europe to the peripheries of the world.

The Punjab of Pervaiz Qazi's time was caught up in the maelstrom of the creation of the world's first global food regime when, within a short period between the 1870s and the eve of World War I, it became possible to map, for the first time, the complexly contradictory and complementary actions and activities of those growing food, those servicing the growing of food, those manufacturing food, those distributing food, and those selling food, for the first time, on a truly global scale: a global food regime with recognizable parameters and processes (Friedmann and McMichael 1989).

At the end of the nineteenth century, Europe was the heartland of developed industrial capitalism. The urban working classes of Bremen, Birmingham, Bratislava and Bordeaux needed food, and the companies that employed them often needed agricultural products that could be used in industrial manufacturing. So many peasants had moved to towns and cities that more food was needed than the remaining peasant farmers of Europe could supply. But they did not need just any food: the working classes were becoming, slowly, better off and wanted to spend more of their money on the luxury of affordable "better" food. They were not adventurous, though; they wanted to improve their existing diet within the confines of their food culture, and thus the European working class wanted a European diet. So, where they had eaten brown bread, they wanted white; where they had used salt, they wanted sugar; where they had eaten potatoes, they wanted poultry; where they had eaten butter, they wanted beef. The European working class was going through something that all societies sooner or later go through as they become wealthier: a "gastronomic transition" from a diet high in starches and low in protein to a diet low in starches and high in protein (Rowthorn and Wells 1987).

The gastronomic transition in Europe required large increases in the production of meat. To increase meat production there had to be large increases in the availability of grain. This had been the main reason for the abolition of the so-called Corn Laws in England in the 1840s, which had restricted food imports and exports in an attempt to maintain food self-sufficiency, and which had, as a result of limited food supplies, kept a tight rein on the growth of the working class (Schonhardt-Bailey 2006). But increasing production of meat and grain, while necessary, was an insufficient condition for meeting the needs of the gastronomic transition, for food also had to get from farm to plate. So the late nineteenth century also saw a profound transformation in the complex of activities around food production as well as the types of food being produced, which started, for the first time, to become standardized in order to simplify agricultural production so that it could be more easily replicated (Clapp 2011, Patel 2007, Weis 2007). Crucially, it was at this time that the entry of capital into food and agriculture took place for the first time.

Between 1815 and 1930 more than fifty million people left Europe for the temperate climate of colonies and former colonies (Baines 1994). When they arrived in the U.S., Canada, Argentina, South Africa and Australia, ethnic and ecological cleansing, along with the impact of earlier episodes of imperialism, allowed them to dispossess any remaining indigenous peoples and to impose European landscapes upon local spaces and places. John Deere's steel plough, in particular, invented in 1837, could cut through the tall grasses of the prairie and the pampas and allow the soils beneath to be captured for agriculture (Weis 2007). It was during the nineteenth century, using these technologies, that there arose, for the first time, large-scale agricultural monocultures imposed by the incoming migrants: enormous farms built on the ruins of the lives of those indigenous people who had been dispossessed, using labour supplied mainly from the family and requiring, because of the size of the farms, large amounts of draft power and that grew, increasingly, wheat or corn or barley over an ever-larger area while still producing garden vegetables and domestic livestock for their own plates (Friedmann 1978). The grains they produced were destined for human and animal consumption, in both the lands of the European settlers and in Europe. John Hrudy's predecessors, who hailed from Ukraine, typified the trend of the transplanted European farmer, allocating their limited amounts of capital and their limited amounts of labour over an ever greater area in order to create a monocultural new Europe in the fields of North America.

The productivity of these farms was, in world historical terms, deeply impressive as they extended their cultivated area. More than enough grain was produced to meet the needs of the urban working class, so large volumes of relatively cheap grain started to be exported from these regions to Europe. European farmers were overwhelmed by this cheap grain, as Engels and Kautsky had both seen; thus, cheap grain contributed to further outmigration from Europe to the continually reconfiguring global agrarian frontier even as European industrialization was consolidated by access to cheap food (Watts 2009).

It was also in the late nineteenth century that the legendary cattle drives of countless cowboy movies were made. Meat became a key defining characteristic of the first global food regime (Weis 2007). These cattle drives had a point: to get cattle to a rail head so that they could be transported to the Union Stockyards in Chicago, where the birth pangs of modern capitalist agriculture and factory farming lie, in the abattoirs where cattle were killed on an industrial scale, processed and shipped onwards.

The contemporary global food regime's organizational and institutional forms coalesced around the fulcrum of Chicago: Chicago had the installed infrastructure needed to handle and transport agricultural commodities in unprecedented quantities over long distances at a cost that was astonishingly cheap; large-scale family farms were supplying the limited numbers of disgracefully unhygienic meat packers based in Chicago (Sinclair 2003) as agro-food capitalism developed, shaped and then reshaped farming to suit its needs; Chicago and its hinterlands were also an important centre for firms to manufacture the farm equipment, including, critically, powered machinery, produced by companies such as John Deere and needed by family farms with sizeable holdings of land if they were to be able to improve their productivity and increase cheap grain and meat exports; and Chicago, in the form of the Chicago Board of Trade, was home to the first futures markets in farm commodities as finance capital started to enter into agriculture (Cronon 1991).

Sprawling outwards from Chicago, the U.S. created a unified domestic agricultural market that spanned a continent, with strong links to industry and finance, and commenced exporting meat and grain to Europe. It demonstrated a future for food that would define the latter half of the twentieth century in the shape of the initial emergence of large-scale agro-food capital capable of regulating on-farm production and in so doing incorporating agricultural production into its search for the surplus value that could be realized as profits (Burbach and Flynn 1980).

The origins of contemporary agro-food capital also lie with technical innovations in canning, freezing and chilling (Toussaint-Samat 1992). Much of the meat processed in Chicago was canned and shipped to England; so too, Australian meat was canned and shipped to Europe. Canning developed throughout the nineteenth century, but it was in the 1870s that the Massachusetts Institute of Technology, following the work of Louis Pasteur on bacteria, developed the requisite heat and time applications for a range of food products and for different sizes of containers; canning finally became safe, and cheap meat for the masses possible. Canning was also used to transport fruit and vegetables.

Freezing technology was also a product of the nineteenth century; from its origins in the 1840s it was in the U.S. that the principle of mechanical refrigeration and freezing was developed as a means of inhibiting enzyme activity and microbial growth, and by the 1870s the commercial application of this technology came on stream (Heldman and Nesvadba 2010). In 1877 the first shipment of frozen meat carried by ships with ammonia compressor freezers arrived in Britain from Australia; later, they came from Argentina. By the early 1880s meat processed and packed in Chicago could be shipped, either canned or frozen, from the ports of the U.S. to urban workers in Europe. The far cheaper cost of these meat imports undermined European meat production and further encouraged the migration of livestock farmers from Europe to the peripheries of the global food regime (Friedmann 1992, Watts 2009).

John Deere's Illinois-built gasoline-driven tractors were widely used by 1900. But as the farms of North America started to reap the substantial rewards of using mechanical draft power and saw their land and labour productivity increasing astronomically, and as capitalism in agriculture started to produce, buy, package and distribute ever more agricultural inputs and farm products, due diligence was not paid to the foundation of what Tony Weis (2007) has memorably called the "temperate grain-livestock complex": fragile ecosystems where grasses had protected the soil and held in moisture were replaced by exposed soils that were easily eroded. Grain monocultures were not based on soil conservation, and as farmers strove to meet market imperatives of cutting costs and maintaining their competitiveness in order to improve their family's living standards in a harsh and demanding market-driven environment, increases in labour and land productivity were based upon the mining of nutrients from the soil (Teubal 2009).

Jerry Buckland (2004) has aptly described this farming technology as a treadmill: once you get on, it becomes inescapably incessant. Capitalism offered a technological fix for grain farmers mining the soil when, as we will see in more detail in Chapter 5, the basis of manufactured synthetic chemical fertilizers was discovered. When later used in conjunction with mechanized farm machinery and, later still, chemical herbicides and pesticides, the pre-conditions for a revolution in temperate farming were set in place. In this twentieth-century agricultural revolution, market imperatives similar to those faced by John Hrudy decades later undermined the soil conservation skills of farmers; they increasingly resorted to using a hydrocarbon intensive petro-chemical arsenal designed to artificially restore diminishing soil fertility. With agro-food capital commanding the production of a vast array of farm inputs that were increasingly purchased by market-dependent farmers in markets that could be defined by the extent of corporate control, the contemporary parameters within which farming could take place were established. As a consequence, agro-food corporations started to take control of agriculture by subordinating temperate large-scale family farmers to its own profitability dictates, all in the rhetorical quest for cheap food for the urban workers in Europe, North America and beyond.

But the workers still needed to be able to buy the food they needed, and hence the birth pangs of industrialized food also lie in New York — and Memphis. In 1859 George Hartford and George Gilman founded the Great American Tea Company, which was based on the idea that if tea was bought directly from the plantation and intermediaries in the food chain were cut out then the company could charge a lower price for their tea, sell in greater volumes because of their price competitiveness and hence be more profitable. Hartford and Gilman renamed the company the Great Atlantic and Pacific Tea Company, or A & P, in 1870, by which time they were operating a number of stores in New York City. Using the same idea to increase market competitiveness, the range of foods they sold had by then expanded to include coffee and spices, and the company's name reflected its transcontinental aspirations. Between 1869 and 1880, A & P opened one hundred more stores; business was very good. In 1880, A & P took a small step that revolutionized food retailing when they produced their own baking powder, which was then sold under the company name in their own stores. This approach spread to the other foods that A & P were selling, and over the course of forty years A & P became an important commercial food manufacturer of considerable size and market power (Ellickson 2011).

Commercially manufactured food had exploded in the nineteenth century: Worcestershire sauce, chocolate bars, evaporated milk, potato chips and factory-produced sausages all started to be produced over the course of a few decades (Toussaint-Samat 1992). Two iconic food brands were created at the start of the first global food regime, in 1876 and 1886, respectively: Heinz ketchup and Coca-Cola. Yet for the most part, food retailing remained much as it had been for centuries. In grocery stores, customers had to know what they wanted, because clerks fetched food from shelves behind the counter, measured up what was wanted and wrapped it: a labour-intensive and time-consuming process (Simms 2007). A & P offered a different model, but stocked only a limited range of products for sale.

Memphis changed all that, when, in 1916, Clarence Saunders opened King Piggly Wiggly (Patel 2007). Saunders wanted his customers to use a shopping basket to shop by themselves from open shelves in a space where they were sure to see all the branded food products that were available for purchase and, following a tour of the space, arrive at a checkout where they would pay. Saunders was so convinced of his ideas that he patented them, and in so doing can take the credit for the creation of the supermarket that we know today, self-service stores offering a wide variety of food organized into a number of departments where all one's food needs can be sourced. Saunders' ideas spread quickly: A & P adopted them in the 1920s.

The first global food regime was truly revolutionary. It fostered a world where the European diaspora living in former European colonies such as the U.S., Canada, Argentina, South Africa and Australia produced food on the first commercially-oriented large-scale family farms, as well as on plantations and on incipient capitalist farms, exporting grain, meat and other foods for the working classes of Europe. It was a world where capitalism began to make its presence felt through the world's food trade, as food production remained principally confined to family farms, and it was the control of trade that could bring profit.

Toward the end of the nineteenth century a confluence of factors in the U.S., with its vast prairie, rapidly expanding population, infrastructure, technological changes and organizational innovations allowed it to dominate the emerging global food regime as capitalism entered agriculture (Friedmann 1978, Friedmann and McMichael 1989, Weis 2007). Reconfiguring the food complex in order to simplify and standardize, other places and spaces were drawn into the expansion of the global food market; hence, wheat from the Punjab became bread and beer in London.

The first global food regime saw the world's supply of food massively expand, and world trade in food became well-established as large-scale family farmers (like John Hrudy's great grandparents) and small-scale peasant farmers (like Pervaiz Qazi) became inexorably drawn into global circuits of food production, distribution and exchange that were increasingly regulated by corporate interests. The food trade, dominated as it was by cheap food, ended the need for industrial wages to be supported by additional non-wage entitlements, such as community-based mechanisms of reciprocity, and non-market survival mechanisms, such as market gardens, within the working classes of North America, Europe and Australia, amongst others. In so doing, the temperate grain-livestock complex of the first global food regime offered an effective subsidy to labour by depressing the price of food; reducing the cost of labour relative to the value of the products labour was producing had the effect of increasing the amount of surplus value accruing to capital. The entry of corporate interests into the food system was, in this respect, a necessary condition for capitalism to complete its development across North America, Europe and Australia by the start of the twentieth century. But for the small-scale farmers of Asia, Africa and Latin America, the implications of this capitalist transformation were stark — incorporation into a global food regime for some, along with the dispossession by displacement and dispossession by differentiation identified by Marx, Kautsky and Lenin for others. And as highlighted by Engels, this transformation had profound political implications: small-scale peasants should not necessarily be expected to go along quietly with this transformation. As we will now see, they did not.

4

"TIERRA Y LIBERTAD"

PEASANT RESISTENCE AND THE QUEST FOR LAND REFORM

Abdul Hussain is sitting on a charpoy, a wooden-framed string-laced bed that is a pretty common sight in the rural areas of Pakistan and north India. It is 1989. He is an older man, with a trim white beard elongating his elegantly gaunt face. White cloth, which is wound around the crown of his head in a way that looks like a flattened turban, serves to both cover and frame the sides of his face: I cannot see his ears. On the lower half of his thin frame is a white dhoti, which is now a pretty rare sight in this part of South Asia: a loose sheet wrapped around his waist and lingering down to just above his thin ankles, tucked in so as to stay in place, straight at the back but with folds of cloth in the front. Over the dhoti is a long white shirt: not the shalwar pyjama-style shirt that most Pakistani men wear. Covering his shoulders, draped around his arms and flowing down his back is a thick red and white blanket-like shawl. On his feet he wears blue plastic sandals.

We are sitting in front of his whitewashed, brick, single-roomed home, within a high walled compound where, separated from his home, in different dwellings, with him live his two sons and their families. The compound also holds the small barns were they keep their farm animals: a lone buffalo — that produces deliciously sweet, white buffalo butter — and some hens. The barn, along with the numerous, playful young children of his son's families, gives the compound the sensory feel of a menagerie. Abdul Hussain's home is in a village so small and insignificant that it, like Noor Mohammad's, does not have a name, just a number. It is about forty-five minutes to the southwest of Faisalabad, which in colonial times used to be called Lyallpur, a city that is famous for its widespread use of child labour in brick kilns, but which still has the lingering feel of a dusty, if overgrown and densely overcrowded, colonial town, particularly in the cantonment part of the city. The well-irrigated fertile plains of Pakistan's Punjab province spread lushly but flatly out from the village; this region has some of the most productive farmland in the country, and in South Asia.

With not only the look but also the air of a graciously pious man, Abdul is speaking slowly, deliberately, respectfully — indeed, perhaps too respectfully; I'm not sure I deserve it. "The farm is sixteen *jareebs* [about four hectares], in twelve separate plots. Some plots are better than others. I have worked on this land since I was a boy; my father farmed the same land before me and before him, his father. Now I am old, and when I am gone, my sons will work this land, as they now do."

I ask Abdul what crops he grows, and I am not surprised by the answer — I was expecting it. "Sugarcane. Some goes to the mill. Some of it I make into gur[1] that I can sell. It is from sugarcane that we get the money we need." I recall looking inside the house; I had surmised that most of their money went to basic food. Beyond a tea set, an old radio and a rickety bicycle, they did not appear to have much other than their farm equipment, and even that was pretty elementary. "The rest of what we need we get from the land, from the other crops we grow and from the animals we have."

We got up and walked out of the compound; within a few minutes we were out of the village, walking down a dirt path beside a hand-dug irrigation channel that sat next to fields of green, toward a copse of trees. The sun was bright overhead and the heat so strong that the air was hazy in the distance. It felt like a timeless setting, that the rhythm of life was as it had been through countless centuries.

Speaking quietly, Abdul Hussain said, "I don't own this land — I am a *kisan*. Like my father before me, and his father before that, the land belongs to the khan [the landlord]." I knew this; the landlord was my great-uncle, and the land had been vested in our family by the British when Pervaiz Qazi's son had joined the police force and worked for the imperial state. It had been a pretty common tactic of the British, both here and throughout the Empire, and it had fundamentally transformed the relationship of the mass of the small-scale South Asian peasantry to their single most important means of production: the land. The effects linger still. "To work it I have to pay half of my crop to the khan; that's the rent that I pay to be able to farm, to be able to feed and clothe and house my family. The khan comes twice a year to collect his share." Indeed, this was the ostensible excuse for our visit: I was with my great-uncle, and he was collecting his rent. I asked Abdul Hussain what would happen if he didn't pay his share. "If I didn't pay, I would be evicted," he said flatly.

Abdul Hussain is, like his father and his grandfather, a sharecropper. As we have seen, sharecropping is a particularly malicious form of land tenure. It was practiced in ancient Greece and is still far too widespread today: in exchange for being allowed to work usually quite small quantities of land, the sharecropping peasant must divide their crop with the landlord in fixed shares. Throughout the history of sharecropping, the most common division has been fifty-fifty: half goes to the farmer that does the work and half to the landlord who provides the land but does none of the work. No one knows why this division has been so common (Byres 1983). One could say that the long history of sharecropping is based on the ability of the landlord to use it to make the peasant work as hard as they can to produce the food they need, which at the same time will maximize the amount of the crop that the landlord can appropriate. By controlling the land, the landlord receives an income while at the same time maintaining a powerless, servile peasantry that is wholly dependent on the landlord for their access to that land. Noor Mohammad is, like Abdul Hussain, a sharecropper; and, following the *Tenancy Act* imposed by the Raj, so too were many of Pervaiz Qazi's neighbours.

Abdul Hussain does not look or act like a servile man, but that is the reality of his life. He has always had to rely passively on someone more powerful to provide him with the land he needs to make a living for himself and his family, and he knows in the fiber of his being that challenging the power of the landlord is dangerously foolhardy. I can recall being told a story in a hamlet in northern Pakistan, quite close to where Noor Mohammed lives. The story may have been apocryphal, but, knowing Paktuns, it sounded real enough to me. In the hamlet lived seven families; they were not sharecroppers, because they paid their rent in cash, but like sharecroppers they depended on the landlord to provide them with land to rent. The families made, at best, a very marginal living; if the yields were good, they would be able to put away a small amount of cash, but if the yields were bad, times would be hard, very hard indeed.

At the beginning of a planting season a few years back the landlord announced to the seven tenant families that their rents were going up; they were going way, way up. The families panicked; the land gave them a living only in good years, and if the rent went up it would be harder to provide what they needed for themselves, as more would go to the landlord, even in good years. The men in the hamlet sat in the *hujra* — a dark, dank, mud-walled hut that was found in every rural community in the area because it was the place where the men could sit with each other, smoke and talk — and, after discussing it for several hours, during which time every man was given the opportunity to speak, decided that they would go to the landlord as a group and appeal that he rescind the rent increase. So, off they went. They presented their case to the landlord, who, as a fellow Pakhtun, listened politely as they drank tea together; hospitality must be shown if you are to be Pakhtun. After a cordial talk, the men returned to their homes.

A few hours later strangers appeared in the hamlet armed with

Kalashnikovs —AK-47s are everywhere in the area between Peshawar and Mardan, and they were a common sight in villages and on the roads. The armed men went into the compounds of each of the seven families, into their private, inner sanctums, forcibly, without permission, chasing the immediately-shamed men, the dishonoured women and crying children out of their homes and into the open shared space of the hamlet. The families were told they had to leave, to get out without taking anything, immediately, or they would be killed. The families knew the landlord's goondas were deadly serious; the armed gunmen were under orders to dispossess them as an example to other tenants and to other poor, non-landowning families in the area. So they all left, with nothing.

When I was told this story the man who was telling it said that the hamlet in which we were sitting was not the one that they had been chased from; that was fifteen kilometres away, and they had never gone back. Such was — and is — the power of the owner of the land in a rural community where a few have a lot and the many have but a little. It was a power that my great-uncle had over Abdul Hussain.

Like Abdul Hussain, Emiliano Zapata, the early twentieth-century Mexican peasant revolutionary, was a sharecropper, and in the photographs I have seen of Zapata I see a look, an apparent manner, like that which I saw when I looked at Abdul Hussain's face. It's in the eyes.[2] Deeply set under his brow, Zapata's eyes look as jet black as his moustache. Of course, this is a result of the photos being in black and white. However, in those photographs when he is looking directly into the lens, and thus directly to the person look-ing at the photograph, it is as if Zapata can peer right into you even as he himself is unfathomable. I see that too in Abdul Hussain.

Zapata had a long, thin face, dark, weather-beaten skin, a shock of thick black hair and a substantial, expansive, yet neatly trimmed mustache. Much of the time you would not have seen a lot of his head, for it was hidden under a large sombrero that cloaked most of his face in darkness. Tall and thin, Zapata always appears immaculately well-dressed in his photographs: when a peasant of his time and place wanted to look good, he dressed as if he was going to church. In his photographs Zapata is usually wearing a buttoned-up white shirt, an unbuttoned waistcoat, dark jacket, trousers that hugged his legs, and boots. Sometimes he is photographed wearing a long white neckerchief, adding a touch of elegance to an otherwise fairly common if elaborate suit of cowboy clothing.

Zapata had a reputation for being a reserved but unflinchingly polite and fair man of his word who was still able to keep a sense of humour. Vigorous but cautious, determined yet patient, Zapata, in appearance and in manners, more than anything else, reflected his origins as a child of Mexico's soil. Being of mixed European and indigenous ancestry, Zapata was mestizo, the ninth of ten children born to a peasant family in the small central Mexican state of Morelos just south of Mexico City. Morelos today is a state of contrasts with rugged peaks rising starkly up behind flat fields from which indigenous farmers try and eke out a living. They were not always able to, though.

When Zapata was born in 1879, as Pervaiz Qazi's life was being transformed by the dispossessive edicts of the British Empire and the ongoing establishment of a global temperate grain-livestock complex, Morelos was one of the largest producers of sugarcane in the world, having had North America's first sugar mill, which was established in the early sixteenth century. Sugarcane is intricately bound up with the history of imperialism, slavery and the primitive accumulation discussed by Marx, Engels and others, and it shaped the history of Morelos and its entry into the global food regime. Sugarcane grown in Morelos always had to compete against sugarcane produced in the Caribbean with slave labour, and to compete, Morelos had long used a hacienda system in which a few powerful individuals had huge estates of land that they farmed as plantations. It was a system of vividly glaring inequalities that the wealthy hacienda owners made worse: in the 1880s, with sugar booming as it started to become an everyday food for the European working class, the wealthy started to grab additional ejido, or communal, land, as well as private land, from the small-scale peasants that surrounded them, knowingly dispossessing through displacement many small-scale peasants and concentrating land in fewer and fewer hands. In this, the agrarian elite had the support of the Mexican state, which at the time was led by the longstanding dictator Porfirio Díaz.

The agrarian elite continually strove to assert their total control over the small-scale peasantry, much as the landlord in the Pakhtun hamlet did or Haji Shahrukh Khan did, trying to crush the spirit of independent communities of indigenous and mestizo farmers such as the ninety households in the village of Anenecuilco, where Zapata's family lived. Some farmers (*peonaje*) were forced by debt to work on the haciendas and were treated as slaves; some farmers did not go into debt but were still unable to manage, as they did not have enough owned or rented land and became resident labour (*gente de casa*) on the hacienda and treated as serfs; and some — like Zapata's mother and father — managed to hold on to their own meager holding of land (*rancho*) and their independence by supplementing their livelihood through other, financially far more important, activities, acting, in a sense, like the semi-proletarians identified by Lenin. Zapata's father Gabriel trained and sold horses, for example, which gave the family the extra income they needed to sustain their farm production and thus remain free of both the poverty that was always threatening them and the Hacienda del Hospital, the dominant sugarcane plantation around Anenecuilco, which was actively encroaching upon and forcibly enclosing the land of small-scale peasant farmers like Gabriel Zapata.

Following the death of his parents in the mid 1890s Zapata brought up his three sisters by taking up farming on sharecropped land and, like his father, trading horses. So Zapata was, like Abdul Hussain and Noor Mohammad, a sharecropper. While it must have been a difficult life, Zapata seems to have been both fairly good at what he did and increasingly respected and trusted within his community, because in 1905 Zapata along with some of his neighbours represented his village in a meeting with the governor of Morelos and the manager of the Hacienda del Hospital. Their purpose: like the dispossessed Pakhtun peasants, to bring to the attention of the powerful the increasingly precarious position of a more than ever marginalized peasantry. The meeting was not a success; nothing came of it.

Zapata knew that the villagers felt *cariño* for him: they liked and admired him, and with this, they recognized his ability to lead them, if he so wished. So, in 1909 Zapata allowed himself to be elected to the position of head of the "defence committee" of Anenecuilco. When elected, Zapata, unlike others, did not forget where he was from or who he was. Confronting the dependence of sharecroppers and other small-scale peasants on the more powerful, he used his position to try to not only defend the collective rights of the peasantry but indeed to have returned to them ejidal and private land that had been grabbed by the Hacienda del Hospital; to that end, Zapata began leading a series of non-violent occupations and re-divisions of land that had been grabbed, which brought him a further measure of esteem amongst the small-scale peasants of Morelos and notoriety amongst its agrarian elite. Aware of the threat that Zapata posed, the elite had him forcibly conscripted into the federal army, where he served for six months.

Eventually returning to Anenecuilco in mid 1910, Zapata saw that the situation of the peasantry remained desperate and that the need for land was stark. Zapata organized around eighty armed villagers to march out with him to reclaim land that had been occupied by the Hacienda del Hospital. When the hacienda farm hands and guards did not oppose the occupation, it succeeded; Zapata learned that armed occupations could work, while his fellow villagers learned that they did not have to accept dispossession by displacement and that they did not have to accept enforced deprivation, but that they could instead reimagine and recreate the village society that they wanted to live in. Then, when a local judge surprisingly supported the peasants in their occupation, other villages began to follow their example, in llano de Huajar, Villa de Ayala and Moyotepec.

With the support of his neighbours and neighbouring villages, Zapata began to organize peasants into revolutionary bands when a northern landowner, Franciso Madero, who had lost a rigged presidential election to Díaz, declared a revolution that included the return of land grabbed by the haciendas to the dispossessed. Zapata began to implement Madero's revolutionary plan, riding with his comrades from village to village and opposing the agrarian elite by tearing down the fences of haciendas and encouraging peasants to reoccupy their seized lands. When, on November 20, 1910, Díaz started to have Madero's followers arrested, the declared revolution became a real one; Zapata, a sharecropper and horse trader, had become a fully-fledged agrarian revolutionary, leading an army of fellow peasants determined to restore their rights and the rights of their communities.

Zapata built his army of followers and fellow travellers quickly; they became known as Zapatistas. When the revolution turned violent, Zapata's peasant revolutionary army was able to seize control of the town of Cuautla. With the legendary Pancho Villa's army fighting in the north, Díaz resigned, installing an interim president who remained firmly sympathetic to the agrarian elite; in 1911, though, this man gave way to Madero. Shortly thereafter, Madero met with Zapata, who asked him to meet the demands of the peasantry to restore lands taken from them; Madero refused, and nineteen days after Madero's assumption of the presidency, Zapata decided to reignite the peasant insurgency.

With some assistance Zapata formulated the Plan of Ayala, which, under the slogan "tierra y libertad" (land and liberty), declared a revolution based on the forcible confiscation with compensation of one-third of all land controlled by the elite *hacienderos* so that it could be given over to the peasantry. Zapata said it clearly and cogently: "The land belongs to those who work it." Hacienderos that refused to comply with the Zapatista demands would have the entirety of their lands forcibly confiscated by the revolutionaries without any financial compensation. An interim government was also declared, pending free elections. In April 1912, Zapata began the redistribution of ejidal lands in Puebla, before moving on to Moderos and Tlaxcala; what today is called "pro-poor redistributive land reform" in Mexico had begun.

Zapata's redistribution of confiscated land began a sixty year cycle that Eric Wolf (1999) has called the time of the "peasant wars of the twentieth century." In his book of the same name, Wolf closely examined social revolutions in Mexico, Russia, China, Vietnam, Algeria and Cuba, revolutions in which small-scale peasant farmers, challenging the processes of dispossession and deprivation that they were confronting as the global food regime consolidated, had played a critical role in decisively shaping the outcome. To this list could easily be added struggles in southern and eastern Europe, Bolivia, Peru, Mozambique and Nicaragua, amongst others. Wolf was particularly interested in understanding how the everyday lives of peasant farmers, like the followers of Zapata, bound as they were by the season, the weather and the peasant conservatism identified by Marx, could produce such significant social upheaval: under what circumstances might men like Abdul Hussain and Noor Mohammad follow men like Zapata?

In trying to understand this, Wolf focused upon how labour and land, those two essentials that every small-scale peasant farmer around the world cannot do without, could be transformed from being essentials that were used by them into being Polanyi's fictitious commodities that could be bought and sold. Wolf, like Polanyi, believed that this transformation was quite unique in human history, and indeed for most agrarian societies such a transformation would be wholly anathema to their way of life. He believed that in Vietnam, in Russia and in Mexico, amongst other places, land was not a resource but was a part of the community, burdened with social ties and obligations, and was not something that should or could simply be bought and sold. It was, as Pervaiz Qazi's friends and neighbours believed, a mother. Only by forcibly stripping land of these social responsibilities could it be turned into something that might be bought and sold.

This "great transformation," to paraphrase Polanyi, configured the parameters of the temperate grain-livestock complex, established the first global food regime and resulted in human subsistence becoming secondary to the process of buying and selling, which is, as I have said, very recent and has never before been the case in human history. The promotion of the market and its imperatives to buy and sell, at the expense of social ties of reciprocity and obligation that could ensure at least a modicum of security, has produced over the years an accumulation of human suffering that, especially through the eyes of the mass media, was far too widely witnessed in the late twentieth century. It has been witnessed because all too often, like the circumstances that were inflicted upon Pervaiz Qazi, this promotion has not been entered into freely but has been forcibly imposed by the better off in the countryside or in the state, whether they be landlords, colonizers or peasant proto-entrepreneurs seeking to improve their position by eliminating any socially-sanctioned ties and obligations that they might have to their neighbours. As I have noted, Marx called this forcible expropriation of the small-scale peasant producer by the better off "primitive accumulation," and it resulted in what he called "alienation": alienation from a guaranteed existence if you worked what you had; alienation from the crops that you produced, which were not used by the family but which would disappear into an anonymous market; and alienation from the work that you undertook, as increasingly people of the land viewed themselves not as the repository of knowledge and of skills but as merely a source of muscle-power and brawn for others to use. Alienation is a fundamental precondition of the development of capitalism in agriculture. It is also fundamentally rapacious.

The peasant wars of the twentieth century tried to combat this alienation. As land and labour was transformed into objects to be bought and sold, small-scale peasants like those following Zapata tried to reinforce the social bonds that connected the members of a community to each other by questioning and confronting the powerful forces that were attempting to tear these ties asunder. Peasant revolutionaries tried to do this in two ways: by reasserting forms of community and processes of human interaction that resonated with historical memory even if they did not challenge the inequalities that are ever present in peasant communities; or by trying to conceive of a new form of society capable of providing shelter against the vicissitudes of primitive accumulation, in part by disputing the inequalities and enclosures that are ever-present in peasant communities and beyond. This latter path was the path of the Zapatistas, who tried to creatively erect a radical and egalitarian democracy on the basis of rural communities that were inextricably divided by power and privilege.

A key to peasant resistance was land: for small-scale peasants like Abdul Hussain, Noor Mohammad and Emiliano Zapata, land provided a right to food, a right to work and a right to survive, and thus dignity and daily bread. In the first three-quarters of the twentieth century, small-scale peasants around the world were witnessing the forces of modernity eviscerating their world, as rural elites used legal and illegal methods to forcibly evict peasants from their territory, fence it in and enclose it for their own private use. In so doing, peasant land was transformed from being a mother into being a commodity to be bought and sold. This was passively and actively resisted by peasants, who called instead, in their hundreds of millions, for pro-poor redistributive land reform, by consent if possible, by force if necessary.

Pro-poor redistributive land reform involves changing property owner-ship and access rights in land. In a canonical but apocryphal example that nonetheless mirrors the circumstances faced by Abdul Hussain, a miniscule class of predatory landlords have a larger class of small-scale peasant farmers work their land, deriving income from the peasants, by force if necessary, in the form of crop or cash rent or tribute that is used to maintain a com-paratively lavish lifestyle and the ability to impose their will upon the class of small-scale peasant farmers. This Faustian form of "agrarian structure," in which a small rural dominant class lives off the work of the mass of the rural population, has been extremely common in Europe, Asia, Africa and Latin America, even though it is a structure based on the oppressive exploi-tation of the majority by a minority, and so is economically undemocratic and socially unjust. The most wretched example of this is sharecropping, which, like the lives of Abdul Hussain and Noor Mohammad, is based on sustaining an enfeebled peasantry completely dependent on the landlord for access to their land.

Peasant movements around land sought to overthrow these pernicious agrarian structures even as those very structures were, during the course of the twentieth century, being captured by and transformed into more capitalist forms of agricultural production as the global food regime matured. Using the slogan of "land to the tiller," land reform can generally try to do one of three things (Warriner 1969, Borras Jr. 2007). First, it can try and consolidate scattered plots of land — like the twelve plots worked by Abdul Hussain — into one holding so that peasants do not have to spend their time going to and from plots but can rather devote their time and their energies to working their land. Secondly, land reform can try and provide protection for tenants, whether they pay in cash or in crops: protection so that small-scale peasant farmers like the Pakhtun families displaced from their hamlet by their landlord do not have to face such circumstances because they have obtained enforceable security over their access to land even if they do not own it. Third, land reform can be redistributive and pro-poor, trying to ensure that the effective control of landed property in rural communities is rearranged: land is reallocated from the rural elite to those markedly poorer, insecure smallholders who, being freed of the exactions of rent and tribute, are able to improve their livelihood security by having real and substantive power over the land they work, the labour they possess and the crops they produce.

Both economic and socio-cultural reasons can be given for supporting land reform in any one of these three guises. Economically, it is argued by many that small-scale peasant farming is more productive per piece of land than other forms of farming (Berry and Cline 1979). In other words, small-scale peasant farms produce more surplus per unit of land than large-scale farms. Huge reams of data, and much money, has been spent in trying to substantiate this claim, which nonetheless remains hotly contested, for it provides the kernel of a populist rationale to sustain peasant farming in the face of changing agricultural production practices. Simply put, people that support this so-called "inverse relationship" between farm size and farm productivity eagerly believe that smaller farms, by producing more per unit of land, will generate higher incomes than larger farms, and in so doing will have a greater anti-poverty impact in the countryside (Eastwood, Lipton and Newell 2009).

Socio-culturally, it is argued that land was and is the basis of any peasant's right, exercised or otherwise, to choose a way of life. Land is a territorial space where peasants, even in conditions of extreme inequality, can choose to exercise their autonomy and their agency, and hence assert their individual dignity. Peasant identity is rooted in a profound psychological and spiritual relationship with the land, a source of autonomy and agency from which flows an array of intimate identities, interdependent kinship relations, individual notions of honour, deep-rooted understandings of meaning and indeed life itself.

The relationship of the peasant to the land is, however, more than just the foundation of the household and its intimate relations. The land of the peasant is also the basis of the peasant's community, which can witness both greater and lesser degrees of equality since land, as I have already shown, provides a territorial space in which power can coalesce into social relations and conditions of identity, privilege and poverty. After all, land is the basis of the power of the landlord over the community as well as the relative disempowerment of the sharecropper and tenant. These social conditions and relations are affected by and reflected in the ties of extended real and fictitious kinship, socially-sanctioned obligation and reciprocity and the implicit horizontal and vertical trust that is rooted in a collective cultivation of land that not only produces the subsistence needs of the family and the community but also produces the collective imaginations that are found within the community.

Collective imagination has its greatest expression in myths, rites, folklore and popular religion — land in a peasant community is interwoven into all of the practices carried on around it, being a receptacle of the sacred and the secular, accommodating diffuse forces through which the gestures of tradition are created, the symbols of power are configured and the investiture of authority that land gives to those who effectively control it, whether lord or peasant, is conferred. So, land gives prestige and influence that is far beyond that of the merely economic, being closely connected to a peasant and a peasant community's sense of identity, justice and equality.

Land, or more precisely the growing alienation of the small-scale peasant from the land as commodification and a global food regime were established, fuelled the peasant wars of the twentieth century. The Mexican agrarian revolution was but the first of a series of powerful peasant movements that sought to dispossess predatory landed property and distribute reallocated land to the tiller, movements that took on an increasingly nationalist and anti-colonialist hue as the century progressed. In the early and middle part of the century, peasant movements were commonly allied to revolutionary socialist movements, as in Russia, China and Vietnam. This occurred because the Soviet Union in particular had a clear prescription for how to deal with insurgent peasantries: as Engels had suggested, turn peasant demands for the redistributive expropriation of land from landlords into a means of mobilizing the countryside in support of revolutionary and anti-colonial nationalist movements, carrying movements for independence, self-determination and socialism into the countryside through the tool of expropriation. This prescription led to the rapid growth of socialist-led, peasant-based nationalism in Asia, Africa and Latin America, a growth that in the end put the question of the peasant's access to land on the table for the United States.

For peasant-based, socialist-led movements the initial advocacy of land to the tiller through redistributive expropriation was to be but a first step in the creation of much larger socialist farms that usually adopted one of two forms: state farms, in which land that had been confiscated from predatory landed property but that remained after the redistribution of land to tillers was formed into single-unit large-scale farms managed by state-appointed directors, funded from the state budget and worked by landless residents who were recruited to work a wage, producing crops in accordance with the dictates of centralized planning; and collective farms, which were essentially agricultural producer co-operatives based on combining small-scale farms into much larger, commonly-owned pools of land, labour and other resources, and with incomes that were similarly pooled (Swain 1985). These forms of socialist farm production have, since the collapse of the Soviet Union, all but disappeared: their demonstrated ability to improve farm productivity was poor, and as a result their ability to enhance food production weak (Nolan 1988). They have disappeared because of a counter-reform, in which state and collective farms were broken up and redistributed to the farmers who worked them, leading to the creation of a "post-socialist" small-scale peasantry, most notably in China but also elsewhere (Nolan 1982, Akram-Lodhi 2005a).

American foreign policy advisers were well aware of the rise of peasant-based, socialist-led movements that put land to the tiller at the centre of their political demands. During the 1950s it became increasingly obvious to political and business leaders in North America and Europe that the only way of suppressing militant peasant movements for land was in fact to give them land as a means of quelling their militancy (Ladejinsky 1977). This pre-emptive and co-optive reasoning was fuelled in particular by the rise of militant peasant movements and tenant unions in Italy and Japan following the end of World War II; the U.S. won the war, but the peasant-led land occupations that swept southern Italy between 1944 and 1949 made it appear that the U.S. might lose the peace in the countryside to forces supportive of the USSR. This logic was but further propelled by the victory of Mao Zedong and the Chinese communists, who during the mid 1950s rapidly introduced collective farming, seemingly creating an alternative form of rural economy with implications for many that lived in the sprawlingly diverse and desperately poor countrysides of Asia, Africa and Latin America (Nolan 1976). Moreover, when, under U.S. military occupation, land reform was introduced in Japan and then later in Korea and Taiwan, it clearly served not only to placate the peasantry but also to create a conformist foundation upon which re-established conservative governments could rule (Lipton 2009). So, by the late 1950s the need for land reform became quite explicit in the thinking of the U.S. state; officials like Dean Acheson and Charles Brannan supported it, and advisors like Wolf Ladejinsky actively advocated land reform.

The U.S. approach to and understanding of land reform in the 1950s and 1960s turned the ideas of the Bolshevik Revolution on their head (Johnson and Barlowe 1954). Drawing on their country's experience in the nineteenth century, and in particular the success of Abraham Lincoln's 1862 *Homestead Act* in energizing the creation of self-sustaining family farms across the American West, the U.S. rhetorically sought to propagate not the collective farms of the Soviet Union but rather a small-scale peasant-based "family farming" model that offered a stable and unadventurous basis on which to configure a food and agricultural policy in developing capitalist countries, a model that was predicated upon small-scale peasant farms operating within a deepening and broadening capitalist economy subject to the dictates of the market imperative that was increasingly inserted into the global food regime (Friedmann 1978). It was a model that was not based upon redistributive expropriation, as was the Soviet and Chinese approach, but rather redistribution with financial compensation to the landed classes whose land was to be confiscated, along with a series of exemptions that would allow certain rural groups to not have their land taken away. Such compensation meant that if land was to be lost, the powerful would not be emasculated; rather, their power would assume a new form.

So it came to be that in both the socialist world and the capitalist one, between the 1950s and the 1970s land and agrarian reform was introduced to accommodate the increasingly assertive demands of revolutionary and nationalist peasantries. Whether it was attempted socialist transformation in Algeria, Mozambique and Ethiopia, capitalist transformation directly under the U.S.-led Alliance for Progress in Latin America and South Vietnam, or capitalist transformation under state-led nationalist regimes in countries as diverse as Bolivia, India, Egypt or Iran, efforts at introducing land and agrarian reform were widespread (Akram-Lodhi, Borras Jr. and Kay 2007). However, for all the efforts that went into redistributive land and agrarian reform in this thirty year period, the result was surprisingly disappointing for the rural landless and small-scale peasantry.

In Latin America and the Caribbean, despite attempts at land reform in Bolivia, Chile, Colombia, Guatemala, Mexico and Peru, and then later in Nicaragua, three-quarters of all farmers had access to only 10 percent of all arable land by the 1990s: a striking indictment of the continuing ability of landed classes and foreign-owed plantations to shape and capture processes of state-led land and agrarian reform in Latin America that, outside revolutionary episodes in Mexico and Cuba, failed to bring about a more equitable distribution of land and a more equitable society (Weis 2007). In Latin America the principle beneficiaries of land reform were the already-dominant agrarian elites (Petras and Veltmeyer 2005).

In Asia, notwithstanding successful agrarian reform in Japan, Korea and Taiwan, along with the much later process of decollectivization and the resulting establishment of small-scale peasant family farming in China and Vietnam, India, Indonesia, Pakistan, the Philippines and Sri Lanka, all witnessed, at best, modest land reforms that in many instances served to paradoxically redistribute land from the land- and asset-poor to the landed classes. Large parts of Asia witnessed what was in effect a counter-reform dressed up in the rhetoric of land reform and which no doubt contributed to poor agricultural performance in grain production in the 1960s (Bremen and Mundle 1991). Even in Iran, which did redistribute land to small-scale peasants in an attempt to create a basis of support in rural society for the Shah's dictatorship, large landowners were able to retain the best quality land, access to state support and, critically, access to adequate and timely supplies of water. So in Asia redistributive land reform was captured to benefit rural dominant classes, not the landless and small-scale peasantry.

Some success was witnessed in tenancy reform: in West Bengal, India, and in particular with Operation Barga, which commenced in 1978 (Dasgupta 1984). Operation Barga recorded the names of the *bargadars* — sharecroppers — that constituted the majority of West Bengal's rural population, as well as educating sharecroppers about their cultivation rights under the law. Recording was necessary because Operation Barga made sharecropper rights hereditary and thus perpetual; in addition, the state government guaranteed the *bargadars* a fixed share of the crop, which was set at 75 percent if the sharecropper supplied the non-labour farm inputs; and lastly, anti-eviction measures were enacted in order to prevent landlords from forcing *bargadars* off the land. In 1979 Operation Barga was reinforced legally: the onus of disproving a claim to bargadar rights was put onto the landowners rather than the tenant, as had previously been the case, while the ability of landowners to claim exemptions from the programme was made more stringent.

Between 1977 and 1990, the registration of sharecroppers in West Bengal rose from 23 percent of the sharecropping population to 65 percent of the sharecropping population (Ghatak, Gertler and Banerjee 2002). As sharecroppers had to register, and thus openly challenge their landlords, this is an indication of the extent to which Operation Barga collectively empowered them. Moreover, agricultural growth in West Bengal improved, rural poverty declined and both food intake and wages in the countryside increased (National Centre for Agricultural Economics and Policy Research 1996). Operation Barga was possibly the most successful land reform carried out in the north of post-independence India or possibly in the developing capitalist countries of Asia, barring those reforms in Japan, Korea and Taiwan.

In Africa, where much of the continent still had large tracts of land available for cultivation, anti-colonial political leaders in central and western Africa that had mobilized rural populations on the basis of the need for political independence and agrarian transformation were either overthrown or assassinated and replaced by leaders more interested in pillaging the state or accommodating emerging rural dominant classes and former colonial overlords. At the same time, colonially-created inequalities in access to land in the export-oriented agricultures of Kenya, southern Africa and northwest Africa were not tackled except in the case of Mozambique and Algeria (Borras Jr., Kay and Akram-Lodhi 2007). Ethiopia's attempt at creating state farms without laying the foundations of a technological transformation in agriculture, along with the extreme degree of coercion used in the program, resulted in dismal failure even as it engendered famine conditions in much of the Wollo region (Githinji and Mersha 2007). Egypt's land reform under Gamal Nasser was reversed under Anwar Sadat (Bush 2007), as were reforms in Syria first introduced under the Ba'ath Party and later reversed by the same party. In short, for much of Africa and the Middle East, access to land changed very little following political independence. Landless and land-poor small-scale peasants continued to need land, in the face of increasingly inequitable agrarian structures.

So land reform between the 1950s and 1970s failed to bring rural social justice to large swathes of the world's small-scale peasantry. Lengthy delays by politicians charged with passing the legislation allowed predatory landlords to develop ways to evade the law, often through the fictitious re-registration of land to family members or indeed to smallholding peasant tenants who then had no power over the land they were only theoretically assigned (Borras Jr., Kay and Akram-Lodhi 2007). Exemption provisions commonly allowed large landowners to evade redistribution, often on the basis of being able to demonstrate that they were "efficiently" "self-cultivating" their holding. Even in the absence of these factors, landlords could simply alter land title documents so as to maintain their control of land. Together, large landowners in much of Asia, Africa and Latin America were able to escape provisions designed to bring about pro-poor redistributive land reform.

The ability to evade reform was enhanced by the fact that some land reform provisions required that tenants make claims upon their landlords, and tenants might not only be intimidated by landlords or local state officials in their pay but might also not necessarily understand their rights or the processes and procedures through which such rights might be enforced (Borras Jr. 2009). Indeed, the mere registration of a title could be a time-consuming process in which small-scale peasants could be subjected to intimidation or worse by rural landed classes. Operation Barga was a success precisely because these practices were turned on their head. For the majority of the world's small-scale peasantry, though, the legal system did not help; often courts were beholden to landowners and even if the courts were not, landowners had the ability to use the courts to delay implementation of tenancy and redistributive reform.

The result was that tenancy reform and pro-poor redistributive land reform lost its momentum by the mid 1970s. While it succeeded in lanc-

5

THE FATHER, THE SON
AND THE HOLY GHOST MAKE
UNLIKELY REVOLUTIONARIES

PEASANTS AND THE
GREEN REVOLUTION

Few people have heard of Fritz Haber, but those who have think that he was one of the most important people of the twentieth century. Haber, whose photographs from middle age show a man that cultivated the genteel air of a central European aristocrat, was born in Breslau, Germany, or what is now Wrocław, Poland, in 1868, the son of one of the oldest Jewish merchant families in the town. His mother died from complications arising from his birth, and while Haber's father remarried when he was seven, growing up motherless had a lasting impact on the ambition and anxiety that shaped his later life (Charles 2005).

In 1891 Haber got his Ph.D. in chemistry, having been a quite undistinguished student. He worked briefly in his father's chemical business and at the Swiss Federal Institute of Technology in Zürich before assuming in 1894 a teaching post at the University of Karlsruhe where he worked until 1911. In 1900 he married Clara Immerwahr, two years his junior, who was also a member of Breslau's Jewish community and whom he had known since childhood. Immerwahr was notable in her own right: she was the first woman to obtain a doctoral degree in chemistry from Breslau's university. But when she married Haber and joined him in Karlsruhe, her own efforts to pursue an academic career were stymied by her position as Haber's wife, and she was forced to give up her own research, becoming Haber's unrecognized English translator. In 1902 Haber and Immerwahr's son Hermann was born, but their marriage does not appear to have been a particularly happy one: Immerwahr once said to a friend:

> It has always been my attitude that a life has only been worth living if one has made full use of all one's abilities and tried to live out every kind of experience human life has to offer. It was under that impulse, among other things, that I decided to get married …

[But] the life I got from it was very brief ... The main reasons for that was Fritz's oppressive way of putting himself first in our home and marriage, so that a less ruthlessly self-assertive personality was simply destroyed. (Cornwell 2003)

In the first decade of the twentieth century, as the temperate grain-livestock complex consolidated, Haber was one of a large number of scientists around the world who believed that the world's population was overtaking the world's food supply. This idea has a very long historical genesis but is most commonly associated with the Reverend Thomas Malthus, who, in his 1798 "Essay on the Principle of Population," had written that "the power of population is so superior to the power of the earth to produce subsistence for man that premature death must in some shape visit the human race" (Malthus 1993: 61). Malthus' grim fatalism, which had a strong element of snobbish class antagonism, had long been criticized; yet he had singularly shaped views of the British imperialists that had forced Pervaiz Qazi to export wheat and shaped the views of European bourgeois elites across the continent — including in Breslau, Berlin and Karlsruhe.

The best way of increasing world food production and preventing widespread starvation lay in decisively accelerating the amount of food produced on each and every piece of farm land: in other words, by ever-increasing crop yields producing ever-larger farm surpluses. And the best way of increasing crop yields was to enhance the fertility of the soil. Small-scale peasant farmers around the world had through history improved soil fertility by using animal manure and human excrement, which contained the nitrogen that promoted plant growth. So, the best way of increasing soil fertility was to augment the application of nitrogen to the soil, and this is where Haber came into the picture. Quantities of nitrogen-bearing sulfer nitrates could be found in nature, particularly in deposits in Chile; but the physical chemistry practiced by Haber had the potential to develop a way to artificially synthesize ammonia, which contained nitrogen, so ending a reliance on nature and ensuring that virtually unlimited supplies of cheap nitrogen could be made available to the farmers of the world (Smil 2004).

This is precisely what Haber was able to achieve. In 1909 he developed a method that employed extreme temperatures, a catalyst — highly pressurized coal, of which Germany had an abundance — and water to fix atmospheric nitrogen to hydrogen, literally synthesizing ammonia from thin air. Haber patented his invention, and the huge German chemical company BASF (which later was absorbed into the Nazi-supporting behemoth IG Farben before regaining its independence after World War II), knowing that the artificial synthesis of ammonia was a licence to print money, bought Haber's patents, making him a wealthy man (Charles 2005). Haber's discovery was a necessary precondition for the widespread introduction of nitrogen-based chemical fertilizers on farmers' fields around the world, which vastly increased the productivity of agriculture: world cereal production increased seven-fold during the twentieth century as a direct result of the use of chemical fertilizers based on Haber's discovery (Smil 2004). Indeed, as Daniel Charles (2005) beautifully notes, half of all the nitrogen in the human body comes from a factory that uses Haber's process. No wonder Haber won the Nobel Prize for chemistry in 1918: we have all been affected by Fritz Haber's revolution.

By 1918, though, Clara Immerwahr was dead by her own hand. The reason: Haber's discoveries were used to wage war. This was true of the Haber process, although in this, Haber was not personally implicated: in 1913 BASF began mass-producing synthetic ammonia and oxidizing it, producing a man-made saltpetre that could be used to make gunpowder. The use of Haber's process for this supported Germany's ability to wage World War I: without it, Germany would have been disastrously defeated in a year. But Haber's role in World War I went far beyond the use of the Haber process. From his base at the Kaiser Wilhelm Institute for Physical Chemistry and Electrochemistry in Berlin, to which he moved in 1911, Haber, still intensely ambitious, fiercely nationalistic and determined to demonstrate his patriotism, at the request of the military began work on a new weapon to break the stalemate of World War I's trenches (Charles 2005).

Haber led a team of chemists working on the development of chlorine gas, a chemical weapon that reacts with water in the mucosa of the lungs to form hydrochloric acid, which, through asphyxiation, can be lethal. Working with IG Farben, which designed and developed the weapon's delivery system in artillery shells so that it could be deployed against soldiers in trenches, Haber's dedication to the project was such that he personally oversaw Germany's first use of chlorine gas at the Second Battle of Ypres on April 22, 1915, when 168 tons of the gas were released over a 6.5 kilometre stretch of the front, killing some six thousand French and African soldiers within ten minutes and blinding many more (Charles 2005). On May 15, as Haber was about to depart for the Eastern Front to organize and order the use of chlorine gas against the Russians, Immerwahr, who had deeply disagreed with her husband's use of chemistry to support the war, took Haber's service revolver and shot herself in their garden (Cornwall 2003). The suicide had little effect on Haber: he departed for the Eastern Front without delay and in 1917 married for a second time.

So, the father of chemical warfare and the creator of the first weapons of mass destruction gained his initial fame developing embryonic chemical processes that were designed to technologically revolutionize world food production. There is, though, another peculiarly perverse connection between Haber, death and food. During the 1920s, teams at Haber's institute worked on research with the potential to use cyanide as a fumigant in grain stores to kill insects, thereby reducing losses in storage. The work had possible applications across the world of farming; storage losses in agriculture are significant in many places. This research resulted in the commercial manufacture by IG Farben of a cyanide gas known as Zyklon B, which was engineered by Haber's research team. Haber's research had led to the death of his wife; now his research would reach out from his own grave and lead to the death of many members of his extended family.

Despite converting to Christianity early in his life so as to show his peers that he was a "real" German, and despite the pivotal and primary role that he had played in World War I in creating weapons of mass destruction, for which he was decorated, Haber was a target of Nazi attacks following their assumption of power in 1933 (Charles 2005). Haber was forced to leave Germany for Cambridge, but did not stay, dying in a hotel in Basel, Switzerland, in January 1934. But a terrifying coda to his life happened in 1942: Zyklon B, which was supposed to reduce grain storage losses, was selected by the Nazis as their preferred method of extermination at both the Auschwitz-Birkenau and Majdanek concentration camps (Cornwall 2003). Haber's research directly led to the mass murder of roughly 1.2 million people at the camps, including the children of his cousins. This may have led Haber's son Hermann to take his own life in 1946.

Fritz Haber, architect of death, was also the intellectual progenitor of the Green Revolution, a phrase which has been used to describe a "package" of seed, fertilizer and water technologies that, when introduced across the developing capitalist countries in the 1960s as the failure of pro-poor redistributive land reform became apparent, led to remarkable improvements in farm productivity in the poorer parts of the world (Ross 1998). In Asia and Latin America, cereal production tripled between 1961 and 2001; even in Africa, a place where many people think a Green Revolution never took place, grain production rose 2.5 times over the forty-year period (Akram-Lodhi 2012). Increased production stabilized, and in many cases, dramatically lowered, the price of food, increased the incomes of some farmers and allowed world agriculture to feed far more than it ever had before. Thomas Malthus was put back in his box by the Green Revolution.

The introduction of Green Revolution agricultural technologies did not occur by accident. Innovations such as the use of chemical fertilizers or seeds that were purposefully bred to maximize farm yields in a given agroecology or the appropriately timed application of water: these had been known for decades. Where the Green Revolution was different was in its systematic state- and philanthropic-led effort to coordinate technological changes in world farming so as to boost yields and thus ensure that such changes were widely adopted by both small-scale peasant farmers and by large-scale capitalist farms and plantation estates in developing capitalist countries. The reason for the need to boost yields was easy to see: in the wake of growing food shortages in the 1960s the ineffectiveness of capitalist and socialist land and agrarian reform to redistribute adequate amounts of land to land-poor and landless small-scale peasants meant that new attempts had to be made to increase agricultural production and productivity on already existing farms and within existing, inequitable, agrarian structures. That this was coordinated must be stressed: the Agricultural Development Council, funded by the Rockefeller Foundation and to a lesser extent the Ford Foundation, in 1966 commissioned the writing of *Getting Agriculture Moving*, a paean to the logic of the Green Revolution, and freely distributed the book across Asia in order to encourage an acceptance of the need for a technological transformation of Asian agriculture (Mosher 1966).

Haber's role in the Green Revolution was to provide the cheap nitrogen that was necessary for chemically-responsive so-called "modern varieties" (MV) of wheat and rice to grow to their full potential. Norman Borlaug's role was to provide the chemically-responsive MVs of wheat upon which the nitrogen could be used. Like Haber, Borlaug is widely unknown, although some credit him with saving more lives than any other person in human history (Hesser 2006). If Fritz Haber is the "ghost" from whom the distant origins of the Green Revolution can be traced, Borlaug is undoubtedly its "father."

Norman Borlaug, the eldest of four children, was born in rural Iowa in 1914, just before Fritz Haber introduced weapons of mass destruction into World War I. Borlaug worked on the family's fifty hectare farm raising maize, oats, hay, cattle, pigs and chickens from the age of seven to age nineteen, by which time he had become intimately aware of how the dust bowl was wreaking havoc on the farms of neighbouring states in the rural midwest. The agrarian depression wrought by the dust bowl led to the creation of a state program, which Borlaug took advantage of and which led him to the University of Minnesota. Interrupting his university education several times during the 1930s in order to make the money he needed to pay for his education, Borlaug worked on several New Deal projects to assist the unemployed; many of those he worked with were not getting enough to eat, and from an early age, with his background in farming and his experience of social provisioning, Borlaug understood the savage permutations of hunger, which undoubtedly affected him deeply. In 1938 Borlaug attended a lecture by Elvin C. Stakman, a plant pathologist, which encouraged him to switch from forest management and into plant pathology; in 1942 Borlaug obtained his Ph.D. in genetics (Hesser 2006).

In the early 1940s Mexico was heavily dependent on wheat imports, mainly from the U.S. Henry Wallace, Franklin Delano Roosevelt's Secretary of Agriculture and formerly of the Pioneer Hi-Bred seed company family, had been unable to get any money from the U.S. Congress for agricultural aid to Mexico. Wallace approached the Rockefeller Foundation, a huge U.S. philanthropic organization funded by some of the proceeds of the Rockefeller oil fortune, which had a long history of promoting rural development, particularly in China during the 1920s and 1930s when, reflecting John D. Rockefeller's Baptist upbringing, an evangelical missionary boom into the country was underway in support of Chiang Kai-shek's authoritarian anti-communist Kuomingtang.

The Rockefeller Foundation in turn approached Elvin Stakman about leading an Office of Special Studies, to be housed within the Mexican Ministry of Agriculture but paid for and directed by the Rockefeller Foundation (Ross 1998). The Office of Special Studies was to conduct research on soil development, maize and wheat production and plant pathology. Stakman chose J. George "Dutch" Harrar to lead the project, and it was Harrar who enticed Borlaug to leave a good job at the DuPont Chemical Company and begin work in Mexico, in 1944 (Hesser 2006).

Borlaug joined the Cooperative Wheat Research and Production Program. Its objective was to increase Mexican wheat production by doing research in genetics, plant breeding, plant pathology, entomology, agronomy, soil science and cereal technology. Drawing on his experience of the dust bowl, Borlaug believed that the problem facing Mexico's agriculture was that it was not adequately using the abundant science of plant breeding, in which he was trained. Borlaug applied his knowledge of genetics and of the importance of agroecological context to breed a series of high-yielding, disease-resistant semi-dwarf varieties of wheat that became the harbingers of the Green Revolution (Byres, Crow and Ho 1983).

Modern seed varieties are bred to absorb more micronutrients from the soil while simultaneously expending less energy on the growth of a shorter, thicker and thus stronger inedible stalk, resulting in uniformly smaller plants with larger kernels of grain, which contributes to yield increases (Kloppenburg 2004). It is precisely because they absorb more micronutrients from the soil that MVs require the application of chemical fertilizers designed around Haber's process: soils depleted of nitrogen need to be restored, and can be, chemically. MVs also require, critically, timely and appropriate quantities of water, which requires in turn substantial irrigation and drainage systems to supply the water necessary to refashion an agroecology so that chemically-responsive MVs can work: this was a key reason why Borlaug's plant breeding efforts worked. Borlaug, moreover, cross-bred his semi-dwarf wheat varieties with disease-resistant wheat varieties: so-called "shuttle breeding" increased the spread of immunity amongst different strains of wheat; increased the efficiency with which plants captured available sunlight for the purposes of photosynthesis; were less sensitive to the amount of light that they received; and allowed more than one generation of a wheat crop to be grown a year (Hesser 2006). Together, Borlaug's plant breeding brought forth three remarkable innovations in the history of world agriculture, while disease resistance and enhanced photosensitivity also meant that Borlaug's MVs were suitable for an array of agroecological conditions.

Borlaug was indeed the father of a revolution: in 1956 Mexico became self-sufficient in wheat for the first time in its history (Hesser 2006). His work became well known, disseminated worldwide through the offices of the Rockefeller Foundation but also through a number of national agricultural research centres that were trying to replicate what the Cooperative Wheat Research and Production Program had achieved. In 1963 his program became the International Maize and Wheat Improvement Center (CIMMYT in Spanish), and while it remained within the Ministry of Agriculture its remit became global. In 1964 Borlaug became director of the CIMMYT's International Wheat Improvement, and in 1966 CIMMYT was given its autonomy from the Mexican government, being located within the newly-established World Bank-led Consultative Group on International Agricultural Research (CGIAR), a global network of international research and training institutes funded largely by the Ford and Rockefeller Foundations (Ross 1998). CGIAR had an explicit mission: spread the Green Revolution.

To spread the Green Revolution, in 1963 the Mexican state, supported by the Rockefeller Foundation, sent Borlaug to India (Byres, Crow and Ho 1983). As I have said, wheat has long been grown in India, but despite the best efforts of the British to turn northern India into the Empire's granary, yields were well below those recorded elsewhere, and so wheat was relatively expensive unless distributed through rigged markets that benefitted the imperial overlord. Borlaug set out to change that, strongly believing that wheat production in India could rapidly expand in the wide array of Indian agro-ecologies and that MVs could supply India with significant increases in food calories (Lipton and Longhurst 1989). Borlaug supplied one hundred kilos of seed from each of the four most promising wheat strains that CIMMYT had developed and 630 promising selections in advanced generations to the Indian Agricultural Research Institute in October 1963 (Hesser 2006).

Borlaug's MVs in India went through extensive piloting in test plots, where they appeared to work well, but widespread distribution of the seeds was slowed by resistance to them within the state-owned seed companies that dominated the Indian seed market and by a war between India and Pakistan. But when, in 1965, an MV wheat crop was finally sown, late in the season, which resulted in it germinating poorly, it still showed a 70 percent increase in yield, the highest yield recorded in the region at that time. With such success, and the wartime emergency, Borlaug was given the go-ahead to bypass the state-owned seed companies entirely and supply MVs on a much larger scale. So in 1966 India imported 18,000 tons of MVs, the biggest single purchase of seed that had yet been recorded; and then in 1967 Pakistan imported almost 2.5 times that amount, enough to seed the entire area that the country cropped in wheat that year. The results, in both countries, were dramatic: in 1968 Pakistan became self-sufficient in wheat, and in 1974 India achieved a similar feat; wheat production increased more than 60 percent in both countries in six years without any significant expansion of farmland (Smil 2000). Higher yields and greater surpluses transformed rural society in both countries: there was not enough labour to harvest the crops when they had to be harvested; there were not enough bullock carts to take the harvested crop to the threshing floor; there were not enough bags to transport the harvested crop; there were not enough rail cars to do the same; and there were not enough storage facilities for the wheat that was being harvested, leading some districts to use schools for grain storage.

Labour shortages in South Asian agriculture in the late 1960s as a result of the adoption of the new agricultural technologies had an important impact on the course taken by the Green Revolution. We now know that the ability to adopt new agricultural technologies in Asia, embodied in the MV–chemical fertilizer–water complex, are not related to the size of the farm: in other words, large, medium and small-sized farms have all adopted the MV–chemical fertilizer–water complex, in part because peasants can buy just what they need to make existing farm land more productive; Green Revolution technologies, in a sense, "save" land (Feder, Just and Zilberman 1985). MVs also require extra labour during planting and harvesting, which, because of multi-cropping, become shorter periods of time and thus could positively affect the demand for waged labour; and the rapid emergence of labour shortages indicate that this did happen. Together, it would appear that the MV–chemical fertilizer–water complex is not biased toward any particular form of farm; but such an appearance is deeply deceiving because of the rapid responses of some small-scale surplus-producing peasant farmers to their changing circumstances in the early years of MV adoption.

Let me put it simply: the labour shortages that occurred in the early years of MV adoption led some small-scale surplus-producing South Asian peasant farmers to reinvest some of their increased earnings in mechanizing, to a lesser or greater extent, their farm operations (Byres, Crow and Ho 1983). Mechanization was seen in the spread of gasoline-powered two-wheel tractor-tillers, four-wheel tractors, mechanical threshers and water pumps capable of drawing up from the aquifer the water needed for the MVs to work. Somewhat later, mechanization was seen in the spread of combine harvesters (Binswanger and Donovan 1987). Mechanization proceeded remarkably rapidly amongst some small-scale surplus-producing peasant farmers, particular in northern South Asia, as they reconfigured their process of farm production away from the messy complexities of allocating petty stocks of capital and family labour toward far more capital-intensive practices.

Within one year of a 1973 ban on tractor imports by the Indian government (local production of tractors began in the early 1960s), 24,000 tractors were being produced annually in the country (United States Agency for International Development and International Rice Research Institute 1986). Also, up until 1975 the government allowed the price of food grains to rise more rapidly than the price of tractors, making tractors relatively cheaper over time, in order to encourage mechanization by those farmers that had most successfully adopted the new agricultural technologies (Ghosh 1988). The most extensive mechanization took place in Punjab, Haryana and western Uttar Pradesh, where the Green Revolution sank its deepest roots: by 1975 threshing across Punjab was almost completely carried out by the 160,000 motorized threshers found in the state, and some combine harvesters had started to be introduced (Byres, Crow and Ho 1983).

In neighbouring Pakistan the speed of adoption was similar: 18,000 tractors were imported between 1966 and 1970, financed initially by the World Bank (International Rice Research Institute and Agricultural Development Council 1983). With the state supporting local crop prices at levels above those of the world market, with tractor purchases being subsidized through state-backed loan schemes and with tractors relatively underpriced relative to other farm tools and equipment because of differential state taxes, the state clearly encouraged mechanization amongst some small-scale surplus-producing peasants that were beginning a process of transformation along more capital-intensive methods and modes of production (Hussain 1988). Even newly-independent and comparatively impoverished Bangladesh the early 1970s saw aid-financed power-driven farm equipment and machinery imported into the country: over a twenty year period more than 6,000 two-wheel tiller-tractors were imported and sold at below-market prices, subsidized by the state and donors, to small-scale surplus-producing peasants that were slowly transforming how they were farming along more capital-intensive lines (International Rice Research Institute and Agricultural Development Council 1983).

The process of mechanization promoted by the states of South Asia did not improve farm productivity; mechanization did not significantly alter cropping intensity, yields or the production of farm surpluses (Binswanger 1978). What mechanization did do, though, was displace agricultural labour (Byres, Crow and Ho 1983). The methods can be difficult to unravel, but in Pakistan in Punjab some transforming farms saw very significant increases in their operated area through the repossession and direct use of previously tenanted land (Hussain 1988). Tenant circumstances were made all the worse because their displacement from their farms was accompanied by an overall reduction in the total use of waged labour as a result of mechanization; tenants were twice marginalized. Bangladesh also witnessed tenant displacement as small-scale mechanization took place, and while the use of family labour, particularly women's field labour, dropped, the effect on the use of waged labour was more mixed; in some cases it went up, but in other cases tenant displacement was accompanied by a reduction in the use of waged labour (Rahman 1986). In India, tractors brought little in the way of material gains to adopters. True, mechanization made labour more productive, which meant that some waged labour was displaced as labour needs per acre were cut; but at times this was offset by increases in the use of waged labour for rural non-farm activities.

Why adopt labour-saving mechanization if the material benefits, in terms of farm productivity, are not apparent? The answer is again deceptively simple: those that mechanized could use markets to acquire the resources of those that were dispossessed even as the dispossessed were compelled out of the need for a job to work for those that mechanized. Mechanization demonstrated a bias against those that could not afford to mechanize: small-scale peasant farmers who had problems growing a surplus. In this way mechanization was part of and contributed to dispossession by differentiation as capitalism began to emerge in South Asian farming, which consequently started to undergo the initial processes of capitalist transformation (Byres, Crow and Ho 1983).

The bias in favour of what I shall call emerging proto-capitalist farms that was apparent in mechanization was not surprising: when two-wheel tiller-tractors were sold at a concessional price in Bangladesh, those able to take advantage of the scheme would not have been the poorest; it would have been the relatively better-off, surplus-producing small-scale peasant farmer. Similarly, when tractors were sold in India, those able to buy more expensive locally-produced tractors would have been those with the cash earnings from farming to make the large payments needed to purchase farm equipment; it would have been the relatively better-off, surplus-producing small-scale peasant farmer. In Pakistan, state policy was explicit: farm mechanization should be directed at relatively better-off surplus-producing small-scale peasant farmers, who received credit subsidies to buy tractors and who, through their mechanization, were able to start to shift to the large-scale farm operations that more closely resembled that found in capitalist agriculture.

So the Green Revolution was biased toward those surplus producers that had the financial and physical resources needed to take advantage of the benefits it offered: they became the first movers in a process of agrarian change toward capitalist agriculture. Resource-bias meant that the beneficiaries of the Green Revolution were those who could afford to use, as a package,

MVs, chemical fertilizers, water and farm machinery to cumulatively and dramatically improve their farm productivity, their cash flow and hence their economic standing relative to many of their neighbours, in part by starting to use the land and labour-power of some of their neighbours. In this way the Green Revolution ushered in a period of deepening social and economic differentiation between the relatively richer and the relatively poorer in the countryside of South Asia, which is the reason that many believe the Green Revolution penalizes the poor: not just in South Asia but around the world many were eventually rendered landless by the intimate exclusions carried out by neighbours and kin that were propelled by the Green Revolution (Shiva 1989).

The Green Revolution has also been criticized for its impact on agro-ecological biodiversity. The work of Borlaug and his colleagues resulted in an ever-smaller and narrower number of seed varieties being planted around the world (Weis 2007). Diverse local food systems that had adapted over the centuries to space- and place-sensitive needs and preferences were replaced with monocultures produced on an increasingly large scale (Shiva 1993). Green Revolution monocultures relied on ever-larger quantities of inorganic fertilizer, herbicides and pesticides, which, by degrading the ecology within which farming took place, had profound implications for the sustainability of the agricultural techniques and technologies that had been introduced.

Three final points have to be made about the Green Revolution. The first is that it was not led by private capitalists: it was led by the state and the international philanthropic and financial institutions of the era (Ross 1998). It was the philanthropic and financial institutions that paid for the research and propagated the technologies; it was the international financial institutions that encouraged adoption through the transfer of new agricultural technologies or through support for national research and the provision of training for farmers in the use of the new agricultural technologies; it was the state in developing capitalist countries that built and maintained the irrigation and drainage facilities that were of critical importance to the ability of the Green Revolution to deliver; and it was the state in developing capitalist countries that created the local circumstances that would encourage a particular class of surplus-producing small-scale peasant farmers to adopt MVs, chemical fertilizers and mechanization.

The second point is that the outcome of this profound rural change was to draw tens if not hundreds of millions of small-scale peasant farmers into monetary markets, often for the first time in their lives (Akram-Lodhi and Kay 2009). Seeds that small-scale peasant farmers had acquired from portions of their previous harvest now had to be bought; fertilizers that had been provided by the animal and human detritus of life now had to be bought; increasingly, energy had to be paid for; and farm machinery and equipment not only had to be bought but had to be maintained at an additional cost. All of this required cash, and getting cash required an increasing reliance on selling the crops that the farm produced. But the need for cash did more: it was not that peasants wanted to sell their crops; rather, peasants had to sell their crops in order to continue farming. The market imperatives of the capitalist economy became binding. This was, of course, true of emerging proto-capitalist surplus-producing peasants benefitting from the package as they slowly transformed toward more capital-intensive methods of production, but it was also true of poorer small-scale peasants simply wanting to try and improve their meager circumstances. The Green Revolution resulted in swathes of peasants around the world having, for the first time, to compete with each other, in terms of price, delivery conditions and quality. In short, and notwithstanding the genuinely philanthropic impulses felt by many involved in its propagation, the Green Revolution caused market dependence to be built in a slowly emerging capitalist agriculture in parts of South Asia, East Asia and Latin America.

Lastly, if state intervention in the introduction and dissemination of new agricultural technologies facilitated the emergence of market dependence and the integration of peasant farmers around the world into market relations in a way that had hitherto not been the case, then the concurrent effect of the Green Revolution was to shift the same peasant farmers away from local food systems and local food provisioning into an increasingly globalized food regime in which clear differences of power and privilege are witnessed.

These differences of power and privilege apply not only to the emerging differences between peasant farmers within communities, but also to differences in power and privilege between farmers and non-farm actors in the food regime. A source of these differences is obvious if one thinks about it: for millennia peasants had retained and shared seeds (Friis-Hansen 1995). In the 1960s and 1970s, for the first time in human history, peasants came to rely on buying the seeds without which they cannot produce anything. So the reliance on having to purchase MVs placed the manufacturers of seed in control of the "commanding heights" of the farm economy: the seed became the basis for effectively controlling the entire crop production process (Kloppenburg 2004). In order for this to happen, two things had to take place. First, the role of the state in the farm economy of the developing capitalist countries had to change. Second, the ability of private capital to exclusively control seeds would have to be enhanced.

So, the role of the state in rural development changed during the 1980s. Encumbered by private and public debts, a consequence of overborrowing in developing capitalist countries and overlending in developed capitalist countries, developing capitalist countries in the 1980s were forced by a lack of alternatives to turn to the World Bank and International Monetary Fund to provide them with the temporary financial support that would allow some debts to be partially paid while complete financial meltdown was prevented. These programs of financial support came to be called "structural adjustment" and continue to be extremely common in developing capitalist countries, although they are now called "poverty reduction strategies." A structural adjustment program sees a country receiving concessionary loans from the IMF or the World Bank on the strict condition that they implement wideranging, deep-seated and significant changes in economic policy: changes that have the effect of altering the "structure" of the economy in favour of markets, exports and accessibility to transnational capital (Mosley, Harrigan and Toye 1995). As a consequence of structural adjustment in agriculture, states withdrew their support of agriculture and farming: the budgets of agricultural research centres compressed; agricultural extension services by the state withered; state-owned seed, fertilizer and herbicide manufacturers were closed or privatized; trade was liberalized in order to encourage national and global markets to set the prices that farmers received for their crops; state-owned marketing boards were privatized; and rules on the entry of agro-food transnational corporations into developing capitalist countries were eased substantially (Sarris 1990). The result was that the state, as a provider of support to agriculture, was functionally and operationally replaced by globalized agro-food transnational corporations in food and agriculture. Agro-food transnational corporations looked to farming not as a livelihood for farmers but as the source of profits to be distributed to shareholders.

The ability of transnational corporations to control seeds required that it be able to exclusively control the input characteristics of the seeds, so that seed responsiveness could only be guaranteed with the use of other, interdependent farm inputs such as particular herbicides. This is exactly what happened: Monsanto, for example, a very large American agro-food chemical company that in 1982 became the first firm to genetically engineer the characteristics of a plant cell, began marketing Roundup Ready seeds, first in soy and then in maize, sorghum, canola, alfalfa and cotton (Robin 2010). Roundup Ready seeds were called that because they were genetically engineered to be tolerant of glyphosate, the most widely used herbicide in the U.S., which was the key ingredient in a Monsanto-owned herbicide called Roundup. So Monsanto used genetic engineering to ensure that its herbicide would be applied with its seeds, giving it the broader capability to shape on-farm decisions in its interest.

The strongest mechanism by which agro-food transnational corporations can control seeds is by eliminating the seeds' ability to germinate: rendering seeds sterile means plants do not flower or grow fruit after the initial planting; consequently, farmers have to continually buy the seeds that the company exclusively controls. This was precisely the purpose behind so-called "terminator technology": developed in the 1990s by the U.S. Department of Agriculture and Delta and Pine Land Company, acquired by Monsanto in 2007, terminator technology has not yet been commercially introduced because rural civil society around the world has highlighted the potential for abuse that such technologies would likely engender.

The transformation of seeds into exclusively-controlled commodities was the cornerstone by which agro-food transnational corporations such as Monsanto consolidated their position within the world's food and farming systems and the global food regime (Kloppenburg 2004). Monsanto — founded in 1901 in St. Louis, Missouri, the creator of saccharine, the former owner of aspartame and the creator of DDT and Agent Orange — split in 2000; its agricultural chemical business became the only segment to continue in the footsteps of the twentieth-century company. That "new" Monsanto made a gross profit of $5.1 billion in 2010 on net sales of $10.5 billion, and seeds and genomics products accounted for the majority of Monsanto's profitability (Wikinvest 2012).

In the absence of the use of terminator technology, the key to Monsanto's ability to enforce its exclusive ownership of branded seeds, herbicides and more was through the patent protection afforded by the intellectual property rights regime of the U.S. and other countries. So, from the late 1990s onwards Monsanto filed repeated lawsuits against farmers in Canada and the U.S. that argued that the sale of seed containing Monsanto's patented genes required farmers to take steps to prevent the seed being carried by the wind into neighbouring fields operated by farmers that had not purchased the seeds, because they might germinate without the farmer having to pay Monsanto (Robin 2010). This litigation has repeatedly been found in favour of Monsanto in both Canada and the U.S. and has led to large fines for the large-scale family farmers found to have infringed Monsanto's patent.

Widely-held worries about biotechnological engineering and "Frankenfoods" should be seen in light of the ability of agro-food transnational corporations to control the commanding heights of the global farm economy and the global food regime (Weis 2007). Biotechnological research creates products for transnational corporations — like Monsanto — that are based on transferring specific genes or sequences of genes within or across plant species in order to create varieties with a set of predetermined characteristics deemed useful by the company. Unlike the Green Revolution, which saw plant breeders carefully selecting genes across species in order to replicate specific traits as has been done for the history of agriculture, the gene revolution sees chemical companies genetically modifying plant characteristics within but more commonly across species in order to produce specific traits (Fukuda-Parr 2007). The technology treadmill continues to roll: this quest to reconfigure gene sequences across species is why the gene revolution creates "transgenic" crops.

Arguments around transgenic crops are fiercely partisan but are usually based on faulty knowledge. Many argued that transgenic crops will increase food production and avert hunger in developing capitalist countries (Herring 2008). But the world already produces enough food, and in any case transgenic crops need not be more productive per unit of land than non-transgenic crops. So the proposition that the world needs transgenic crops to prevent the recurrence of a Malthusian nightmare is fallacious. What transgenic crops do is put much more effective and efficient private control of farm research, development and marketing in the hands of agro-food transnational corporations so that potentially profit-enhancing products and applications are created and disseminated, thereby boosting the bottom-line of agro-food transnational corporations such as Monsanto (Fukuda-Parr 2007). Transgenic crops are not about improving small-scale peasant productivity; they are about monopolistically consolidating the profitability needs of agro-food transnational corporations (Rossett 2006).

The Green Revolution saw widening social inequality around the world, both within and between communities. The transgenic gene revolution threatens to do the same by extending the control by corporations of the food system into a yet deeper, more all-encompassing realm. The principal mechanism by which this is being done now is the creation of the Alliance for a Green Revolution in Africa (AGRA). Funded to the tune of $150 million by the Bill and Melinda Gates Foundation and the Rockefeller Foundation, AGRA says that it will rely on conventional gene selection to try and create sustained increases in yields of African crops. AGRA even sought the sage advice of Norman Borlaug; despite his receipt of the Nobel Prize in 1970, deep doubts about the efficacy of the Green Revolution had made him something of a pariah amongst the international rural development institutions, particularly as the backlash against chemical- and water-intensive hybrid monocultures deepened.

The commitment of AGRA and the agricultural development arm of the Gates Foundation to a non-transgenic approach to creating an African Green Revolution must, to some degree, be doubted. This is because in late 2006 the Gates Foundation hired Robert Horsch, a former vice-president of Monsanto who had worked at the company as a committed transgenic partisan for twenty-five years as its Director of Agricultural Programs. Indeed, Horsch was part of the team that developed Roundup Ready. Another senior program officer at the Gates Foundation also has a long-standing record of involvement in cattle genetic improvements. And of course Bill Gates has substantial private investments in genetic research, being a shareholder in Genomics, the Craig Ventnor company that first decoded the human genome and is currently archiving an array of gene sequences for use in a variety of profitable ways.

If Fritz Haber is a ghost in the history of the Green Revolution, Norman Borlaug is its father and through AGRA continued to be so until his death in 2009 at the age of ninety-five. But despite his best intentions, the Green Revolution was not about solving the riddle of food-based social inequality in the countryside of developing capitalist countries. No: by drawing slowly transforming, surplus-producing proto-capitalist peasants in different and complex ways into an increasingly global food system the Green Revolution facilitated the gradual emergence of capitalism in agriculture in developing capitalist countries. But for this transformation to be complete there was a need to expunge the possibility of small-scale peasant farmers sustaining any kind of self-reliance. This, which we will excavate in the next chapter, fundamentally contributed to deepening global inequality in access to food.

Technological transformations in agriculture are not neutral with regard to the methods of farm production: they are part of their evolution. So AGRA cannot be divorced from the parameters of the global food regime: AGRA and the continuing quest for a Green Revolution in Africa are about laying the groundwork for the further and deeper opening of African agriculture to the market imperatives promoted by transnational seed, chemical and fertilizer corporations seeking dominant positions in profitable and potentially profitable markets. Bill Gates' philanthropic efforts may indeed be well-meaning, but the practical implications of the deepening of the market imperative in the global food regime suggest that he has become the "son" to Borlaug's father and Haber's holy ghost. A more unlikely trio of capitalist revolutionaries would be hard to find, but the meaning of what they have done and are doing for the small-scale peasantry around the world is clear enough, as corporate-led dispossession by displacement and differentiation continues its untrammeled course, with, as we will see, implications for the food upon which we all rely.

6

A FEW GRAINS OF RICE

THE FARM PROBLEM AND THE CREATION OF FOOD IMPORT DEPENDENCE

Bob Miller is sitting at his kitchen table. It is a functional, formica-topped table, in a functional, formica-topped kitchen that has lots of natural light streaming in from the outdoors. It is 2008. A stout man who looks like he's in his forties but who is probably in his fifties, Miller has an upper body that looks like it has been ever so slightly squashed; he is a man who keeps fit through hard work. Under his blue checked cotton shirt are the large, muscular arms and thick forearms that I would expect of such a man; the forearms are resting on the table. His head is oval and his wide eyes are offset by thick, dark eyebrows. In his hands he holds a few grains of rice that he has picked out of the bag in front of him on the table.

"I'm the fourth generation to farm this land," Miller says to me, his face expressionless, "and this is what we farm." He rolls the grains of rice between his thumb and forefingers. "In 1890 Horst Mueller was farming in Indiana when he saw an ad in the newspaper. It advertised good land for sale in several parishes here in southwestern Louisiana, including land around Crowley. Horst's doctor had told him that he needed to move to a warmer climate, so he took his doctor's advice and in 1890 moved his family down here and bought the first 150 hectares of this farm for fifteen hundred dollars. Jess still has the ad somewhere.

"When he came down, he didn't know anything about growing rice — he had been a wheat farmer. Still, that first year he managed to make nineteen hundred dollars. He never looked back. Horst learned the ins and outs of rice farming, and as he produced more, the farm became more profitable, and he and my grandfather Hubert plowed the money back into the farm, buying more land and machinery and creating the farm that we work.

"Today we farm about 300 hectares. In the late fall the land is plowed and the levees are made. It's hard work, but it would be even harder if we didn't have all the machinery that we have. In late January the land is plowed again, twice, and then flooded before the water is levelled. In late March the seed is broadcast by plane — we use Cypress and Bengal varieties of long grain rice. Once that is done, we apply the fertilizer. When the seed germinates, the water is let off the field, before being flooded again during the season. Just before we harvest, which is three and a half or four months later, the water is drained off the field. We usually start cutting the crop in early July and finish in late August. Although we use a combine to cut the stalk and thresh the grain it's still a really busy time: you can't lose any time when you are trying to get the crop out of the field. We have to get up way before daylight, have lunch under the shade trees in the fields, and usually don't get home until at least nine pm. I always put in at least a seventeen hour day. Our boy, Sam, helps out, driving a tractor pulling a rice cart. So do some of our relatives and friends. If we're lucky, we don't have to hire any help. It's always better to work with people you know. Besides, that helps Jess balance the books. If all goes well, we'll cut thirty to thirty-five dry barrels. More is a good year. Less a bad one."

Bob Miller farms a plant that has been cultivated for at least 7,000 years (Smith and Dilday 2003). Rice is a grass, with long stems and long, green leaves that can be grown in dry soil or, more productively, in wet rice fields, called "paddies." Out of the stem grows the panicle, where the richly nutri-tious grains cluster and which can become so top-heavy that it can cause the stem to lean. In the unhusked grain, under the hull and the subsequent layers of bran, lies the starchy endosperm which, when milled, we think of as "rice." It comes in a number of varieties: long, medium and short grained; aromatic; and glutinous. These various varieties of rice have, over the millennia, become exceedingly important to humanity; in some societies the word for "food" is "rice," and rice is the most important basic food for almost one-half of the world's population (Latham 1998).

As is abundantly clear from Miller's story, rice is also a very labour- and water-intensive crop, requiring hard work in land preparation and the setting of seedlings, water, nutrient and pest management, as well as harvesting and processing. Consider the act of transplanting rice seedlings, an activity that has been a central part of rice cultivation for two millennia: between twelve and fifty days of work by an individual are needed to transplant one hectare of rice by hand (World Bank 1967, Barker, Herdt with Rose 1985). For Miller this need for labour-power meant that his farm is highly mechanized, with tens of thousands of dollars of farm machinery sitting in his barns.

Requiring lots of labour and lots of water, rice was best suited to be first grown in those places where people were plentiful and rainfall was abun-dant, so its earliest cultivation was in China, India and parts of West Africa. Consequently, rice played a critical role in the establishment of early civiliza-tions: the use of communities of peasants to construct water drainage projects or irrigation works, including dams, canals, conduits, sluices and ponds, led to the rise of pre-capitalist states in China and India, where peasants paid tribute to their overlords and patrons in rice (Kipple 2007, Fraser and Rimas 2010). Rice was also responsible for some of humanity's earliest technological advances, which occurred in China: the oxen-pulled iron plow was introduced before the birth of Christ; the use of animal manure to increase the nitrogen in the soil and so boost yields also dates from that time; and purposive seed selection to boost rice yields, which has been supplanted by the market as a result of the Green Revolution, is 2,000 years old.

Rice produces more food energy and protein per hectare than wheat and maize, and so can support more people per unit of land (Smith and Dilday 2003). This is the reason why the popularity of rice cultivation amongst farmers of all stripes spread far and wide around the world, including to the United States and Bob Miller's predecessors. Rice cultivation in the U.S. possibly began with a trial planting in Virginia around 1609; by 1690 rice farming was well established in South Carolina and Georgia, using seeds brought from Madagascar (Carney 2001). Rice farming in the eighteenth century American southeast became deeply entangled with slavery: 40 percent of all the slaves imported into the U.S. passed through the port of Charleston, South Carolina, and its slave markets (Allen 2009). Rice farming's need for lots of labour started the slave plantation era in the South, because even with ox and mule-drawn equipment rice farms of a hundred hectares or so required from one hundred to three hundred workers to prepare the soil, plant, harvest and thresh the crop. Slaves from West Africa, notably the Senegambia region, brought the highest prices because of their extensive knowledge of rice culture, which slave owners appropriated and put to use on their rice plantations (Dusinberre 2000, Carney 2001).

Slavery made rice a major agricultural business in the early and mid nineteenth century in the U.S., and the antebellum South was a major rice exporter, setting the international standard for quality (Smith 1991). But with the end of the Civil War the rice plantations of South Carolina and Georgia lost ownership of the slave labour that was so central to their profitability; rice cultivation in the southeastern U.S. withered away to next to nothing.

Starting around 1850, though, rice farming had begun to shift westward, partly to avoid hurricanes and partly to avoid competition from other crops like cotton. Rice farming moved into southern Arkansas, Louisiana and eastern Texas, where land was parcelled out to soldiers returning from the Civil War, and it remains there to this day — Arkansas produces 45 percent of all the rice grown in the U.S. (Dethloff 1970, Daniel 1984, Livezey and Foreman 2004). At first, the extremely labour-intensive character of rice farming meant that those farming it in the Arkansas Grande Prairie, Mississippi Delta and the Gulf Coast were small-scale family farmers, producing enough for their own needs but little more. They were, in many ways, little different from Pervaiz Qazi or Abdul Hussain or Noor Mohammad. By the time Horst Mueller arrived in Acadia Parish, where Crowley is found, rice in southwestern Louisiana was only beginning to be grown for commercial sales.

But the decade following Mueller's arrival in Crowley saw a boom in rice farming as it started to become commercialized. Acadia Parish had its own advantages: shallow ponds and levelled prairie lands, which, when levees around ponds and marshy places were elevated to collect rainwater, were well-suited to the water needs of rice farming (LSU AgCenter 2012). These natural advantages were reinforced by the coming of the railroad into southwestern Louisiana in the 1880s, and both, together, were underlined by the land speculators that had, acting as real estate agents, attracted Midwestern farm families like the Muellers to the Parish. So, the number of rice farmers and total rice production swelled dramatically (Post 1940). Family farmers like Horst Mueller were able to make a good living from rice, which of course served to attract more farmers into the area and into rice farming.

But the rice farmers of southwestern Louisiana in the 1890s faced a risk: the market. That the market imperative was — and is — an incessant risk for farmers is not widely appreciated in our world. Think about it, though: farms are isolated and physically set apart from each other. This means that small-scale and large-scale family farmers often work alone, having limited interactions with non-family members for extended periods of time. Isolation means that transporting your crop for sale can be hard; it means that communication with others can be difficult. Together, these mean that the information available to family farmers about opportunities — and threats — can be poor. Consider this: family farmers wouldn't know who was paying the best price for their rice or whether a bumper crop in Texas might affect the amount they could earn for their rice. Or this: physical isolation from rice markets means that family farmers often have very little choice about from whom they buy or to whom they sell, in which case the very act of buying and selling is complexly embedded within sets of interpersonal relationships between people; like Sam Naimisi selling to John the middleman, you sell your crop to a trader because there is no one else to sell to, and you have always sold to that trader, but that exclusivity is bound to affect the terms and conditions of the sale.

So these "personalized transactions" mean that who you are can affect what you get; transactions are not between supposed equals who rationally and anonymously weigh up the pros and cons of a sale (Akram-Lodhi 2001c). Instead, one actor can dominate a sale, deliberately setting its terms and conditions so that they reap the lion's share of the benefits — for example, by buying at a price that is lower than that paid in a neighbouring parish. Economists call the expressions of power that can congeal around these types of market transactions "monopsonistic exploitation," and they lead to an ever-smaller share of every dollar of the final price paid by the consumer going to actual farmer. So the markets faced by farmers around the world are highly imperfect institutions through which asymmetries of power and privilege can be refracted and the use of which can be a costly proposition, even though peasant and family farmers may have no alternative.

The risks of the market for the rice farmers of Acadia Parish in the 1890s were especially pronounced in three areas: seeds, labour and marketing (Post 1940). When Horst Mueller arrived, the rice farmers of Acadia Parish relied upon buying seeds that were imported from Japan and Honduras and which were not, in the views of the farmers, especially well-suited to the needs of southwestern Louisiana, being less productive when in the ground and less hardy when in the mill. That they had to buy their seeds placed family farmers like Horst Mueller in a riskier position than they would have liked and gave the seed sellers, as we saw in the last chapter, a stronger position for determining the price that would yield the most money possible for themselves. After all, as I have already said, a farmer without seeds is not going to have a crop and so has very little choice but to pay the price regardless of what it is.

Rice farmers also had to rely on the market for waged labour. Southwestern Louisiana had a low population density, which meant that it could be costly to get the right number of farm workers at the time they were needed; yet if farmers did not do so they might not be able to plant their crop, let alone harvest it, at any price. Again, relying on the labour market to meet their needs for farm workers placed family farmers in an inherently riskier position.

The final risk was milling. When Horst Mueller arrived, rice milling, which removes the chaff and the outer husks of the grain, was concentrated in New Orleans, the lone market for the Louisiana rice crop; local family farmers were compelled to send their rice crop to New Orleans to be milled and the farmer would either have to pay the company for having milled the rice or allow the miller to deduct an amount from the final price paid to the farmer to cover the cost of the milling. Farmers believed that the New Orleans mills made too great a profit and that family farmers had to pay too high a price for milling, but with limited choice, rice farmers were at the mercy of those that dominated the market.

Salmon Lusk "Sol" Wright solved the imported seed problem, for a time, for the farmers of Acadia Parish (Lee 1996). Arriving in Crowley at the same time as the Muellers, from Oregon by way of Indiana, Wright was, like many of his neighbours, unhappy about his need to rely on imported seed. Although he knew nothing of rice, he spent the next several years naturally selecting and cross-pollinating seeds in order to breed one that was not only more suitable for local conditions but which could also be produced locally, eliminating the need to rely upon imports. It took him more than a decade of work, but when he finally developed Blue Rose rice it quickly spread throughout southwestern Louisiana and beyond.

Labour was a far greater problem. The risks inherent in relying on the labour market were without doubt the main constraint confining the expansion of the commercial production of rice. This risk began to be addressed in the 1870s, when Joseph Fabacher introduced the first ox-drawn rice-threshing machine, which did the work of a number of men. Next, in the mid 1880s the twine-binder was first used in rice harvesting, dramatically cutting labour requirements; local farmer Maurice Brien refined the twine-binder in order to make it more suitable for rice farming, and in 1890 twenty-two cars loaded with three hundred binders designed specifically for rice were shipped to Lake Charles, in southwestern Louisiana. Some Midwestern wheat farmers who had migrated to southwest Louisiana also found that their wheat farm machinery could be fairly easily adapted to suit rice farming (Millet 1964).

Slowly, field operations began to be mechanized, and, as we have seen with the case of the Green Revolution in South Asia, the labour needs of farm production in southwestern Louisiana started to be cut. Even as Horst Mueller increased the size and scale of his farm operations he was able to work the farm with the help of his wife, two sons and daughter and only occasionally had to hire local farm workers, who were mostly African-American (Post 1940, Millet 1964). With machinery, Mueller was able to configure a more capital-intensive family farm.

The reliance on the rice mills in New Orleans was all but eliminated with the establishment of local rice mills. Seaman A. Knapp, a balding, portly farmer who had moved into the area and developed a large-scale farm on which he implemented a number of innovative farming techniques, raised money in New York to build a rice mill in Crowley (Bailey 1971). By the end of the 1890s six rice mills had been established, with a milling capacity equal to half that of more distant New Orleans mills. Knapp also developed a system whereby local rice farmers were given money if they demonstrated to their neighbours the new farming techniques he had developed (Millet 1964). This system, which is now widely used around the world, resulted in Knapp becoming employed by the U.S. Department of Agriculture (USDA) to promote better agricultural practices across the South.

Cumulatively, innovations in rice farming during the 1890s reduced the dependence of family farmers on waged labour and increased their dependence on oil-driven farm machinery and equipment. These innovations increased rice production per acre, and with increased productivity came the increased farm profitability that families like the Muellers needed if their lives were to improve. In the early 1890s the yield of rice per acre under the most favourable conditions was about fifteen dry barrels, and with a market price of $3 a barrel the gross return per acre was $45. Deducting production costs of $1 per barrel, rice farming generated a net profit of over $30 per acre, giving farmers like Horst Mueller and Sol Wright a good living (Cary 1899).

So, in the short period between 1890 and 1893 Louisiana saw a five-fold increase in production; by 1899 Louisiana farmers were cultivating 201,685 acres of rice, producing 172,732,430 pounds valued at $4,044,489, and by 1903 Louisiana was producing 70 percent of the total American rice crop (Cary 1899). For fifteen years following his arrival in Crowley, Horst Mueller and his family did very well out of their farm, and over the following sixty years, acreage, production and the value of rice production tripled in southwestern Louisiana, the self-styled "rice capital of America," as the commercialization of rice production allowed its increasingly capital-intensive large-scale farms to be run by families like Horst Mueller and his descendents (Daniel 1981).

The remarkably rapid expansion and continuing commercialization of rice production in Louisiana took place behind protective tariffs that taxed imports of rice from East Asia in an effort to protect Louisiana farmers from the risk of having to compete with imports from the international rice market. But even with these tariffs, imported rice could still compete on price with Louisiana rice, and, at the turn of the twentieth century, the U.S. continued to be a net importer of rice as it had been ever since the Civil War. Imports meant that despite the rapid rise in commercial rice production in Louisiana, the demand for that rice, mainly in the southeastern U.S., grew much more slowly than the expansion of production, and the period between 1903 and 1913, which were the last years of Horst Mueller's life, saw many farmers in Acadia Parish forced to quit farming by the bust that followed the boom.

Horst Mueller was involved, to a small degree, in helping found the Rice Association of America (RAA) in Crowley in 1901 (Cline 1970). During this first difficult decade of the twentieth century, under the leadership of Henri Gueydan, a French-educated politician-businessman, the RAA attempted to offset weak American rice markets by trying to find export markets for Louisiana rice, initially promoting exports to Cuba, Puerto Rico and the Philippines (Dethloff 1970). Those sales finally began in 1910, and Gueydan became manager of the RAA from his home in Gueydan, Louisiana (named after his father). But with production rising, domestic consumption stagnant and the export market underdeveloped, the rice industry faced difficult times. So World War I was a blessing in disguise for the family farmers of Louisiana: widespread food shortages in Europe galvanized increased demand for staples such as rice. The U.S. government encouraged larger-scale family farmers to increase production in order to sell abroad, which they did, but when supply did not keep pace with demand the price of rice rose dramatically, and rice farming had a short-lived boom.

This boom led the U.S. Food Administration to regulate the sale and distribution of rough and milled rice in 1918. The Southern Rice Growers Association, which had been a farmers' marketing cooperative that altogether controlled 60 percent of the rice grown in Louisiana and Texas, was compulsorily transformed by the state into a federally-controlled purchasing agency know as the Southern Rice Committee (Daniel 1986). The committee was given the authority to establish maximum prices for rough rice along with the responsibility to negotiate contracts with producers and millers. This little-noticed intervention began the era of strong state intervention in the U.S. rice industry, which would have profound effects not only on the lives of those working the Mueller farm but also on other farms that were far, far away. Indeed, the creation of the Southern Rice Committee has arguably affected world agriculture for the last ninety years.

The end of World War I saw a rapid drop in rice exports, and the Mueller farm, now run by Horst's son Hubert, who had had his name anglicized to Miller by his father, faced a difficult time. Like other U.S. rice farmers, the Millers had become increasingly reliant upon international sales of their rice — indeed, the U.S. was now a net rice exporter — and the price of rice fell every year between 1919 and 1926. U.S. government tariffs introduced in 1921, 1922 and 1930, which were partly designed to insulate farmers, including rice farmers, from international competition in the domestic market, failed to remedy the problem.

In another round of rural restructuring, some of Herbert Miller's neighbours reduced the area they farmed, and others were forced to quit agriculture altogether. So during the 1920s the area in Louisiana under rice cultivation fell; rice farmers like the Millers, as well as processors, needed more direct assistance to cope with low rice prices and the rising cost of living, and, through their farmer associations, they called for the introduction of a national agricultural program that would increase domestic rice prices, stabilize incomes and promote the sale of rice surpluses on international markets at the lower world market price (Daniel 1986). In 1929, when the stock market crashed, the price of rice, like other agricultural commodities, fell through the floor; rice farmers in Louisiana were in crisis, and the Millers felt it personally: Hubert Miller's health suffered during the "dirty thirties," which no doubt contributed to his death in 1943 at the relatively young age of fifty-eight.

The hardships the Millers faced during the 1930s simply compounded those that they had experienced during the 1920s: for family farmers in southwestern Louisiana the Great Depression began in 1921. The hardships of the 1930s happened despite the fact that in May 1933, a mere nine weeks after

FDR's inauguration and following more than a decade of calls by farmers for state intervention to support their livelihoods, Congress passed the *Agricultural Adjustment Act* and created the Agricultural Adjustment Administration (AAA). While a "New Deal" for agriculture was supposed to be underway (Daniel 1986, Sheingate 2001), it was not until 1938, when a second Act was passed to overcome political and judicial challenges to the AAA, that the New Deal actually got started in Crowley.

The new Act included a basic rice support program, providing growers with several types of assistance. To the import controls that had been created in the twenties and thirties were added marketing quotas that regulated the domestic market, including that of rice. In addition, through the Commodity Credit Corporation (CCC), which had been created in the wake of the AAA, farmers became eligible for soil conservation payments, loans for the storage of crops and parity price payments if they restricted the acreage they farmed. Parity payments, which farmers had demanded since the early 1920s, offered farmers a modest state-guaranteed price for their crop relative to its purchasing power in the period 1910–1914: if the parity price was not offered in the open market, the CCC would buy up their crop at that price. Parity prices were designed to maintain the living standards of families like the Millers by stabilizing prices and markets.

Hubert Miller, and other rice farmers in Louisiana, benefitted from acreage quotas, conservation payments and parity price payments, although on the Miller farm more productive seed varieties and continually improving farming practices resulted in steadily higher yields per acre, which limited efforts to reduce production and get some of the compensation offered by the CCC. So the Act did not achieve its goal of stabilizing the farm incomes of families like the Millers (Sheingate 2001). In yet another round of restructuring, many of Hubert Miller's neighbours left farming in the 1930s, and the number of rice farms in Louisiana was reduced; some of Hubert Miller's neighbours, but not Hubert himself, benefitted from this, buying up more land at rock-bottom prices and seeing their farms grow bigger both in size and in scale. Restructuring facilitated the emergence of capitalist rice farms.

It was in 1942 that Bob Miller's father, John, whom Bob Miller described to me as quiet, took over the running of the family farm, at the age of 28. World War II, and the worldwide food shortages it caused, ended the twenty year depression in Louisiana's rice farming industry: the war effort required rice, and lots of it, for the Allies (Daniel 1986). The U.S. increased its control over rice production: prices paid by consumers were kept deliberately low, domestic rice consumption was discouraged and exports to the Allies strictly controlled under wartime planning. In order to encourage the maximum production of rice, the parity price administered by the CCC was increased in 1942 to 90 percent of the 1910–1914 price — it had been 81 percent two years before. Rice production, and food production generally, rocketed: U.S. farmers, who were less than one percent of the world's population, soon produced nearly half the world's food.

Because the war effort needed rice and because large numbers of farm workers had left to fight in the war, further, deeper and more extensive mechanization of farm activity was supported by loans from the CCC: combine harvesters were first used in rice farming in Louisiana in the early 1940s in order to increase production and productivity in the face of labour shortages (Daniel 1986). The first beneficiaries of further mechanization were the larger-scale, capital-intensive and more directly capitalist farms that had emerged during the dirty thirties and which continued to grow through the 1940s; John Miller's farm would not get a combine harvester until the 1950s, which helps explain why John married relatively late: he had to work, because he and rice farmers of his ilk benefitted relatively less from the war than neighbouring larger-scale capitalist farms.

In the decade that followed the end of World War II, U.S. government intervention in agriculture in general and rice farming in particular deepened (Sheingate 2001). Under a system of parity price payments, production controls, marketing regulations and import tariffs, what was later called "the farm problem" was created: farmers increased production, market prices dropped, parity price payments kicked in and farmers were encouraged to "overproduce" because they knew that the CCC would buy up their "surplus production" at the parity price (Gardner 1992). At the same time, though, the share of the consumer's dollar that was directly received by farmers was dropping: in 1946 the share was fifty-two cents out of every dollar, but by 1955 it had dropped to forty-two cents out of every dollar spent. A result of increasing retail distribution costs, the implication was that the U.S. food regime was starting to tightly squeeze farm incomes, as falling farm prices were not reflected in falling retail prices and increased domestic food consumption. In the context of a farm income squeeze that an increase in state spending could not offset, only the most efficient large-scale family farms were capable of managing, in tandem with the rapidly-consolidating capitalist farm sector (Friedmann and McMichael 1989). So during the 1950s the number of rice farms declined and the size of rice farms increased: while commercially-oriented, capital-intensive, large-scale family farming tried to consolidate their position in rice, classically capitalist farms were increasingly tightening their dominant position within the rice industry, and some of these farms were coming to resemble industrialized farm production. Differentiation was taking place in the production of rice.

The way in which the problem of farm overproduction and falling incomes was addressed in the middle of the 1950s would bring benefits to John Miller and his family over the remainder of his life. It would also have consequences that resonated around the world. A first hint of how this would happen can be seen in a June 1947 meeting of sixteen European nations in Paris. The object of their discussions: the assistance they were seeking from the U.S. to rebuild their war-shattered countries (Hogan 1989, Mikesell 2009). The group's first request was, not surprisingly, for food and agricultural commodities, including rice: three-quarters of the $22 billion that was requested under a proposed four-year plan would go to buy products from American farmers. Such a request was not novel: since the end of the war Germany had been in receipt of substantial food aid, in the form of U.S. surplus food held by the CCC. The proposal came at a good time for U.S. farmers: 1947 had seen the biggest wheat harvest in U.S. history, and many other agricultural commodities, including rice, were being produced far in excess of what the U.S. market was capable of buying. When Congress approved what became known as the Marshall Plan in the spring of 1948, food and agricultural products started flowing across the Atlantic, being paid for in money supplied by the U.S. During its four years, the Marshall Plan would see $11.8 billion in development aid and $1.56 billion in development loans being extended to the states of Europe, which were used, for the most part, to purchase U.S. goods and services, including food.

The Marshall Plan increased worldwide demand for U.S. agricultural products, and farmers, including the Millers, responded by increasing farm production. In order to deal with continuing and sustained overproduction, in 1948 the new Secretary of Agriculture, Charles Brannan, was given additional powers to use purchases, loans and marketing quotas, as well as, later, acreage allotments and support prices, to stabilize agricultural prices. The result was that state-controlled stocks of food increased. When the Korean War began, though, farm prices, and particularly rice prices, strengthened, CCC stocks were sold, consumer food prices rose and farm incomes reached a historic high. But the cost of this agrarian historic compromise was high: by mid 1950 the U.S. government was spending $11 million a day financially supporting farmers (Sheingate 2001). That figure would only rise.

War-stimulated global food demand led U.S. farmers to expand production. Faced with mounting surpluses and the increased costs of government programs — by 1954 the CCC had acquired one million tons of rough rice — in 1954 the Eisenhower Administration introduced a flexible price support program, in which parity prices were allowed to fluctuate between 75 percent and 90 percent of the 1910–1914 reference price (McClenahan Jr. and Becker 2011). The fluctuating parity price was supposed to reflect supply and demand: when demand was near supply, support would be high; when supply exceeded demand, support would be less. Despite the new scheme, though, in 1955 farm production controls again became necessary when the value of the U.S. food surplus held by the CCC reached $7 billion. With farmer programs costing the taxpayer $4.5 billion a year for the period between 1956 and 1958, it is little surprise that the government in 1956 introduced the Soil Bank program, which provided direct payments to farmers if they reduced their acreage of crops supported by farm programs (Ragatz 1960). The desired effect of these cost-control programs was largely offset by improved farm technology, however, which made it possible to greatly increase yields per acre, sell at the parity price and still collect direct payments for reducing the cropped area. Like many other family farmers, John Miller was able to take advantage of the system, but not as much as the dominant capitalist and industrial capitalist farms, which financially benefitted far more.

The ongoing U.S. farm problem had two possible solutions: farmers could adjust to a world in which global appetites for U.S. food were diminishing; or a world in which global appetites for U.S. food were diminishing could adjust to better meet the needs of U.S. farmers. Clearly, the former would have been borne heavily by family farmers such as John Miller, while the latter had the potential to benefit family farmers like the Millers. More to the point, though, the latter would benefit the now-dominant industrial capitalist farms.

It was clear that if the latter was the route that was going to be taken global adjustment to U.S. farm interests would require a mechanism that would greatly reduce the surplus food held by the CCC. Enter the 1954 *Agricultural Trade Development and Assistance Act*, or Public Law (PL) 480, which became known as the "Food for Peace" program under President John F. Kennedy (Barrett and Maxwell 2005). PL 480 made U.S. grain — mostly wheat, but also rice — available to countries to buy at a very low cost. This was done in three ways. Title I PL 480 assistance allowed countries to buy U.S. food surpluses using long-term, low-interest loans provided by the U.S. on very generous terms, usually including a long grace period in which no repayments had to be made. Such "concessional" sales — concessional in the sense that the price paid was below the market price — became the basis of accusations that the U.S. was engaged in "food dumping": selling food outside the U.S. at less than the cost of production (Friedmann 1982, Weis 2007). Such food was most commonly made available for distribution through state-owned enterprises controlled by the borrowing state and was usually resold to the citizens of the borrowing country, with the receipts from the resale accruing to the borrowing state. With much of world eating rice as a basic staple, Title I provisions of PL 480 had the potential to benefit John Miller by increasing the state-sponsored market for his long-grain rice.

Title II PL 480 assistance made some food surpluses available to countries without charge, as humanitarian and non-humanitarian aid, delivered through private relief agencies, non-governmental organizations and international institutions such as the World Food Programme (Schultz 1960). Title

II provisions also had the potential to benefit rice farmers like the Millers by increasing demand for their crop. Title III PL 480 assistance provided bilateral state to state grants to the poorest countries to boost farming production and productivity in developing capitalist countries, principally through infrastructural investment and the building of deep and liquid private-sector led food markets. Later, in 1986, Title V PL 480 assistance was introduced in order to link American volunteer farmers with farmers in developing capitalist countries so that U.S. farmers might work with their counterparts to improve food production, marketing and distribution. Titles I and II of PL 480 together created a mechanism whereby below-cost concessional food sales and food donations could be used to at least partially liquidate CCC-held farm surpluses (Barrett and Maxwell 2005).

Not surprisingly, Title I and Title II programs became the most important components of PL 480. The advantages of Title II programs to the receiving country were obvious: they didn't have to pay for food. The advantages of Title I assistance to the receiving country was that initially loans could be repaid in local currencies without converting them into hard-to-get dollars, a formula that lasted until the mid 1970s; repayments were deposited in local banks in local currencies, where they could then be used by the U.S. In many instances the repayments were used to pay for U.S. development projects and programs in the country as well as military aid; in other circumstances repayments would be returned to the borrowing government as an outright grant; and in a third set of instances repayments would be used to support the entry into and activities of U.S. transnational corporations operating in the borrowing country — Cargill, Ralston Purina and Bank of America were among the 419 corporate subsidiaries in 31 countries that had benefitted from this by the early 1980s (Burbach and Flynn 1980). So, Title I PL 480 assistance brought direct benefits to U.S. transnational corporations, facilitating their entry into markets and building their global networks of clients, particularly as the USDA worked with U.S. grain transnational corporations to expand their presence in other countries.

PL 480 has had a significant impact on global food flows, including rice. Between 1954 and the early 1980s some $30 billion of agricultural commodities were shipped internationally as a result of PL 480 (Barrett and Maxwell 2005). Indeed, during the first twelve years of the program, something on the order of one quarter of all U.S. agricultural exports were financed under Title I provisions alone; Title I allocations peaked in 1963 at $1.7 billion (Burbach and Flynn 1980). Later, between 1974 and 1990 some 5 percent of U.S. agricultural exports were financed under Title I. In contrast, between 1954 and 1990 some $10 billion was allocated through Title II, and when PL 480 allocations peaked in 1985 at $2.2 billion, Title II allocations had become the more important, as they would remain to the present day when around 80 percent of PL 480's $1 billion plus annual allocations are assigned to Title II.

The effects of PL 480 on U.S. farmers was rapidly felt: having been broadly stable for the forty years following the start of World War I, starting in 1954 foreign agricultural markets, particularly in developing capitalist countries, started to rapidly open up for U.S. farmers, and food exports from the U.S. soared. The bulk of these exports were not shipped under the provisions of PL 480 assistance, but nonetheless PL 480 allocations were critical in opening up foreign markets for U.S. food exports: between 1956 and 1960 more than 30 percent of the entire global wheat trade was funded by U.S. food aid through PL 480, which rapidly opened up global food markets to U.S. agro-food transnational corporations (Friedmann 1982). That was to be expected: an explicit objective of Title I was that it had to pry open food markets outside the U.S. to commercial food sales, which were dominated by the U,S.

So PL 480 was not just about liquidating CCC-held farm surpluses; it was also about building international markets for U.S. food products, and this brought real and immediate benefit to the Miller family. Over the course of the late 1950s and through the 1960s, long grain rice from the Miller farm increasingly found its way to far-flung places in Latin America and the Caribbean, either through PL 480 or through commercial U.S. rice traders operating in the region (Weis 2007). The Miller farm came to rely more and more on rice exports, albeit indirectly, a characteristic that has not changed to this day; Bob Miller does not know for sure — he cannot know for sure — but he thinks that possibly half of his crop is exported, because half the U.S. rice crop is exported. He's proud of this; in his view, American rice feeds the hungry of the world.

PL 480 opened up food markets particularly in countries with which the U.S. was allied. Important early recipients of PL 480 assistance were Japan, South Korea, Taiwan and Brazil; all had, by the late 1960s, become commercial buyers of U.S. food exports (Burbach and Flynn 1980). As these early recipients of U.S. food aid no longer needed it, PL 480 assistance was channelled into new priority countries such as South Vietnam and Cambodia, who received 75 percent of Title I allocations in 1974. Later in the decade, Egypt under Anwar Sadat, after he signed a peace treaty with Israel, became the largest single recipient of Title I allocations: it is well documented that PL 480 was used as a geopolitical lever by the U.S. and thus, unbeknownst to them, the rice farmers of Louisiana became indirectly embroiled within the geopolitics of the Cold War (Friedmann 1982).

Despite biotechnologically-driven increases in farm productivity as a result of the Green Revolution, in developing capitalist countries export markets for U.S. food continued to boom as more and more food was shipped around the world. The market imperative meant that emerging proto-capitalist farmers in developing capitalist countries had to compete with subsidized U.S. exports; the Darwinian metric assumed a new form. Booming export markets also meant that in the early 1960s farm gate prices for farm products in the U.S. were on the up-and-up: the farm problem appeared to have been answered, in that farm incomes were rising. But because of the ongoing process of farm differentiation and consolidation that had aggressively deepened since the late 1940s as commercially-oriented market-dependent industrialized capitalist farms were built, rising farm incomes in the early 1960s did not benefit all farmers. By 1964 the most productive 9 percent of U.S. farms accounted for half of all farm production, and the most productive 3 percent of U.S. farms produced as much as the least productive 80 percent of U.S. farms (Cochrane 1993). An ever-increasing share of U.S. farm output was thus being produced on big, large-scale, heavily-capitalized industrial capitalist farms; these were the farms with which large-scale family farmers such as John Miller had to compete, as his dependence on selling his rice meant that he had to be able to match the lower costs of the industrial capitalist farms.

For industrial capitalist farms the parity price support system was a golden opportunity: parity prices that covered the production costs of family farms like the Millers' offered the chance of increased profitability for the far more efficient industrial capitalist farms. Thus, when in 1964 payments from the U.S. state accounted for 20 percent of the $13 billion in net farm income, these payments were not evenly distributed across farms: they disproportionately benefitted the industrial capitalist farm sector (As They Saw It 2012). Similarly, when the *Food and Agricultural Act* of 1965 reduced parity price supports on major farm commodities so that farm incomes could be protected through direct income support payments based on controlling the supply of certain farm commodities, not all farmers gained: again, its benefits were disproportionately directed toward the industrial capitalist farm sector. So government support for farming during the 1960s acted to ensure the dominance of industrial capitalist farming in the U.S. at the expense of family farms, whose economic circumstances became over time more suspect (Cochrane 1993). This is not to say that John Miller received nothing; Bob Miller does not know the details, but he does know that his father received state support while he worked the farm.

Rapid growth in food exports meant that by the late 1960s the U.S. had become the world's largest exporter of rice, and it is in this perspective that the 40 percent increase in world rice consumption per capita between 1960 and 2000 should be viewed: rice exports from U.S. farmers like John Miller helped reconfigure diets around the world away from local staples and toward rice (Food and Agriculture Organization 2002). Small-scale peasant farmers in Asia, Africa and Latin America could not compete with cheap, subsidized American rice, and the market for their food products diminished, reducing their ability to sustain any kind of self-reliance. The growth in rice consumption was mirrored by a threefold increase in world production of rice, to 600 million tonnes, between 1960 and 2004 (ChartsBin 2011). A significant component of that growth was accounted for by the U.S. rice industry, which is, at seven tonnes a hectare, the most productive per unit of land in the world; the U.S. is the tenth largest rice producer in the world (Snyder and Slaton 2001). However, unlike China and India, who are much larger rice producers but who do not export large quantities of rice, the U.S. is a major rice exporter; almost 50 percent of all U.S. rice is exported, and the U.S. remains the fourth largest exporter in a global rice market that is estimated to only be around 6 percent of total production (United States Department of Agriculture 2011). Most exports of American long-grain rice go to Latin America, while exports of medium-grain rice go to Northeast Asia and the Middle East. Even as late as 2004, food aid through Title II acquisitions accounted for 6 percent of all U.S. rice exports (United States Department of Agriculture 2004).

In the early 1970s, in the wake of the onset of the last global food crisis, international demand for U.S. farm products took off dramatically. With rising prices, the U.S. tried to restructure its system of farm support, maintaining a lower parity price of 75 percent of the 1910–1914 price, while making direct income support payments to farmers that reduced the amount of land they cultivated and thus restricted production increases. However, for the large industrial capitalist farms that dominated the receipt of these government subsidies, with 20 percent of farms in 1972 receiving 60 percent of all U.S. subsidies, it was more logical to collect direct income support payments for taking land out of production and then increasing farm yields on their remaining acreage so that they could collect the support price on their remaining production (Cochrane 1993). Moreover, the continuing parity price system encouraged exports, in that it led to the CCC continuing to buy surpluses and having to try to sell them on world markets at below the cost of production because U.S. farm prices were too high for world markets. So food dumping continued, and by 1975–6 the U.S. shipped 55 percent of all coarse grain exports in the world. The 1970s as a whole saw the value of U.S. agricultural exports grow at 20 percent a year, and the volume of U.S. agricultural exports doubled (Friedmann 1982). Rice exports though grew by only 14 percent over the decade and became far less important in total U.S. agricultural exports. This relative decline in the importance of rice in U.S. agricultural exports continued through the 1980s, although the total amount of rice that the U.S. exported continued to rise.

Part of the reason for the continued growth of U.S. agricultural exports was that in the late 1970s the U.S. began selling wheat and other agricultural commodities to the Soviet Union. This had the effect of rapidly depleting the stocks of grains held by the CCC and led to the growing dominance of increasingly global commercial food markets and transnational corporations involved in the global grain trade. As a consequence, PL 480 became less of a tool to dispose of surpluses; as I have noted, Title I allocations reduced dramatically, and Title II allocations became more important. Thus when, by 1983, various export subsidies equalled the value of 18 percent of all U.S. agricultural exports, of these only 18 percent were associated with the PL 480 program (Congressional Budget Office 1983).

In 1996 the U.S. Congress passed the *Federal Agriculture Improvement and Reform Act*, which ended supply controls in agriculture and "decoupled" income support from current production. The Act also reauthorized PL 480, although Title I allocations remained comparatively small, at around $175 million in 2000, while Title II allocations are large, at around $800 million that same year (Barrett and Maxwell 2005). Title I PL 480 allocations, along with export credit guarantees offered by the CCC, still amounted to 7 percent of all U.S. agricultural exports of $53 billion in 2002. The U.S. state was continuing to try to build markets for its agricultural exports, including rice.

In theory, Bob Miller's rice production is now subsidized on the basis of the 2002 *Farm Security and Rural Investment Act* and the 2007 Farm Bill. The former provides for: direct income support payments on the basis of historic acreage and yields; countercyclical price-based payments when the state's calculated "effective price" falls below its "target price," implying that the lower the domestic market price the higher the countercyclical payment; and marketing assistance loans that allow farmers to use their rice production as collateral, with forfeit loans being repaid in their entirety if the current rice crop is transferred to the CCC (United States Department of Agriculture 2012). So Bob Miller receives price support in return for complying with acreage allotments; not only is the amount planted by Miller effectively determined by government policy but so is the price he receives for his product; and Bob Miller's rice is indirectly subsidized through import tariffs. The independent family farm is now little more than a modern-day myth, as the state, not the market, has a critical role in the array of production decisions made by family farmers.

The effects of these state interventions are far-reaching: between 1995 and 2010 rice subsidies amounted to $12.9 billion; government protection and subsidies amount to half the income of rice farmers such as the Millers; and rice farmers are the most heavily subsidized group of farmers in the U.S. (Environmental Working Group 2011a). Certainly, Bob Miller and his family have benefitted from farm subsidies: between 1995 and 2006 Bob Miller received over $700,000 in subsidies, while his wife Jess received almost $650,000. These figures are admittedly somewhat misleading: while the Millers each received amounts in excess of $100,000 in 2000, 2001 and 2003, for the remaining years during the period the average amount received each year totalled around $30,000 — enough to make a difference to Bob, Jess and their family, but hardly a king's ransom. This is not surprising. In Acadia Parish, as in agriculture across America, it is usually the landowning nonfarmers and industrial capitalist farms that receive the bulk of rice subsidies. In Acadia Parish, for example, the largest 3 percent of farm producers received 54 percent of state subsidies between 1995 and 2010, while the smallest 80 percent of farm producers, including the Millers, receive a mere 7 percent of state subsidies (Environmental Working Group 2011b).

State intervention in the rice industry of Louisiana has become ever more deeply entangled since World War I. In seeking to solve an ongoing farm problem of overproduction and falling incomes, the U.S. state brought in a range of direct and indirect subsidies for agriculture while at the same time using the surpluses acquired by the CCC to create international markets for U.S. farm exports. The effect has been perverse: the number of farmers has declined, and the ability of family farms such as the Millers' to survive has become more difficult while industrial capitalist agriculture receives the lion's share of the government support that is on offer. What is particularly galling, though, is that the effects of these policies have not just affected the Millers, who in comparative global terms are relatively affluent. In opening up export markets for the Millers' rice, PL 480 drove down the price of locally-produced rice and other staples in a large number of developing capitalist countries. Food dumping undermined the sustainability of small-scale peasant agriculture around the world, and helped create the global agrarian crisis that we are now witnessing.

You can see this if you travel southeast across the Gulf of Mexico to Haiti. Travelling from the rice fields of Crowley to the port of Saint-Marc, on the western edge of the island of Hispaniola, sitting on the Gulf of Gonâve in the Caribbean, is like travelling back to an earlier decade. Saint-Marc is a small, bustling, decrepit, chaotic town that exists because at the beginning of the twentieth century a railroad was built that connected it with the capital, Port-au-Prince, one hundred kilometres away. That connection to the capital meant that following the catastrophic 2010 earthquake, refugees from Port-au-Prince came to Saint-Marc seeking relief, as the town itself was not seriously affected.

Like much of Haiti, the centre of Saint-Marc was to the outsider, even before the earthquake, much the worse for wear: whether in the central market or on the waterfront, rusty tin-roofed rickety wooden buildings that had not been whitewashed in an age looked like they were on the verge of falling down; brightly coloured trucks that had been converted into rough, uncomfortable buses, called tap-taps, plyed the roads, overflowing with cargo and people, many of whom sat on the roof; petty traders, selling a few bananas or cigarettes or the like, were all around; garbage was everywhere, having been casually thrown into the dusty streets; and open sewers let off a foul smell. As in the rest of Haiti, in Saint-Marc poverty is an ever-present lived fact.

Yet despite the circumstances, women and men, girls and boys continually smiled as they went about their business, shopping for cooking oil and rice from the many street-side petty vendors, going to school in remarkably clean and well-pressed green uniforms or just sitting by the side of the street, hanging out. Perhaps it is because some of them live on the outskirts of the town, as it rises toward the green hills that encircle it, where there is more space, and well-groomed whitewashed two-storey cement brick homes offer respite from the confusion of the centre of the town, but I doubt it. Haitians tend to have a garrulous disposition; whether it is because of their pride in their revolutionary heritage (Haiti was the first country in the world to have a successful slave rebellion, which resulted in the country's independence, in 1804) or because of the need to maintain humour in continually difficult times (Haiti is the poorest country in the western hemisphere and has been badly governed by a venal and corrupt ruling class for decades), I know not.

Saint-Marc was the principal outlet for agricultural products produced in Haiti's fertile Artibonite Plain, which sits flatly between the imposing Black Mountains and at the foot of Terrible Mountain, and that is why I am here. Sipping a Prestige beer just outside the Hotel Belfort, where I am staying because it has simple but clean rooms and reasonable plumbing for only $16 a night, I am talking to Maxime Auxilaire, a fairly thin man wearing used non-descript jeans and a used lime-green polo-necked shirt with a meaningless label over the right breast. It is 2010. Of indeterminable age but probably in his thirties, his angular face is sharply drawn because of his very short hair and the close-cropped goatee that surrounds his mouth. Auxilaire is a stevedore in Saint-Marc's port, and while I am interested in that, it is not the main reason I am talking to him.

Auxilaire takes a swig of beer from the bottle he is holding in his hand and speaks to me in Kreyol-accented French. "My father was a rice farmer in the Artibonite Valley, about forty kilometres from here, along highway 109. We had always been rice farmers, as long as anyone could remember. And why not? After all, it's what everyone eats.

"My father was a pretty typical farmer, farming land as it had been farmed for decades. He had about half a hectare, quite close to the Artibonite River, and irrigation canals sluiced the water into his fields. So we had land, and we had water. The only other thing a farmer needs is workers, so we all worked on our farm, growing rice: my mother, my brother and me, although my mother also did lots of work around the house, which my father never did. It was hard and, because of the mud, dirty work — much harder than unloading ships! You see, we did everything by hand: we prepared the land, we flooded the fields, we planted the seedlings, we harvested the rice, we threshed it — we did everything. Whenever we needed help, we could ask our neighbours — we had a system there where we shared work in each other's fields; it's called *konbit*. That's why everyone was a member of the local peasant association — we wanted to help each other. It was a hard life — fertilizer was expensive, because it came from America, and the managers of the irrigation system were corrupt. So the costs of farming were always going up, and many farmers were very, very poor. But it was worth it. The land was fertile enough that even a quarter hectare would feed all of us and leave a little left over that we could sell, if local thugs didn't come and steal it. We managed, which is more than many of our neighbours did."

Rice has been grown in Haiti since before Toussaint Louverture led the slave rebellion. All through the intrigues and coups that characterized the first seven decades of Haitian independence, small-scale peasant farmers toiled away on their plots of land, growing rice for themselves and their countryfolk, especially those living in the cities (Girard 2010). During the relative stability and peace of the years between 1867 and 1911, when the sugar and rum industries were developed in Port-au-Prince and Haiti was widely seen as a successful model of post-colonial development, peasant farmers continued to grow their rice. During the twenty year American occupation, peasants grew rice. Through the long years of the brutal Duvalier dictatorships, Haitian peasants grew rice (Abbott 1988). Such a history meant that rice was more to the average Haitian than merely a food: the country was desperately poor, over two-thirds of the Haitian population was engaged in or dependent upon agricultural production and some 20 percent of households directly engaged in rice farming and processing; it was deeply embedded within the culture of the country (Howard 1997). Yet in the 1980s something happened that dramatically changed the place of rice in Haiti, possibly forever (Abbott 2011).

Until the 1980s most rice eaten in Haiti was grown in Haiti. But starting in 1985 U.S. rice began to be imported, as the insolvent post-Duvalier military government, seeking $24.6 million in loans from the International Monetary Fund, dismantled some of its controls on imports. Comet Rice, an American rice exporter, quickly became Haiti's biggest rice supplier (Cox 1997). Maxime Auxilaire remembers the anger that Comet Rice's imports caused: when the first imported rice entered the Artibonite Valley, it was in a heavily armed convoy, in order to avoid attacks from enraged peasant farmers. It would appear that they had reason to be angry: imported rice rapidly came to dominate Haitian rice consumption. In 1991, U.S. rice imports exceeded Haitian rice production for the first time. With the exception of a single year, that has been the case ever since. Moreover, there has also been an increasing disparity in the rice that Haitians eat: a larger and larger share of the rice that is eaten in rural and urban Haiti is imported U.S. long grain rice — the type grown by Bob Miller. Rice imports in Haiti, mainly from the United States, increased fifty-fold between 1985 and 2006. Conversely, between 1985 and 1995 Haitian rice production dropped from 110,000 tons to 80,000 tons; within two years of the first so-called "Miami rice" imports, small-scale Haitian rice farmers could no longer compete with cheap, subsidized U.S. rice imports (Street 2004). By 2006 three out of four platefuls of rice eaten in Haiti were grown in the U.S., and cheap rice has replaced other locally-grown staples such as cassava, cornmeal and millet. Haiti has become the third largest importer of U.S. rice, despite being the poorest country in the hemisphere.

In 1994 the government of Haiti — led by recently-restored President Jean-Bertrand Aristide, still insolvent and facing up to the severe economic circumstances caused by a 1991 military coup — as part of an agreement with the U.S. government, turned once again to the International Monetary Fund for financial assistance, entering into a structural adjustment program. One extremely common component of a structural adjustment program is trade liberalization: countries reduce tariff and non-tariff barriers to international trade, making it easier for companies to import from and export to the country that is adjusting, as well as lowering any restrictions on the operation of transnational corporations into or out of the country. This makes a country far more exposed to international markets and transnational corporations, which, from the perspective of the IMF and the World Bank, is a good thing, because it forces a country to pursue those economic activities that are most appropriate to the resources that it has in light of market imperatives and inflows of global capital.

As a consequence of Haiti's program, in 1995 the tariff on rice imports dropped from 35 percent to 3 percent (Howard 1997). Tariff reductions made it even more difficult for local rice producers like Maxime Auxilaire's father Maurice to compete with imports. Imported rice reduced the price of rice for Haitian consumers, leading to an increase in rice consumption, but also reduced the price paid to small-scale Haitian rice farmers, who were, as I have indicated, a substantial share of the population, meaning that still more of the rice consumed in Haiti was imported. The decline in the demand for Haitian rice amongst both urban and rural Haitians was devastating for small-scale peasant farmers like Maurice Auxilaire. As Maxime put it to me, "rice farmers wanted a better life. They worked hard for it. But when they got their rice to market they were bombarded with an invasion of cheap imported Miami rice, so they had to sell at any price that a buyer was prepared to give. Inevitably, the price was less than the cost of growing the rice. How could my father compete against the big guys?"

Recall the circumstances under which Bob Miller and his large-scale family farm produce rice in Acadia Parish. U.S. rice production is subsidized through a variety of domestic and export support mechanisms that enable the Millers' rice to be sold internationally at a price that can be far less than the cost of production. So, in 2003 it cost on average $18.43 to grow, transport and mill one hundred pounds of rice in the U.S.; one hundred pounds of U.S. rice was then exported for a price of $13.68, which was only 74 percent of the cost of growing it (Institute for Agriculture and Trade Policy 2003). Subsidies made up a large part of the difference. Conversely, the contracting rice industry in Haiti received no support from the state; this was eliminated under structural adjustment, meaning that small-scale peasant rice farmers did not and do not receive domestic support or export subsidies. The "competition" that takes place between Haitian and American rice growers is far from fair; a more apt characterization would be to say that it is rigged in a way that expunges the possibility of small-scale peasant farmers sustaining any kind of self-reliance and in so doing deepens the grinding poverty that encompasses the countryside.

Remember though that the biggest beneficiaries of U.S. subsidies are the large U.S. industrial capitalist farms as well as agro-food transnational corporations engaged in the global business of buying and selling farm inputs and outputs. These modern-day behemoths dominate U.S. agriculture; and they dominate the global food regime (Patel 2007). These companies include Erly, Inc, the owner of both Comet Rice and the later-established Rice Corporation of Haiti, the companies which, awash with U.S. rice subsidies, were able to totally undermine the livelihood of Maurice Auxiliare.

Rice imports made the already poor peasant farmers of the Artibonite Valley desperate. Maxime's younger brother was taken out of school by his father, because he could no longer afford to pay for the school fees that he, like Grace Muchengi, had to pay as a result of structural adjustment. Maxime remembers that the family of one of his neighbours couldn't get enough food to eat; for a while the family tried to manage by eating mud cakes, which have an unfortunately long provenance amongst the desperately poor of Haiti, but were eventually, with few alternative employment choices, forced to leave the land in search of work in the neighbouring Dominican Republic. At first, it looked like Maurice Auxiliaire and his family would manage. But, continually unable to sell enough rice at the right price to meet the family's needs, household income fell precipitously, and they became vulnerable. Maxime clearly remembers the days in the mid 1990s when all he ate was some of the rice that his father couldn't sell; there was nothing else, because they couldn't afford to pay for anything else. In the end, Maurice Auxiliaire became just as desperate as his neighbours. When Maxime turned twenty, Maurice Auxilaire sold his plot of land, left his wife, Maxime and his brother in the town of Petite Rivière de l'Artibonite in the Valley, and paid $1,000 for a place on a boat to take him to the U.S. "He had to do this because he could no longer support his family by growing rice," explained Maxime. Maxime never saw his father again: the boat was one of the many that sank trying to make its way to the U.S., and his father died.

Maxime was left with his mother and brother. Without money or land, there was no way that they could go back to farming. So, they made the decision to move to a shantytown in Saint-Marc; it was much bigger than Petite Rivière de l'Artibonite, so there was a better chance of finding work. For a long time, Maxime's mother worked selling fruit for a pittance by the side of the road, but in 2001 Maxime was lucky enough to be able to bribe someone to get him a job unloading ships in Saint-Marc's harbour, and the family is now better off than they have been in more than a decade. He even offers to pay for another Prestige.

"The first day on the job I had to work long and hard unloading a Panamanian freighter that was full of Miami rice. I tried not to think about it: I was unloading the very thing that had killed my father. But what else could I do? After all, we eat Miami rice; we have no choice, because it's the cheapest. If I could, I would prefer to go back to rice farming: it's better being your own boss. But rice farmers aren't their own boss anymore. They have no incentive to grow rice anymore. It's almost impossible to make a profit."

As rice farming families, a few grains of rice would bring the Millers and the Auxiliares together, but those same few grains of rice mark out the profound separation between them. Like Maxime Auxiliare, Bob Miller simply wants to make a living, faces uncertain and risky markets and is happy to take any help that is offered by the U.S. state, which he often feels is inadequate. One could say that Bob Miller has very little choice in the matter: without the support of the U.S. state, he would not be able to continue to farm. Certainly, if he were to think about it, which he does not, Bob Miller would not like to know that the conditions by which he makes his living directly prevent Maxime Auxiliare from going back to rice farming: that small-scale Haitian peasant farmers, like peasant farmers around the world, are directly affected by the agricultural policies of the U.S. Those policies bring some benefit to the Millers; they allow the Auxiliares to buy cheap "Miami" rice; but the biggest benefits of these policies go to U.S. transnational corporations. Global corporations like Erly, Inc, which is engaged in the business of corporate agriculture, are profitable for their shareholders because Maurice Auxiliare was dispossessed through cheap imports and his family thrown into the limbo of the squatter camp slums of Saint-Marc. The prosperity of the pension funds, endowments and sovereign wealth funds that own the shares of agro-food transnational corporations are perversely predicated on the lurid construction of a global food regime that disempowers the already dispossessed.

It was not the market imperative that overwhelmed Maurice Auxilaire. Rapidly escalating state intervention in the world rice industry by the U.S. after World War I reconfigured farming in both America and Haiti: small-scale peasant farmers could not manage; large-scale family farmers had difficulty making ends meet; and the lion's share of the benefits of these arrangements went to the industrial capitalist farms that spewed forth cheap rice into the world market and the agro-food transnational corporations that provided the inputs and the marketing channels through which that rice could be sold. In apparently seeking to solve an ongoing farm problem of overproduction and falling incomes, the U.S. has sutured together a global food regime that has culminated in the dispossession through displacement and differentiation of relatively small-scale farms such as the Auxiliares' and the Millers' so that agriculture can become a source of the surplus value required by capital to be realized as profit if the system is to continue to reproduce. The process by which the reproduction of capital takes place creates entire populations that are surplus to requirements, or what Marx called "relative surplus populations": the Noor Mohammads, the Grace Muchengis, the Abdul Hussains and the Maurice Auxiliares are immiserated as the overwhelming forces of extreme poverty collide with the rapacious wealth of the few. This is our global food regime: a regime that recreates the crisis of the many. And it is, unfortunately, simply a normal part of how the regime works.

7

ADI SEREVI BUYS SOME FISH

SUPERMARKETS, PEASANTS AND THE CONTRADITIONS OF THE CONTEMPORARY FOOD REGIME

The rain had just stopped, temporarily; it was Suva's usual tropical midday downpour, and anyone who had been caught out in it was now soaking wet — a warm wet, but wet nonetheless. They were likely to stay wet, too, because the humidity in the air was, as usual, extraordinarily high. Rain is one of the defining features of life in Suva, a place that had been, prior to the infamous military coups of the early 2000s, a relaxed, laid-back town of 100,000. Suva is the capital of Fiji and in the mid 1990s its centre retained its colonial atmosphere and ambiance; in Suva it often felt like it was raining on a place that had stood still over time. I can recall one period when it rained on thirty-eight consecutive days. It always remains a mystery why the English, when they colonized the Fiji islands in the nineteenth century, eventually settled on Suva, in the rain-drenched and perpetually cloud-covered southeastern corner of Viti Levu, to be the capital. The western part of this rugged, emerald-green tropical island has clear, azure blue skies, beaches where the sand is nearly white and vibrantly bright sunshine. It can be the paradise of people's dreams. Local people say it's because the English wanted to be reminded of home.

It was 1992. I had come from an office in the Reserve Bank of Fiji, a greying modern office block that for many years had the distinction of being, at more than ten stories, the tallest building in the country and having the country's only escalator; indigenous Fijians from the villages considered the escalator a tourist attraction when they visited Suva. At the Reserve Bank I had met a friend, an ex-patriot economist funded by Britain's Overseas Development Institute; afterwards, I ducked down the street and under the covered sidewalks that were still found in Suva's commercial centre. I was lucky that day; the rain had missed me. I kept walking, to Morris Hedstrom, to do some grocery shopping for the evening.

For a country as off the beaten path as Fiji, Morris Hedstrom, or "MH"

as it is known locally, was a supermarket that Clarence Saunders would recognize. The arrangement of the space within it was like any in the world:
on entering I followed an architecturally-determined option of shopping
paths engineered to unconsciously persuade me to place products into my
shopping basket. I was treated, as Raj Patel (2007) memorably puts it, like
"rats in a maze." So, even though they can be damaged during a prolonged
stint in a supermarket, fresh fruits and vegetables were placed first when I
walked in because people like me shop in a better mood when they see fresh
food. Eggs, fresh imported meat and milk reconstituted from powder were
at the back, so that I would have to go through the store in order to get to
them. So too were the freezers: frozen food is cheap compared to fresh food
in Fiji, and so a more "everyday" item. In between the entry and the back
of MH were aisles of dried, tinned and processed food, all of which have a
longer shelf life, along with skin care and beauty products and household
products. Even along the aisles, the shaping of space by science was at work:
higher-cost items from the big transnational food and household product
producers were put at eye-level, while lower-cost items produced by local food
and household companies were below eye-level. Off to one side of the store
there was a bakery that used pre-prepared frozen dough to bake bread, cakes
and other items — I was very fond of the onion rolls. It would have been
far more cost-effective to have a larger bakery off-site that serviced multiple
MH outlets, but food scientists tell us that the smell of freshly baked bread
can make people feel hungry and thus encourage them to buy (Lindstrom
2008). Truth be told, it usually did it to me. Finally, at the crowded checkout
tills were the temptations: chocolate and sweets for children standing in line
with parents — at the eye level of the child.

In the past twenty-five years, supermarkets have come to dominate the
global food regime. More than the agro-chemical companies that emerged
to stride across the world during the Green Revolution, supermarkets are
the face of agro-food transnational corporations in the twenty-first century.
In 2006, global food spending was $6.4 trillion. The ten largest food retail-
ers in the world captured $1.1 trillion — some 17 percent — of total global
food spending (von Braun 2007). Such is the unchallenged domination of
the supermarket in our times that all the world's farmers produce a value
added, which can be defined as the difference between the farm gate sales
price minus the cost of production, of only $1.6 trillion. Walmart, Tesco,
Carrefour and Metro are the four biggest food retailers in the world, having
rapidly globalized in the 1990s (United Nations Conference on Trade and
Development 2009); these four firms alone sell more than 10 percent of the
world's food and employ more than three million people.

Supermarkets have come to drastically dominate our food for four
reasons, as suggested by Wayne Roberts (2008) of the Toronto Food Policy

Council. Supermarkets bleed abundance: there is food, and there is lots of it, and this makes us feel emotionally secure and stable. With abundance comes an aura of choice and selection — who would have thought that in a little IGA outside Collingwood, Ontario, I could get fresh basil. But behind the apparent choice that is offered in supermarkets lies a reality of ten types of baked beans and five brands of corn flakes, a phenomena that I earlier called "standardized differentiation" — things appear different but are in reality basically the same (Hatanaka, Bain and Busch 2006). Moreover, the imposition of rigorous quality standards by supermarkets, in terms of colour, shape and size, means that all our tomatoes are uniformly bland, all our bananas have the same curvature and it is impossible to find purple-sprouting broccoli in any North American supermarket; it will remain so until the supermarkets teach North Americans not to be afraid of it. Thirdly, supermarkets are convenient: they allow you to do all your household shopping in one location at the same time; whether I am in Suva, Seattle or Santiago, time is money in the twenty-first century, and convenience pays. Fourth is affordability. Food in supermarkets is cheaper than that found in High Street or Main Street grocery stores. As I write this, a current Walmart marketing campaign is touting the probably true tale that a standard fifty dollar basket of indistinguishable groceries is 10 percent cheaper in Walmart.

Of these reasons, two stand out. The basil in Collingwood is an example of how supermarkets efficiently manage their ability to obtain, distribute and sell their products, which in the case of MH is made more complex by the comparative isolation of Fiji. Modern supermarkets tightly manage the logistics of their food supply chain by centralizing their buying, working with specialized wholesalers that supply a single category of products to quite demanding quality and safety standards specifically for that supermarket, while using demanding contracts with suppliers to ensure on-time delivery of adequate quantities of products as and when needed (Bevan 2006, Blythman 2007, Fishman 2007, Simms 2007). The organization of procurement this way significantly reduces the cost of doing business for the supermarket, as it does not have to continually search for suppliers or keep inventories of products, while the terms and conditions of the contract offload the risk of the market onto the supplier. In the language of economists, the "transactions costs" — essentially, the costs of actually doing business — are reduced for the supermarket at the expense of the supplier. So, if the supplier is unable to buy oranges that meet the supermarket's quality standards, it costs the supplier money and not the supermarket, in that the supermarket is under no contractual obligation to take delivery of sub-standard "product" as well as the fact that the supplier will face contractual penalties for non-compliance, including reduced payment or indeed non-payment for some offsetting future deliveries.

Information technology has been a boon for procurement, enabling much tighter and more rigorous real-time management of the food supply chain, which allows the supermarket to reduce its stocks while making suppliers hang on to unsold stocks. Likewise, the marked improvements in global transport have had a profoundly positive effect: Martinair planes taking off from Jomo Kenyatta International Airport in Nairobi, Kenya, are full of freshly cut flowers, not people. Arriving in the Netherlands, the flowers are transported by trucks to the flower markets in the Westland, auctioned, returned to Schipol airport, and put on board KLM 747s in which the middle half of the plane's cabin does not have seating but instead carries cargo, having been set aside to transport flowers to the U.S. On arrival in America, the flowers are shipped to the central distribution point of the buyer, from which they can be trucked to specific supermarkets. The whole process from cutting to final sale can now take less than 36 hours, during which time each individual flower, bar-coded, can be tracked by computer to ensure that it is in-store as rapidly as possible (Perlez 1991).

Similarly, the refrigerated ships that allowed meat to be shipped from Australia and the U.S. to Europe in the late nineteenth century have now been replaced by container ships that can stack containers in their thousands — 9,000 containers are not uncommon. The astronomical increase in the capacity of the ships has dramatically cut the cost of shipping food and agricultural products long distances, including to more remote places like Fiji. This applies not only to food for people, but also food for animals: increasingly, the food that is grown around the world is being used to try to satiate the world's insatiable appetite for meat. As I have said, the world grows enough food; one part of the reason why people do not have enough to eat is that a lot of the food that is grown is fed to animals, not people, so that we can eat voluminous quantities of meat — bought overwhelmingly in supermarkets (Weis 2007, Patel 2010).

Efficient logistics is critical to the capacity of supermarkets to respond to the market imperative. In order to stock a chain of supermarkets, it is necessary to buy in far larger volumes than a smaller grocery store; all the flowers in the 747 can be for one supermarket chain. The vast majority of the food on the container ships arriving in Fiji is for MH. The bulk buying of supermarkets allows them to impose contractual terms and conditions, including prices and penalties, on their suppliers; the suppliers cannot alienate what is often, contractually, their sole customer, because they would lose access to the retail market on which they ultimately depend. Imposing low prices on suppliers allows lower prices to be passed on to customers, who, of course, are happy that the prices they are paying are being "rolled back," to use a phrase made popular by Walmart.

Paradoxically, though, low prices are also good for the supermarket;

while the profit margins for global supermarket are typically quite low — in the U.K., for example, profit margins over thirty years were broadly flat at around 5 percent (Thanassoulis 2009) — the way in which they are able to make an awful lot of money is by shifting large volumes of an astonishing array of ever-changing products. Tesco, for example, stocks more than 55,000 products (*Economist*, September 13, 2007). A wide variety of products can be sold in high volumes by making products as cheap as possible; this encourages people like me to buy, especially those non-necessary impulse purchases that look tantalizing or that we've heard about on television. That's one of the reasons supermarkets continue to sell so much industrially-processed mass-produced food: it's cheap. Selling cheaply in high volumes also allows supermarkets to undermine small-scale grocery stores, driving them out of business as they are unable to match the market imperative of price competitiveness imposed on them by big-box supermarkets.

The same forces of lower prices, higher volumes and tight food supply chain management are also true of MH, which, while a global minnow, dominates the food system of Fiji, operating in a way that shows, in a microcosm, the power of the modern supermarket. With a reported turnover of more than F$140 million, a staff of more than 1,100 and a chain of 24 stores, of which 19 are supermarkets, MH is the largest wholesale and retail organization in Fiji (Sporting Pulse 2012). Starting from a colonial general merchant store and trading company founded in 1910, it was acquired in 1956 by WR Carpenters Ltd, a firm that started out as a colonial commodity trader and eventually turned into a diversified conglomerate that was — and is — the largest private-sector enterprise in Fiji, with interests in cars, shipping, finance, property and other areas, including supermarkets. Currently owned by MBf Holdings, a diversified Malaysian conglomerate, Carpenters has an annual turnover of over F$400 million, provides over 2,200 jobs, and pays a substantial share of the corporate taxes and duties received by the state (Carpenters Fiji Group 2012). So it is an important part of the Fiji economy and is close to the state.

The business of MH, like the business of the global supermarket giants, is based around its logistical capacity, its ability to control its key suppliers by being the most important outlet for its supplier's products, by offering standardized differentiation, by dominating the retail food market through the offer of cheaper prices and thus selling in large volumes. As a result, MH has, unlike its rivals in Fiji, been able to benefit from the market imperative, capturing an ever-larger share of the retail food market across the country's four largest islands.

Going down the canned meat and fish aisle of the MH that day in 1992, I spotted Adi Serevi. Adi was a large woman: with her thick curly black hair cropped closely around her round face, her head seemed disproportionately small when set on top of the rest of her body, as reflected in the thick fingers that sat on her large hands. She was wearing an off-white pantsuit with a slightly garish pinkish-purple floral shirt that had a tropical motif; it is a fairly common outfit amongst the indigenous Fijian women that work as low-level civil servants for the state. I only knew Adi because she worked with my friend in the Reserve Bank; it can be pretty difficult for foreigners to get to know indigenous Fijians, even though they, despite repeated military coups and inter-ethnic tensions with the Indo-Fijian people, are remarkably friendly and open. Adi was reaching out to put some tins of Sunbell tuna flakes into her shopping basket; when she turned and saw me, her lips parted in a broad, welcoming smile. She greeted me in that all-encompassing Fiji way: "Bula," she said.

I knew that Adi was from a coastal village in the northeast of Viti Levu, close to the town of Rakiraki. Unlike Suva, there the sun was bright, the sky was almost always clear and the water was a deep aquamarine blue. By Fiji standards, Rakiraki was a major town; by international standards, it was little more than an overgrown village, organized around a colourful colonial-era main street and a long-distance bus and taxi stand, which also doubled as the local wet market. Most people in Rakiraki were going somewhere else; those that lived there either worked in the town's shops, including its MH, or worked a little ways away in the Penang Sugar Mill, one of four mills in the country where sugarcane from the area was turned into sugar, one of Fiji's leading exports, destined mainly for Europe. Growing sugarcane means that the area around Rakiraki is rugged, green and alive under the sparkling sky. Unusually for Fiji, in this area indigenous Fijians grew sugarcane; in most of the rest of the country Indo-Fijians grew the cane and indigenous Fijian cane gangs cut it (Akram-Lodhi 1997).

Adi grew up by the sea, and fishing for coastal communities was, for many, a main source of income and of protein. But it was far, far more than a merely economic activity for indigenous Fijian fishers. Fishing was a daily task, done inshore in nearby waters, and because it was the main source of protein for coastal communities and households, village society was organized around fishing. Fishing was arranged within kin groups by households, with a clear division of labour between men and women (Thompson 1949). As it was always based upon intricate local knowledge and skills, fishing became deeply embedded within the spiritual and material culture of coastal indigenous Fijian communities (Ruddle 1989). Indigenous Fijians have a deeply devout attachment to the sea. So, unearthing a *lovo* — a covered underground barbecue in which, amongst others, fish tightly wrapped in a weave of palm fronds, placed in the bottom of a pit lined with hot rocks and topped with root crops such as *dalo*, cassava and wild yam — is an elaborate communal celebration. Indigenous Fijians also love to share fresh fish drowned in *miti*, a mixture of thick coconut cream combined with onions, chilies, lime juice, salt and pepper and served with boiled cassava and unceasing accompanying rounds of palm-oil fried bread. Such foods — a legacy of a colonially-shaped and supermarket-dominated food system — helped explain Adi's weight. Fish is a central part of indigenous Fijian food culture, and I was more than a little surprised that Adi was buying tins of Sunbell tuna, rather than going down to Suva's central market and buying fresh fish. I asked her about it.

"I use it to make curries," she said in clear yet island-accented English. Inwardly, I groaned. Fiji's food can be a fabulous amalgam of South Asia and the South Pacific, but I was sure she meant "Fijian curries," a pretty common but almost inedible combination of powered tumeric and canned fish. "It's fast, and it's cheaper than the fish in the market." This I know is true: canned fish was, at F$2.50 a kilo, the cheapest source of animal protein that one could buy in Fiji. "And it lasts. I don't have a fridge, so I can't keep fresh fish very long. Tinned fish will keep, for when I need it, so I don't waste my money," she said, with the rolling garrulous laugh that was widely heard on the island.

When I lived in Fiji I always found it remarkable that a people that live by an ocean that, unusually, remains bountiful, with more than enough to sustain them, would settle for tinned fish over fresh fish. The reason that this had happened in Fiji is a microcosm of the global food regime in which we all live today; it is a story of globalization, agro-food corporations, the insecure livelihoods of Maurice Auxiliare and Bob Miller and the obesity of Jessica Carson.

The story begins in the 1980s, when a global campaign started to stop tuna fishing by huge, mile-long purse seine nets, which, trawling through the high seas, caught far more than just tuna, including dolphins, and which led to the rapid depletion of global tuna stocks (Brown 2005). The destructive character of the commercial purse seine tuna fishery was a godsend for the South Pacific tuna fishery; tuna had been caught by indigenous Fijian fishers for time immemorial, using techniques that did not destroy the fishery, so that when Japanese corporate interests began looking for new sources of high grade sashimi in the 1960s, attention turned to Fiji. The Japanese introduced longline tuna fishing to Fiji, in which mile-long fishing lines can catch hundreds of tuna at a time but no dolphins; they also set up an export-oriented processing facility on the small island of Ovalau, in Fiji's bucolic former capital, Levuka, to which was later added a canning capacity. The Pacific Fishing Company, better known as Pafco, became Fiji's biggest fish exporter and an important part of the country's economy, supplying mostly frozen and canned tuna to the U.S., Canadian and Japanese markets and, before 2007, to Europe, particularly the U.K. (Rajan 2005).

The Fiji government bought Pafco in 1986 just as the U.K.'s J Sainsburys supermarket was trying to secure long-term supplies of high quality line-caught canned tuna that they could label as being "dolphin-friendly," differentiating themselves from their competition and possibly gaining a brief competitive advantage. Scouring the globe, they came upon Pafco and signed a typically dense contract with them to supply Sainsburys own-label canned tuna, to be packed in Levuka; I always thought it was mighty odd to be walking down the dusty streets of Levuka and see discarded labels of J Sainsburys tuna blowing haphazardly in the wind. For over a decade, Pafco shipped canned dolphin-friendly tuna from the shores of Levuka to the high streets of Lincoln, Leeds and London (Veitayaki 1995). Then corporate strategy started to change. In 1999 Pafco started to reduce its canning operations and began shipping frozen tuna loins to American Samoa, where it entered free of import duties and was then canned. In this way, Pafco tuna obtained duty free access to the U.S. market, although its share of the total value added from catch to plate — which was, at between 4 and 6 percent of the final product, already quite small — was further reduced (Barclay and Cartwright 2007). Such a move was probably astute: in 2007 the European Union stopped imports of canned tuna from Fiji on the grounds of poor hygiene compared to that of plants found in southern Europe (Kelsey 2007).

So Pafco's canned tuna is now mainly sold in Canada, by John West, a company that originated in Liverpool in 1885 as a purveyor of canned goods but is now wholly owned by Simplot Australia, which is in turn a subdivision of JR Simplot, a transnational agro-food business based in Idaho with annual sales of $5.6 billion (Simplot 2012). One of John West's advertising slogans is revealing: "the best fresh fish doesn't make it to the market." This is because it stays in a food supply chain rigidly dominated by supermarkets and tight contractual relations with single specialized suppliers; like Horst Mueller, John West avoids the risk of markets.

A diversion is in order here, before returning to Pafco and Adi Serevi. Simplot was started by the legendary Jack Simplot, also known as Mr. Spud, who died in 2008 (Martin 2008, *Economist* 2008). Starting out in Idaho at age fourteen and with only $80 from his mother, Jack Simplot was able to ingeniously finance a bank loan that he used to buy several hundred pigs, on which he made $7,800. That money went into farming, a potato sorting machine and the processing and drying of potatoes and other vegetables. By 1940 he had 12,150 hectares of land and was filling 10,000 freight wagons a year with Russet Burbank potatoes. Simplot's eponymous company had become so big that during World War II one-third of all potatoes served in American military mess halls were from Simplot.

Simplot was by then a classic "vertically integrated" agro-food business: owning most of the land on which his company grew Russet Burbanks; fertilizing that land with phosphates from mines owned by Simplot; owning the forests that provided the wood for the boxes in which his vegetables were shipped around the U.S.; and using unsold food and processing waste to feed what in time became the biggest cattle ranch in the U.S., Simplot tried to directly own every stage of the supply chain that was necessary to get potatoes onto American plates.

In 1953, a chemist working for the already very profitable Simplot was able to develop a way of freezing chipped potatoes; by the late 1960s Simplot was the biggest supplier of frozen french fries to McDonald's, facilitating Simplot's transformation into a transnational corporation with substantial presence in Europe, Central America, Korea and, most recently, China, where its activities, as we will see, are dramatically altering the character of Chinese farming (Walden 1996).

But back to Fiji. Pafco's reliance on Sainsburys in the late 1980s and 1990s led to the consolidation of export-oriented longline industrial fishing in Fiji, which is the best developed in the South Pacific region. Industrial fishing is very capital intensive and large-scale, so while some of Pafco's tuna came from Fiji-owned fishing boats that fish in the waters of Fiji and beyond, more of it came from the much bigger Korean, Taiwanese and, more recently and increasingly, Chinese longliners that were licensed by the Fiji state and then chartered by Pafco to supply it with tuna (Barclay 2010). You see, for Pafco to work, whether it be in the frozen loin or canned segment of the market, it needed lots of fish; so the bulk of Pafco's tuna that ended up in cans with Sainsburys or John West labels on them originated from huge Taiwanese freezer vessels that still ply the international waters off the northeast coast of Fiji for years at a time (Barclay and Cartwright 2007). Under contract to Pafco, these vessels have to supply specific amounts of tuna caught in a particular way and of an appropriate quality. So Pafco uses its contractual relations with huge industrial fishing vessels to try and maintain its competitiveness. For the industrial fishing vessels such a relationship is beneficial, as the tuna has an assured buyer, and the longline tuna market can be, in per boat terms, very profitable — even though the share of industrial longline boats, which peaked at over one hundred vessels in Fiji, in the total tuna fishing fleet in the South Pacific is diminishing over time as purse seine boats deplete the stocks (Barclay and Cartwright 2006).

In addition to consolidating export-oriented capital-intensive fishing, Pafco reconfigured the livelihoods of the indigenous Fijians living on Ovalau. The success of its sales to Europe led it to expand in 1992, and by 2005 it employed around 750 people. These employees did not live in Levuka, which only had a population of 1,000; accompanied by their children to attend school, they were transported to Levuka on Pafco trucks from farming villages in the interior of the volcanic island and from the fishing villages that dotted Ovalau's coast. Waged labour became important for household livelihoods;

more particularly, female waged labour, because women dominated Pafco's tuna production line (Rajan 2005). Women that work for Pafco started because it was a steady wage, because they were often the sole income earners in their families — something that was itself something of a cultural revolution in Ovalau — and because patriarchal cultures in the villages resulted in women being told that they had no choice but to work for a wage; but it was a low wage. The hourly wage for tuna production-line workers was about $1 for women, which was ten cents less than the minimum wage for men. Various deductions brought down gross weekly earnings. By all accounts, discipline inside Pafco was very strict; no talking was permitted, workers were deterred from going to the toilet and being late resulted in stringent wage deductions (Leckie 2000). Pafco's success, as a result of contracts with supermarkets, created a cheap and dependent female working class amongst communities of indigenous Fijian peasants and fishers (Emberson-Bain 2001).

Pafco's reliance on Sainsburys also reconfigured indigenous Fijian diets; Adi Serevi's enjoyment of Fijian curries was a direct consequence. Fiji's longline industrial fishing economy needed bait for its lines. Some of that bait came directly or indirectly from the inshore fisheries, depleting that on which coastal villages relied heavily (Rajan 2005). Such depletion meant that food that was caught was replaced with food that was bought — and hence the need for waged work at Pafco in Levuka. It also meant that dwindling catches of fish were replaced, to some extent, by the purchase of fish; in this way Pafco built, for a while, a local market for its canned tuna, a local market that grew quickly enough in urban areas but which also grew in rural and coastal areas as livelihoods changed.

Ironically, though, Pafco was unable to maintain its place in the growing market for canned fish in Fiji that it was so instrumental in creating. Pafco's inability to sustain its market was a result of it being unable to meet the market imperative and compete with rivals on the basis of price: as the market for canned fish expanded, the ever cost-conscious MH began importing tinned fish from cheaper Thai suppliers; as a result, the market in Fiji is now dominated by imports from Thailand. In this way, peasant and fisher communities came to be reliant on cheaper food imports; Fiji's food system had changed.

Pafco also has a place within the turbulent politics of modern-day Fiji. In 1987, Colonel Sitiveni Rabuka led the first in a series of military coups in Fiji that were ostensibly propelled by the question of indigenous rights (Sutherland 2000). As a result of that coup, following the government's takeover of Pafco, the management of it was "indigenized." Indigenization brought little benefit to the women who worked the production line: the benefits went to those who were politically connected within the indigenous Fijian elite, who used their ties of patronage to improve their own position, both materially and culturally (Ratuva 2000). As went Pafco, so went

MH: in order to sustain its position as the only significant supermarket with cross-national presence, MH rented the land on which its stores are located. It rented its land from Fiji Holding Corporation, a state-created vehicle designed to improve the economic position of indigenous Fijians that has in actuality brought disproportionate material and social benefits to the indigenous Fijian elite that controls indigenous Fijian politics (Ratuva 2000). So the material production and distribution of food in contemporary Fiji brought benefits to Fiji's indigenous elite but not to the newly-created, small working class or the preponderance of increasingly marginalized small-scale fishers that could not compete with large-scale industrialized fishing (Rajan 2005). The configuration and organization of food as an industry and its effective control by supermarkets dedicated to working with singular and specific suppliers undermined the livelihoods of rural indigenous Fijians who relied on the fishery.

What is true for the indigenous Fijian inshore fishers is also true for the small-scale peasants of Fiji. The challenges faced by Fiji's peasants differ from those of farmers like Maurice Auxiliare, because rather than trying to grow food Fiji's peasants, like Sam Naimisi, grow a cash crop: the already-mentioned sugarcane. Sugarcane farming, processing and sugar manufacturing were first established in Fiji in the nineteenth century, when the country, as an outpost of the British Empire, was dragged into the global food regime that ensnared Pervaiz Qazi. Sugarcane continues to be the most important crop produced on Fiji's 21,000 farms (Akram-Lodhi 1997). It might seem odd that farmers continue to grow a cash crop and don't really grow much of their own food, but in a way it makes sense: like Maurice Auxiliare, Fiji's farmers could not compete with the prices of the food that is imported into the country by MH, so growing sugarcane and using earnings from it to buy food showed some sagacity.

But the reality is far messier than the theory. This was made clear to me in 1992 when I visited a farm on the western side of Viti Levu, midway between Sigatoka, a friendly, quiet farm town, and Nadi, site of Fiji's international airport and some upmarket beach resorts. Ganesh Prasad, a tall, lanky man with a messy shock of jet-black hair was standing under the awning of his thatched-roof whitewashed wood farm house. Under a clear blue sky, three large trees gave the house shade; it was a welcome respite from the unrelenting heat of the day. Looking away from the house, stretching out across the gently rolling, rising landscape, seemingly all the way to the rugged mountains in the distance, was sugarcane. It was the early part of the season, and the sugarcane was standing about two metres tall, its stout, jointed, fibrous stalk for the most part hidden by its verdantly green leaves that, swaying in the light breeze, resembled nothing as much as the sea: a green sea of sugarcane.

Prasad was a *girmitya*: the descendent of one of 60,595 indentured labourers brought, in this case, from what is now Uttar Pradesh to Fiji by British Governor Arthur Gordon on five year contracts to work on the sugarcane plantations that were the basis of the colonial economy and that were owned by the Colonial Sugar Refining Company (CSR), an Australian firm that at the time was one of the most important in the colonial economy (Lal 2004). When the management of the CSR realized that the real money to be made in sugarcane came not from its growing but from its milling, it started leasing its plantation land to those that had completed their indenture, including Prasad's forebears. By the mid 1990s, 70 percent of Fiji's 21,000 farms were run by the Indo-Fijian population that first came ashore in Fiji as *girmit* then continued to grow sugarcane (Akram-Lodhi 1997).

Prasad had a fairly typical farm: it was about four hectares; seed cane for new plantings was provided by Prasad from his previous harvest; he used small quantities of chemical fertilizers, in part because of the cost; a lot of the draft power that he used was provided by his animals, although he did, occasionally, hire farm machinery; and the farm was worked, for the most part, using only the labour of himself and his family, with the exception being harvesting, when he hired an indigenous Fijian cane cutting gang to get the crop in quickly. Prasad operated a small-scale farm like those I have visited elsewhere; he produced about eleven tonnes a hectare.

The market imperative made it difficult for Prasad, like Maurice Auxiliare, to make a living growing sugarcane. It cost Prasad altogether about F$25 an acre to grow the cane, as well as about F$13 a tonne to harvest it and transport it to the sugar mill for processing. With sugar prices of around F$50 a tonne, Prasad only made around F$12 per tonne as a net return to the work of himself and his family (Prasad and Akram-Lodhi 1998). It was not a lot: the Prasad household's income from farming was only around F$2,900 a year. So the issue for Ganesh Prasad was that, like other small-scale peasant farmers around the world, he had to compete on price with much larger-scale more capital-intensive producers.

I have never been to Queensland, Australia, but when it comes to sugarcane farming and processing it has a global reputation as one of the most cost-effective producers in the world. Australia has 4,800 sugarcane farms; Queensland is home to 4,000 of them, which is far fewer than Fiji (Canegrowers 2012). In the mid 1990s the average size of a sugarcane farm in Queensland was around sixty-eight hectares, which was a lot bigger than that found in Fiji, but this is actually quite misleading, because while there were many sugarcane farms in Queensland operating less than sixty-eight hectares, there were only a few operating more than sixty-eight hectares (Welsman 2011). In Australian cane farming as a whole, which is dominated by Queensland, in the mid 1990s 65 percent of farmers produced less than

7,500 tonnes a year, while 3 percent of growers produced more than 30,000 tonnes a year and 1 percent of growers grew more than 50,000 tonnes a year (Hooper 2008). The result was significant differences in average gross margins: for the farmer growing more than 50,000 tonnes a year, gross margins were A$6.30 per tonne, while for farmers growing less than 7,500 tonnes a year gross margins were A$1.24 a tonne. So there was significant differentiation between sugarcane farms in Queensland and evidence of a trend toward larger-scale and -sized farms, even as Queensland produced far more sugarcane with far fewer farmers on far larger farms than Fiji (Thompson et al. 2010).

The large scale of Queensland's farms is seen in their productivity, their costs and their profitability (Hooper 2008). Queensland's sugarcane farms were almost twice as productive per hectare as those of Fiji, largely because of extensive mechanization at all stages of production, allowing, as in America, Canada and elsewhere, small workforces to operate extensive holdings. Ganesh Prasad's sugarcane farm was small-scale and labour-intensive; the largest sugarcane farms in Queensland are large-scale and capital-intensive. Because of capital-intensive mechanization the cost of producing that sugarcane in Queensland was around A$21 a tonne in the mid 1990s (Hildebrand 2002); that was around $23 Fiji dollars. In other words, Queensland sugarcane cost around F$2 less a tonne to produce than that in Fiji. Being that much cheaper, Queensland sold — and still sells — a lot of sugar, which benefits, in particular, the biggest of the Queensland sugarcane farmers, whom I have just noted have far higher gross margins, gross margins that were far beyond the wildest dreams of farmers like Ganesh Prasad.

It's easy to turn around and say that Ganesh Prasad could not compete with Queensland because he was less productive, and there is an element of truth to this claim. Much of the sugarcane that he grew had not been replaced for several years, and a lack of new plantings of cane reduces productivity. Prasad could not afford to use various farm inputs that would have increased his yield, and his farm was too small to substantially benefit from mechanization even if he could have afforded it. Most importantly, Prasad did not own the land he farmed but rather rented it on a long-term lease, because most land in Fiji is owned by the indigenous Fijian population and administered, on their behalf, through the government-controlled Native Land Trust Board (NLTB). The NLTB, like Pafco and FHC, have not so much spread the wealth around the indigenous Fijian community as much as allowed some within the indigenous Fijian community to become well-off at the expense of the majority of indigenous Fijians (Ratuva 2000). For Ganesh Prasad, his lack of ownership of the land he farmed brought with it insecurity, which reduced his motivation to improve his farming techniques, thereby consigning him to being less productive: Prasad and his family were caught in a vortex of self-perpetuating poverty.

But if he is compared to the sugarcane farmers of Queensland it would be incorrect to say that Ganesh Prasad's lesser productivity was the main cause of his poverty. No: the cause of Ganesh Prasad's poverty was that because of the market imperative, small-scale farmers like Ganesh Prasad and small-scale sugar producers like Fiji had to compete in global markets with large-scale farmers from Queensland that were disproportionately responsible for setting the world price of sugar because they were and are the third largest sugar exporter in the world. It was the market imperative that had the potential to cripple Ganesh Prasad's ability to provide for his family: unless he was provided with some kind of state support to sustain his ability to compete, like that offered Bob Miller, he was not able to compete.

For many years Prasad did receive that support: the Sugar Protocol allowed Fiji to sell most of its sugar in Europe through transnational agro-food giant Tate and Lyle, which sold on to European supermarkets, and receive the same price that sugar beet farmers in the European Union were receiving, which was at least double and sometimes three times the world market price (Prasad and Akram-Lodhi 1998). The Sugar Protocol in effect insulated farmers like Ganesh Prasad from having to compete with farmers from Queensland, enabling him to ensure that one of his children went to university, a family first. But support for small-scale farmers in Fiji like Ganesh Prasad diminished in the 1990s because it contravened the rules governing international trade that are managed by the World Trade Organization (WTO). Under pressure from the WTO to comply with international trade rules, the European Union saw fit to "negotiate" the termination of the Sugar Protocol, replacing it in 2008 with a so-called "Economic Partnership Arrangement," which is little more than a mechanism to force Fiji to substantially reduce the levels of protection shielding the peoples of Fiji from the global food regime and establish in its place a liberal trade system between the E.U. and Fiji, a system that Fiji, a diminutive place of 740,000, cannot hope to sustain as an equal with a bloc of 500 million (Mahadevan and Asafu-Adjaye 2010). With the expiration of the Sugar Protocol and in the absence of the money needed to subsidize small-scale sugarcane-producing peasant farmers, it is becoming more and more difficult for them to manage, and the market imperative is, under the EPA, becoming more binding on farmers like Ganesh Prasad than was previously the case.

Maurice Auxiliare could not compete with imported "Miami" rice. Ganesh Prasad could not compete with Queensland's sugar. Around the world the configuration of the global food regime, and its effective control by transnational agro-food capital, most particularly supermarkets, has reconfigured diets and threatened the livelihoods of small-scale peasant farmers that struggle to compete with large-scale, well-financed industrial capitalist agriculture. This is not only the case between developed capitalist and developing capitalist countries; it is increasingly the case that within developing capitalist countries the relationship between small-scale and large-scale farmers is not the mythical "level playing field" as much as a hilly playing field, with small-scale peasant farmers struggling to stay at the bottom of the hill even as the large-scale capital-intensive capitalist agriculture that has developed in the last thirty years increasingly threatens to push them off the pitch.

As I have stressed, supermarkets and other agro-food companies demand uniform quality, reliable deliveries and large volumes. In order to get this, such companies are increasingly entering into stingily stringent contracts with farmers. These contracts may bring benefits to local communities: in eastern Rajasthan, small-scale peasant farmers grow barley under contract to global beer giant SABMiller so that their barley enters the supply chain for beer production in northern India despite the fact that most peasant farmers still plow their fields with camels, and it is common to find only three tractors for every one hundred farmers (Lamont 2009). Lives have been changed. But if contracts are with small-scale peasant farmers, one purpose of the contract is typically to encourage farm reorganization and consolidation around fewer suppliers, for whom the rigours of the contract will serve as an incentive to remain with the buyer as well as invest in becoming more capable of meeting the precise specifications of the buyer. That is certainly the case in eastern Rajasthan.

It is also the case in China. Remember Simplot? Simplot established a joint venture potato processing facility outside Beijing in 1992 and started producing frozen french fries there in 1993, principally for — you guessed it — McDonald's. By 1997 it was dealing with one thousand suppliers under demanding contracts designed to ensure that suppliers shouldered the risk of disease and poor harvests but which still required extensive monitoring by Simplot of contract compliance. In order to economize on the costs of enforcing contract compliance Simplot encouraged farm reorganization and consolidation amongst its suppliers, particularly stressing that more successful suppliers could lease additional land in order to start to mechanize and begin to reap economies of scale. By 2007 it had reduced its number of contracted suppliers from one thousand relatively small-scale labour-intensive farms to one hundred much larger, more capital-intensive farms capable of delivering increased volumes of potatoes for it, the only transnational potato processor in the country and so a dominant supplier of frozen french fries to global supermarkets and global restaurants operating in China (Dyer 2007).

That contract farming was not for the small of scale was vividly illustrated when, in 2006, I took a group of graduate students to visit the El Moughrabi citrus farm, which was close to Sadat City in the reclaimed desert northwest of Cairo. It was, in many ways, quite remarkable: driving down a parched road, surrounded by the off-brown colour of the barren desert as the wind whipped up the sand, we started driving through groves of orange trees where clearly nothing was meant to grow. The El Moughrabi farm was able to grow orange trees in a thin layer of topsoil, under which was literally the desert, as a result of a costly and complex irrigation system that pumped water up from the aquifer to below ground-level water hoses that ensured that the orange trees always received the right amount of water at the right time. This complemented the climatic conditions, which were good for growing citrus, and thus meant that the citrus grown in the area would ripen quickly. The farm grew some mangoes, but most of its seventy-five *feddan* (31.5 hectare) cultivated area was given over to growing mandarin and Valencia oranges under contract, again, to J Sainsburys; the farm devoted most of its cropped area to the April to December mandarin orange crop, producing about nineteen tonnes per hectare and thus growing four hundred tonnes a year. The rest of the cropped area was devoted to Valencia oranges, grown between July and December; the farm produced about twenty-two tonnes per hectare, one hundred tonnes a year.

The farm also purchased oranges from neighbouring farmers for processing, which was carried out in a large dedicated warehouse behind the main farm offices. The warehouse was a spotlessly modern, machine-driven sorting house, and purchasing was done to ensure that when the warehouse was working it was working at full capacity. Overseen by a male floor manager, the fifty or so young female floor workers, in their pristine blue uniforms and head scarves covering their hair, sorted the oranges as they passed in front of them along conveyor belts into one of three categories: those that fulfilled not only the demanding requirements of the EurepGap scheme (Campbell 2005), which certified that agricultural imports met the food safety requirements of the European Union and were therefore eligible for import, but also the stricter requirements of the J Sainsburys contract for the colour, size, shape and texture of the orange; those that did not meet the highest standards but which were perfectly capable of being exported to the Gulf States; and those that were only suitable for the local market.

Oranges for the local market were placed in grey plastic boxes that had seen better days. Those that were destined for the Gulf were packed into open green, orange and white cardboard boxes with the name of the farm clearly emblazoned in English on the side. Those that were packed under contract to J Sainsburys were placed in small clear plastic tubs that held about six oranges, with Sainsburys labels on their lids, prior to being loaded onto a refrigerated truck for the drive to the airport in Cairo, from where they would be flown to the U.K. and Sainsburys' central distribution centre in Basingstoke. They would be on the shelves of English supermarkets within twenty-four hours.

Egypt's El Moughrabi was a vision of the future of food and farming that Simplot was trying to replicate in China. Operating with machinery that had been imported from the U.S. and capable of meeting the exacting requirements of the E.U., the farm itself was mostly empty of people, with only a few workers tending the groves. Inside the warehouse, though, there were lots of employees, who were mostly young females and thus, according to the general manager, not needing to receive a wage that would support a family. The irrigation system, the farm equipment and machinery, the warehouse: all spoke of money and, notwithstanding state largesse, of which there was a lot, of the investment that the owner — apparently ex-military with ties to the now-discredited National Democratic Party, former President Hosni Mubarak's political machine — had been able to put into this farm in order to get it up and running as a business designed to make money through exporting.

El Moughrabi demonstrated an important facet of farming in contemporary developing capitalist countries: in a land where many did not get enough to eat, food was being exported for those who, globally, were the wealthy. Those that were incorporated into this global food regime were doing well — the general manager of El Moughrabi owned a good car; the young women who worked there made what was, by Egyptian standards, a reasonable wage; the owner must have been making money; and the customers of J Sainsburys in Staffordshire could buy Valencia oranges in December. But the privileges of those that were incorporated into the global food regime were based upon the exclusion of the many that were not: for an operation like El Moughrabi to work, globally, Maurice Auxiliare had to lose his livelihood, and indeed his life, and the future for Ganesh Prasad and his family was tenuous. For one to work, the other had to take place. They were two moments in a continuum of complex and contradictory agrarian change.

This is nowhere more apparent than in the so-called "Republic of Soy," a fifty million hectare area in southern Brazil, northern Argentina, Paraguay and eastern Bolivia (Holt-Giménez and Patel with Shattuck 2009, McMichael 2012). In the past decade tens of thousands of small-scale labour-intensive farms not unlike those of Maurice Auxiliare and Ganesh Prasad have been displaced by large-scale capital-intensive soy estates owned by Brazilian agricultural capital. Brazil is, in doing this, demonstrating why it, along with agrarian capitalists in Argentina, Chile, Mexico, South Africa and Thailand, is an exemplar of the "new agricultural countries," or NACs (Friedmann 1993). The NACs are countries that have a history of exporting food and agricultural products that for the most part were unprocessed. So Thailand has been an exporter of rice for millennia. But the state in the NACs wants to either replace or supplement older agricultural exports with the export of so-called "non-traditional" food and agricultural products. Non-traditional agricultural exports include higher value fresh fruit and vegetables, aquaculture products, horticulture and animal protein. So Thailand's rice exports, while still important, are not nearly as important to the country as its exports of shrimp and chicken — or even tomatoes (Rossett, Rice and Watts 1999). Indeed, this shows a key characteristic of the NACs: in an attempt to retain global cost competitiveness, significant amounts of processing takes place within the NAC to take advantage of lower unit labour costs and the improved efficiency of transport. The NACs are trying to use non-traditional agricultural exports to promote a form of agro-industrialization: agro-food transnational capital dominates a global food regime that has produced its own singularly unique path of agrarian change — the development of capital and capitalism in agriculture (Goodman and Watts 1997).

Brazil is the dominant NAC, being to global agriculture what China is to global manufacturing and India to global offshoring: a powerhouse whose volume of production and efficiency is hard for rivals to match, which means that Brazil has a huge influence on the global price for its food and agricultural products. Although Brazilian soils are not good, the country has a near-perfect agricultural climate, a huge river system to water crops, low land prices, lots of cheap labour and laggard environmental standards. It also has the indigenous research capacity to convert poorer soils into land capable of being used, thus expanding the agrarian frontier. These advantages mean that despite facing very high tariffs for its exports, Brazil is the world's largest or second largest exporter of sugar, soybeans, orange juice, coffee, tobacco and beef, and is rapidly building its exporting position in cotton, chicken and pork (Barros 2009). It is no wonder that the country has the largest agricultural trade surplus in the world and is using these resources to fuel its development. And Brazil is just at the start of its agro-industrial revolution, having the potential to increase its arable farmland by the equivalent of the entire area currently under cultivation in the U.S. — 170 million hectares.

The apparent success of the agro-industrialization "model" in large parts of Brazil has meant that small-scale labour-intensive peasant farms have to compete for land with large-scale capital-intensive industrial capitalist farms under contract to food producers, wholesalers and supermarkets. It is a competition that the small-scale peasant farmers are, for now, losing: while a big farm in Illinois might be 1,500 hectares, in the Republic of Soy a big farm is 15,000 hectares. To get away with this rapid reorganization and consolidation of large-scale industrial capitalist agriculture around the production of a crop that no one in Brazil actually eats while many continue to go hungry, capital in agriculture has had to reforge long-standing alliances with provincial politicians to protect their interests. This, along with state support in research and development around new agrarian techniques and technologies and large private sector investments in industrial capitalist agriculture, both from within and outside Brazil, has resulted in Brazil's farms seeing falling costs of production as scale of production increases, which contributes to increased exports and world market dominance.

In a world of NACs, small-scale peasant farmers face contracting space as large-scale capital-intensive industrial capitalist agriculture tries to increase its cultivated area. Indeed, this is the logic behind private capital-led "land grabs" in much of the world, a phenomena that is affecting a remarkably large proportion of the global cultivated area (Anseeuw, Wily, Cotula and Taylor 2012, Akram-Lodhi 2012). Increasingly the Ganesh Prasads and Maurice Auxiliares of this world have to compete against the products of the NACs and the developed capitalist countries and their place, because of uniform quality, reliable delivery and massive supplies, in the supermarkets of the world.

In the NACs the clear parameters of a global food regime based on a globalized industrial capitalist agriculture are emerging, and the agrarian question as such appears, at last, to have been solved: small-scale peasant farmers will be dispossessed through differentiation and displacement into the cesspools of urban slums, just as Maxime Auxiliare's mother was, being replaced by large-scale capital-intensive industrial capitalist agriculture producing for export, particularly to the developed capitalist countries. The organization and management of agriculture as a capitalist industry has captured the global food regime. Its effective control by supermarkets has contracted the space for small-scale peasant farmers like Maurice Auxiliare or Ganesh Prasad, who have often in any case been undermined by farm subsidies in the developed capitalist countries, as they are completely unable to meet the market imperatives of low cost, uniform quality, reliable delivery and massive supplies. Rural livelihoods for many are under threat as a population that is apparently surplus to requirements is created, which begs the question: for whom is this global food regime?

It cannot be for the small-scale fishers and peasants as well as the marginalized living in the impoverished slums; they are a relative surplus population for the global food regime. Is it for the wealthy consumers that are incorporated into it, who in any event constitute only a fraction of the world's population? Jessica Carson is one of those, but hardly seems to benefit from the ill-health the global food regime creates. Or is the global food regime for the agro-food transnational corporations that control the production, marketing and distribution of food and want to use the control of food to sustain profitability even if it comes at the expense of people's health?

8

"RED IN TOOTH AND CLAW"

CAPITALIST AGRICULTURE VERSUS FOOD SOVEREIGNTY

I have never met Robert Zoellick, but I have known about him for a long time. Zoellick is part of what can only appear to me to be a self-sustaining and seemingly eternal world governing class. A dyed-in-the-wool lifelong Republican from Illinois, following his graduation from Harvard Law School at the age of twenty-nine, Zoellick was well enough connected that he became, only three years later, for the period from 1985 to 1993, a mid-ranking political appointment in the U.S. government under presidents Ronald Reagan and George H.W. Bush, working in the Treasury Department, State Department and, toward the end, the White House itself, with immediate access to the president (Institute for Policy Studies 2011). How Zoellick managed this is not clear, but early in his career he made a key contact while working at the treasury: he worked under James Baker III while he was Ronald Reagan's Treasury Secretary; it was this connection that helped him get into the White House, and it was this connection that got him close to the Bush family.

During the first Clinton administration Zoellick was "exiled" to Fannie Mae, the U.S. housing finance corporation officially known as the Federal National Mortgage Association, a "government-sponsored enterprise" that was nationalized late in 2008 as a result of the U.S. economic crisis; he served as executive vice-president (Harvard Law School 2009). It has more than a touch of the old Soviet Union that a man who would, as we will see, become a key figure in the Republican Party would have, as his longest period of work in a single business, worked for a state-owned enterprise in a senior capacity. During the second Clinton administration Zoellick drifted through academic and business jobs; most notably, he briefly held a post with Wall Street powerhouse Goldman Sachs, the key private sector conduit into the global governing elite based around Washington and New York.

It was during the late 1990s that Zoellick became associated with the Project for the New American Century (PNAC). The PNAC was a Washington think tank with a list of associated persons that read like a who's who of U.S. neo-conservatism. The PNAC was founded in early 1997 by William Kristol and Robert Kagan; within a year it had sent an open letter that Zoellick had signed, along with Donald Rumsfeld and Paul Wolfowitz, to President Clinton advocating a unilateral pre-emptive attack on Iraq because of the threat that its purported weapons of mass destruction posed to the U.S. (Project for the New American Century 2001). Many of the signatories of this letter went on to become the architects of the war in Iraq. Zoellick's attachment to the PNAC demonstrated an idealistic streak that nonetheless had the potential to result in dangerous consequences; this view was reinforced by some of his written articles at the time. For example, in a January 2000 *Foreign Affairs* article he wrote that "the United States must remain vigilant and have the strength to defeat its enemies" (Zoellick 2000).

However, although Zoellick had close ties with senior U.S. neoconservatives he was an unlikely bedfellow because of the long-standing patronage that he had received from Republican realists George H.W. Bush and James Baker. Rather, it is best to explain these ties in connection to the uneasy shifts in allegiances that characterized Republican foreign policy initiatives during the late 1990s. Knowing that Bill Clinton's enduring popularity had implications for Al Gore's presidential campaign, a diverse group of neoconservatives and Republican realists came together in 1999 to collectively advise George W. Bush on foreign policy. The group, which became known as the Vulcans, was clearly full of tensions, including as it did Richard Perle and Paul Wolfowitz under the leadership of the politically quite different Condoleeza Rice, who had been in the National Security Council under George H.W. Bush and who was by this time already very close to George W. Bush (Mann 2004). Bob Zoellick was one of Rice's like-minded colleagues in the Vulcans.

That Zoellick had, with his membership of the Vulcans, entered the heart of the Republican governing elite was vividly demonstrated in 2000. James Baker, who was Chief Legal Advisor to George W. Bush, made Zoellick his second-in-command — "a sort of chief operating officer or chief of staff" — during the 36-day contest in Florida when the unclear election results were recounted, a contest that resulted in Bush becoming president (Tiefer 2004). Zoellick's reward for his astute political acumen was swift: he was named U.S. Trade Representative (USTR) in 2001, a cabinet-level appointment.

This is when I first got to know about Bob Zoellick because he became, at this point, a key player in efforts by the global ruling class to unlock markets and promote more liberal trade relationships through the instigation of the World Trade Organization's 2001 Doha Development Agenda, a wide-ranging set of international negotiations around trade liberalization and market access. As USTR Zoellick did not demonstrate an ideologically-driven commitment to free trade; he was not a WTO partisan (Perdikis and Read 2005). Like his former colleague and boss-to-be at the State Department, Condoleeza Rice, Zoellick was a Republican realist that sought to pragmatically preserve the global political and economic hegemony of the U.S. Such preservation did not require the projection of U.S. military and political power when it was not necessary; the global promotion of U.S. economic interests could preserve the global hegemony of the U.S. So Zoellick argued that while there was no alternative to globalization, it had to be led by the U.S. so that U.S. capital and consumers could benefit from it. For Zoellick free trade is not a philosophy; trade agreements are, in keeping with the Republican realism of George H.W. Bush and Condoleeza Rice, instruments of American national interests (Institute for Policy Studies 2011).

This meant that when the principles of liberal trade relationships could have a potentially deleterious impact on the short-term interests of the U.S. and important political groups within the U.S., Zoellick did not defend free trade; that was part and parcel of his highly personalized dispute with former European Union Trade Commissioner Peter Mandelson. Zoellick is more than anything else a classic American mercantilist, seeking to attract resources into the U.S., if necessary unilaterally, rather than a multilateral free trader. This mercantilism led Zoellick to begin to build a "coalition of the liberalizers" in September 2003: completing a wide-ranging set of bilateral and regional trade agreements outside the purview of the WTO, Zoellick ensured that a number of countries would keep their markets open to U.S. capital and protect U.S. investments in those markets in exchange for continued access to the coveted and crucial U.S. market (Feinberg 2003). This strategy of "competitive liberalization" was in particular designed to weaken the demands of more powerful developing capitalist countries in the WTO such as Brazil and India for access to the U.S. market for food and agricultural products and cuts in farm subsidies (Zoellick 2002). Mercantilism was also demonstrated in the U.S.-led dispute against the European Union in the WTO over genetically modified foods, which attempted to force E.U. countries to accept imports and production of transgenic crops, crops whose production required key inputs that were controlled by U.S. agro-food transnational corporations, as we have already seen (Feinberg 2003).

It's funny that Zoellick was a member of the Vulcans, because to my mind he looks like one. He is thin, as befits a long-distance runner, and his suits fit loosely on his frame. His head is almost quadrilateral as it rises up from his protruding chin. His messy brown hair is receding up his forehead, but clearly slowly, given his age. His ears are like those of Prince Charles, sticking out of the side of his head as if they have been glued on incorrectly. The thick eyebrows that sit on top of his blue eyes are angled away from his nose; perhaps that's the feature that makes him most look like a Vulcan from the *Star Trek* TV series. When he wears glasses, as he frequently does, they are large, and perched precariously on the front of his nose. Like a Vulcan, Zoellick has a reputation for being a fairly charmless intellectual, and certainly that charmlessness comes through aplenty in the numerous snippets of him that are available on the Internet. When Zoellick is photographed in an African village or an Asian school he looks distinctly out of place in his forced casualness; he looks uncomfortable. Unlike a Vulcan, though, he is known to have a bad temper.

Zoellick's Vulcan-like appearance belies the power to which he ascended. In early 2005 Condoleeza Rice chose him to be her number two at the State Department. He only lasted there for a year and a half; apparently he felt marginalized. He went back to Goldman Sachs in as vice-chairman of International Operations, reflecting the Rolodex that he had acquired as USTR, before being tipped, in early 2007, to become the eleventh president of the World Bank, following the resignation of Paul Wolfowitz after he had, amongst other things, improperly intervened in personnel decisions in order to promote his lover at the time. Zoellick resigned from the presidency of the World Bank in 2012.

As president of the World Bank, Zoellick ran the International Bank for Reconstruction and Development (IBRD) and the International Development Association (IDA), as well as three smaller affiliates of the World Bank Group, which are collectively owned by the 185 countries that are members of the World Bank. With a staff of more than nine thousand, many of whom are the best and the brightest, the World Bank is a source of financial and technical assistance to developing capitalist countries trying to claw their way to the riches that they associate with the U.S.

With just one arm of the bank, the IBRD, having total assets of $283 billion in 2010 (World Bank 2010b) and with cumulative lending, commitments and guarantees of $691 billion since 1944 (World Bank 2008), the World Bank is no minnow: it is a powerful institution, particularly for those many countries in sub-Saharan Africa, Asia and Latin America for whom it is a main source of loans or grants. The bank is even more powerful than these figures imply, for two reasons. First, the World Bank coordinates certain anti-poverty programs, known as Poverty Reduction Strategy Papers, with the International Monetary Fund, meaning that money from the fund is conditional upon the approval of the bank. Second, many bilateral donors, including big spenders like the European Union, the United States, Japan, the United Kingdom, Sweden and others coordinate their grant-giving and loan-making activities with the bank, meaning that access to these monies can often be conditional upon having satisfied the dictates of the bank. So the World Bank Group, of which Bob Zoellick was president, is the most important global institution promoting economic and human development in the world. Given that almost half the planet lives on less than two dollars a day (in 1993 purchasing power parities), and that the number of people that live on less than one dollar a day is almost a billion, it's a pretty important mission (Population Reference Bureau 2011).

The World Bank is housed in Washington, DC, on the corner of H and 19th streets; the IMF is across 19th Street. The World Bank is in a large, imposing building, a fairly typical sight in Washington: the vast inner atrium rises from a marble floor thirteen stories to a glass roof, like the dome of a broad modern cathedral. A bronze sculpture of a small African boy using a stick to lead a sightless African man sits next to a tree that rises up through part of the atrium, which also has a pool fed by a waterfall, against which a sign proclaims the World Bank's mission: "Our dream is a world free of poverty." The message seems oddly antiquarian in light of the high modernism of the building.

The World Bank has a vision for the future of the world's farmers. It was not Bob Zoellick's vision, for it was started under his predecessor Paul Wolfowitz, but he no doubt has shared it. It is a vision captured in the *World Development Report 2008: Agriculture for Development* (World Bank 2007). World Development Reports are the bank's annual flagship publication, offering a definitive in-depth analysis of a specific aspect of development. Although World Development Reports commit the bank to nothing, they are usually used by the bank to provide a rationale for specific development policies, either independently or in conjunction with other development donors. They are also used to encourage member countries to adopt a set of policy priorities that are consistent with the analytical recommendations made in the report. The bank invests a significant amount of time and money in producing a World Development Report — someone who should know told me that the 2008 report cost more than $600,000, a figure that does not include the cost of the time of the World Bank staff that contributed to the report.

The 2008 report was the first on agriculture since 1982. It starts, promisingly, with an explicit admission of failure: most poor people in the world live in the countryside and rely, to a greater or lesser extent, on farming to provide at least part of their livelihood, and yet "the share of agriculture in official development assistance declined sharply over the past two decades ... The bigger decline was from the multilateral financial institutions, especially the World Bank." It claims that this decline is a result of "agroskepticism" amongst donors, which is an outcome of "past unsuccessful interventions in agriculture" that were previously "promoted heavily by the World Bank" (World Bank 2007).

So far, so good. We have seen in this book that starting in the late nineteenth century small-scale peasant farmers around the world, usually as a consequence of the imperialism of the time, began to be forcibly incorporated into world trade as a global food regime was constructed. We have seen how dispossession through displacement and differentiation, which was forced upon them by the privileged, undermined rural communities and led to calls for land and agrarian reform around the world, calls that ultimately benefitted the already powerful. We have seen how the failure of land and agrarian reform to improve the lives of marginalized small-scale peasant farmers around the world led to the adoption of Green Revolution biotechnologies, and consequently gene revolution biotechnologies, which have consolidated the emergence of capital in agriculture in many developing capitalist countries, most notably the NACs, while also allowing agro-chemical transnational corporations to squeeze value out of the marginalized, making their poverty a source of profit. We have seen how the globalization of food in the mid and late twentieth century undermined the living of countless millions of small-scale peasant farmers around the world as cheap food provided as aid or imports forced many of them to quit farming and migrate into the planet of slums. We have seen how supermarkets increasingly use developing capitalist countries to source non-traditional high-value foods such as fresh vegetables, fruit, horticulture and aquaculture that are produced not to improve the lives of the marginalized but to allow the relatively affluent of the world to be able to shop the world in their supermarket, while all the while increasing the financial profitability of those same supermarkets and so pleasing shareholders. We have seen how this domination of our global food regime by supermarkets is directly associated with a worldwide obesity crisis, even as hundreds of millions around the world do not get enough to eat. We have created a global food regime that brings hardship to a majority of humanity, profitability for some and which, in terms of its ecological sustainability, probably can't last. The world faces a crisis rooted in the ability of many to access adequate subsistence, so producing a World Development Report on agriculture seems like a good first step in starting to address this crisis.

How, then, did Bob Zoellick's World Bank think that the crisis might be solved? The first thing to stress is that within the World Bank, both in the teams that work on the reports and beyond, there are a wide variety of often quite divergent views. Part of the culture of an institution like the bank is that it has to have processes and practices that allow divergence to be resolved into a uniform and coherent position. The modes by which the bank does this are central to its ability to maintain a consistently homogenous approach. This means, then, that in terms of the bank's approach to the global food crisis, not everyone in the bank supports all or even some of the analysis and recommendations that are on offer; but, critically, key senior personnel will support the overall tenor and conclusions of the report.

The 2008 report begins by breaking down developing capitalist countries into one of three groups, based upon agriculture's contribution to economic growth and the share of rural poverty in total poverty in the country. These three "worlds" are: agriculture-based countries, with the contribution of agriculture to growth being more than one-fifth of the total and the rural poor being at least half of all the poor, and which are typically those countries found in sub-Saharan Africa; transforming countries, with the contribution of agriculture to growth being less than one-quarter of the total and the rural poor being at least six-tenths all the poor, which are typically the larger countries of Asia such as India and China; and urbanized countries, with the contribution of agriculture to growth being less than one-fifth of the total and the rural poor being less than six-tenths of all the poor, which are typically countries found in Latin America. The report presupposes that economic development must see agriculture-based countries becoming, eventually, transforming countries that in turn become, eventually, urbanized countries.

The report argues that each group of countries faces a different set of issues if agriculture is to be transformed, and that, within this, countries within each group face a specific set of issues that they must address if agriculture is to be transformed. But what is striking about the report's understanding of their purported three worlds of global agriculture is that it results in a remarkably uniform triad of pathways out of rural poverty: commercially-oriented entrepreneurial smallholder farming amongst those operating less than two hectares of arable farmland; the rural non-farm enterprise development that creates non-farm waged labour; and outmigration to the cities, where farmers become waged labour. Thus, the bank presents, in a diverse and heterogeneous world, a standardized and homogenous set of paths out of rural poverty across the three worlds of global agriculture, only one of which involves small-scale peasant farmers continuing to farm. The report comes across as being quite pessimistic about the ability of farming as a livelihood to cut rural poverty in the countryside of developing capitalist countries.

The three pathways out of rural poverty across the three worlds of global agriculture require strikingly similar and indeed, to those that have studied structural adjustment in agriculture, strikingly familiar policies: trade, subsidy and price policy reforms in developing capitalist countries that get farm and non-farm prices "right" are the key to achieving poverty-alleviating growth. The role of trade, subsidy and price policy reforms in developed capitalist countries, and the implications of such reforms for the viability of small-scale peasant farming in developing capitalist countries, are inferred but are not systemically addressed. Getting prices right is needed because this will improve the investment climate in the rural economies of the three worlds, particularly by promoting investment in non-traditional high value fresh fruit and vegetables, livestock, horticulture and aquaculture products. It is this investment, according to the report, that will allow commercially-oriented entrepreneurial smallholder farmers to use contract farming or other forms of outgrower schemes to insert themselves in better positions in the global food supply chains organized around the needs of supermarkets. So for those small-scale peasant farmers whose future lies in farming, the report emphasizes the capacity of market-led development and contract farming to generate the economic growth that agriculture and rural poverty reduction needs.

Beyond these reforms, which the World Bank has been pressing on developing capitalist countries since the onset of structural adjustment in agriculture in the early 1980s, the report adds a set of "usual suspects," rural development policies and programs that the bank has been advocating since the early 1990s, including better soil and water management, the rapid adoption of new agricultural technologies and transgenics, improved extension services to disseminate information about the use of these new agricultural technologies, enhanced infrastructure provision to allow farmers to get their crops to market and access to better health care and education, to improve skill sets.

The report pays a great deal of attention to smallholder farming in Asia, Africa and Latin America, but its emphatic support for commercially-oriented entrepreneurial smallholder farming suggests that this support is by and large rhetorical, because commercially-oriented entrepreneurial smallholder farming represents a very specific and distinct form of farm enterprise that is likely to emerge from within the ranks of a larger set of smallholder farmers. Smallholder farming is likely to be: focused on the small-scale production of staple foods, some of which may end up in food markets, and which, together with the fruits from any waged labour that is undertaken, generates the cash income to buy the products that the family does not produce themselves; labour-intensive, using mostly but not exclusively family labour; market vulnerable, in the sense that peasant households are more sensitive to shifts in crop prices and wages; and hence risk averse. Commercially-oriented entrepreneurial smallholder farming, on the other hand, is more likely to seek to take advantage of market imperatives through sharpened competitiveness and become, over time, relatively more capital-intensive in their use of modern farm equipment and machinery and rely upon the purchase of labour-power.

If these distinctions are correct, commercially-oriented entrepreneurial smallholder farming will create problems for the wider small-scale peasant farming community as growth takes place, in that those commercially-oriented smallholder farm entrepreneurs that are successful will need increased access to land, labour-power and other resources in order to continue to grow. These resources are likely to come from the comparatively less successful and more market vulnerable small-scale peasant farmers who are unable to make the leap into commercially-oriented farming and whose farming activity offers at best limited opportunities and lesser productivity. According to the report, such farming is, in global terms, not viable in the long term when set beside commercially-oriented entrepreneurial smallholder farming. So, the inefficient small-scale farmer will, facing a squeeze on their ability to produce and reproduce, be displaced by the more efficient market-oriented farmer: the possibility of processes of dispossession through differentiation in the countryside, market-led appropriation of land and exclusion is implicit in the report's analysis of the prospects for smallholder farming in developing countries (Hall, Hirsch and Murray Li 2011).

The report fails to place the expected expansion of commercially-oriented entrepreneurial smallholder farming — or what should be called emerging larger-scale capital-intensive proto-capitalist farming — within the global food supply chains that, as we have seen, operate to benefit the supermarkets and chemical companies that dominate the chain. Food supply chains are subject to the power of highly monopolistic forms of transnational corporate interests. It is well known that under contract farming the allocation of the added value that is divided between the farmer and the contractor working for or as part of a supermarket or chemical company is not on the basis of real value added but on the basis of asymmetrical power relations between the contract farmer and the agro-food corporations that dominate the chain (Sivramkrishna and Jyotishi 2008). There is, in addition, still a second asymmetry: poorer small-scale peasants are not contracted by agro-food corporations, which instead prefer to work with the already emerging proto-capitalist farm sector because of greater certainty around the monitoring and enforcement of contracts. So the report's advice would not necessarily establish pathways out of rural poverty but rather consolidate the access of emerging proto-capitalist farmers subordinated within food supply chains dominated by agro-food corporate interests.

The point about this is that agricultural markets globally are strongly controlled by agro-food transnational corporations that capture a disproportionate share of the global value added in food and agriculture and that have a decisive capacity to influence the terms and conditions by which sales take place (ActionAid International 2005). Emerging proto-capitalist farmers from developing capitalist countries will be integrating into food supply chains in subordinate positions to the agro-food transnational corporations that regulate the operation of global agricultural markets and the global food regime. So the report's advice does nothing so much as deepen the operation of the very mechanisms of power and privilege that have led world agriculture into the current crisis. Bob Zoellick's World Bank would consolidate a capitalism that, in Tennyson's memorable 1850 phrase, would be "red in tooth and claw" in global agriculture: predatory, violent and unsentimental, it would be one dominated by capital that has been unleashed in order to seek profits at the expense of people who are already marginalized around the world.

While I've never met Bob Zoellick, I have met Rafael Alegría, a couple of times. Alegría is a short, balding, stout man, a peasant farmer whose belly has, in the last fifteen years, started to expand in girth as he has farmed less and acted as an advocate more. Alegría is from Honduras, where he farmed in Olancho, a sparsely populated, rugged, heavily forested region that lies at the end of the eastern road from the capital, Tegucigalpa, and stretches all the way to the Nicaraguan border and north into the emptiness of the fabled Mosquito Coast. Olancho has been an untamed frontier since the first Spanish colonizers clashed with the local population when they were searching for Aztec gold in the early sixteenth century, and today that reputation for resistance continues (Leonard 2011).

Being heavily forested, Olancho has for decades been overlogged by wealthy timber barons connected to the state and the military (Sunderlin 1997). The value of the timber has encouraged the barons to encroach upon the lands of small-scale peasant farmers. Overlogging has also lowered the water table and caused crop failures for the small-scale peasant farmers that need the water, stretching livelihoods and resulting in many having to send family members north to the U.S. to work. But not all families have had to send a migrant north. Farms in Olancho are one of two types: small-scale peasant farms that grow mostly maize and beans; and large-scale livestock farms with beef cattle and dairy cows (Kaimowitz 1996). The intersection between small-scale farmers, livestock farmers and timber barons has generated conflict between the poorer campesinos, the richer rancheros and the timber barons, with the latter two facing the former, with the aid of a corrupt state that is sensitive to the needs of the rural dominant classes (Stonich and DeWalt 1996). Much of the conflict is over land; despite a state-sponsored land reform process that had redistributed some land to small-scale peasant farmers, like Emiliano Zapata's followers campesinos in Olancho tend to be land-poor when they are not landless and in any event do not have secure control of the land that they farm, as the rural elite, with the aid of the state, commonly try to take control of it (Jansen and Roquas 1998). More recently, the conflict is over transgenic crops, as the state, with assistance from the U.S. Agency for International Development, has tried to push the introduction of genetically-modified maize onto the small-scale peasant farmers of the area (Humphries et al. 2012).

The Olanchanos have a saying: "Olancho is easy to get into and hard to get out of." Certainly, being from Olancho, and its long history of resistance to authority, has shaped Rafael Alegría, just as being Olanchanos is reflected in what he does and how he does it: between 1972 and 1975 he was a local organizer for the Unión nacional de campesinos (UNC; National Union of

Peasants), arranging for the establishment of farmer cooperatives and land reclamation in his native village of Potrerillos. It was his UNC membership that resulted in his being able to complete a law degree and better serve his fellow campesinos. But being a member of the UNC was a dangerous thing to do; there is a long history of the state-sanctioned assassination of peasant activists in Honduras in general and in Olancho in particular. One of the worst atrocities was in Olancho and directly affected Alegría; on June 25, 1975, when peasant activists were planning a hunger march on the capital, the military and local landowners attacked the UNC members at Los Horcones, killing fourteen of them. Alegría was subsequently imprisoned for a time his activism.

Peasant activists in Central America have a long history of organizing across the porous borders of the region. Arising in part because migration to the U.S. has resulted in wide-ranging cross-border ties, cross-border mobilization and organization was given further impetus by the victory of the Sandinista movement in overthrowing the Somoza dictatorship in 1979 and the resulting international solidarity movement that the victory created, particularly amongst Central American peasant movements that witnessed the success of the Nicaraguan agrarian reform and then compared it unfavourably to the collapsing attempts at land reform in their own countries.

During the 1980s Alegría continued working to promote land and agrarian reform against a backdrop of U.S.-supported state-sanctioned campesino repression but increasingly carried his work to other countries in the isthmus and participated in peasant-to-peasant exchanges across continents. This cross-border work eventually led him, in May 1992, to the second congress of the *Union nacional de agricultores y ganaderos* in Managua, a meeting of farm activists from Central and North America and Europe. A year later, forty-six farm leaders met in Mons, Belgium, under the auspices of a Dutch non-governmental organization, *Paulo Freire Stichting*, with the objective, which was not known to their hosts, of building an international farmers' movement that explicitly rejected the dominant capitalist agricultural model that was, at the time, being aggressively globalized through the multilateral trade negotiations being conducted under the General Agreement on Tariffs and Trade, the predecessor to the WTO (Desmarais 2007, Borras Jr. 2008). On May 16, 1993, the forty-six leaders issued the Mons Declaration and founded *La Vía Campesina*, the Peasant Way, an organization dedicated to protecting the needs of the world's peasants and small-scale farmers that work the land and produce the world's food. Rafael Alegría became the International Coordinator of Vía Campesina, a post he held until 2004; indeed, the Honduran Coordinating Council of Peasant Organizations hosted Vía Campesina.

Vía Campesina has grown in the past fifteen years into a transnational rural social movement with 148 member organizations in 69 countries representing possibly as many as 100 million people: it is without doubt the largest social movement in the world (Borras Jr., Edelman and Kay 2008). It offers a vision of the future that is starkly different from that proposed by Bob Zoellick's World Bank in *World Development Report 2008: Agriculture for Development*, promoting not a model of emerging proto-capitalist farms subordinated to agro-food transnational capital but rather a model of small-scale family-farm based agriculture rooted in sustainable production processes that use local resources and preserve local culture and traditions (Desmarais 2007). This is the key, suggests Vía Campesina in their pronouncements, to achieving food sovereignty: the right of peoples and countries to set their own agricultural and food policy so that they can produce and consume much of their own food (Holt-Giménez and Patel with Shattuck 2009).

For the members of Vía Campesina, food sovereignty organizes small-scale family-farm-based food production and food consumption around the needs of local communities, giving priority to local farm production for local food consumption. To de-globalize food in this way and rebuild local food economies, food sovereignty includes the right to regulate and protect food and agricultural production and to shield countries from the dumping of agricultural surpluses and low-price imports. Food sovereignty requires that peasants, small-scale farmers and landless people get access to land, water and farm-bred seeds, as well as other natural resources that are needed for sustainable farming, and adequate public services, including education, health and appropriate farm management and marketing support. Food sovereignty takes precedence over liberal trade policies, according to La Vía Campesina (2012).

Clearly, the members of Vía Campesina are working to undermine and transform the prevailing industrialized capitalist agricultural model that dominates the provision of food around the world, subordinates farmers and workers and concentrates economic and political power in the hands of agro-food transnational corporations. Instead, Vía Campesina proposes the reestablishment of highly decentralized farm production in which farming, processing, distribution and consumption are controlled by the people in their local communities and not by transnational capital. In other words, Vía Campesina wants to replace a global food regime "red in tooth and claw" with a series of interconnected and interdependent local food systems that support and sustain communities (Desmarais 2007). As Chavannes Jean-Baptiste, the head of Vía Campesina Haiti has said, Vía Campesina is engaged in "a struggle for the defense of peasant life and agriculture" (Bell 2002).

With the global food regime in a crisis of its own making, there can be little doubt that Vía Campesina is right to be highly critical of the water- and hydrocarbon-intensive industrial capitalist agriculture that is now being offered by the World Bank as the solution to the world's food problems: if anything, it was the expansion of the bank's farming and food production model that created the crisis that Vía Campesina, in suggesting that small-scale peasant-based farming offers a better path to steward the planet's soil, water and genetic resources, as well as meeting the food needs of the globally dispossessed, is seeking to undo. But Vía Campesina's vision does have problems, and one in particular stands out, at least to me.

The agrarian question is about understanding whether or not, and if so, why or why not, capitalism is developing in agriculture. Clearly, the World Bank has a vision of how the agrarian question is to be answered: migration to the cities, rural waged labour and the establishment of viable industrial capitalist farms within global food supply chains. Vía Campesina, though, does not offer an answer to the agrarian question. Its diverse membership, which is a source of its strength, represents a number of alternative forms and systems of rural production under vastly different sets of social conditions that revolve around access to, control over and stewardship of land and other agrarian resources. So we see landless workers in Brazil, richer small-scale peasants in India and dairy farmers in Germany all being members of Vía Campesina. But this diverse membership does not necessarily have consistent interests — even within these groups, men and women farmers will not necessarily have the same interests. The members of the organizations that make up Vía Campesina have differing degrees of insertion into or protection from capitalist social and economic conditions and relations and exposure to market imperatives. The food sovereignty alternative put forward by Vía Campesina — agrarian reform, agroecological technology, fair prices for farmers and greater emphasis on local production — cannot be isolated from the prevailing social and economic conditions and relations, which are currently capitalist, within which the call for food sovereignty is situated. So it is not clear from Vía Campesina whether rural social movements are developing an understanding of the ways by which they can seek to reconfigure the social conditions and relations of capitalism or are in fact forging ahead with the development of a post-capitalist alternative.

In 2006 I heard Rafael Alegría directly chastise staff members of the World Bank, the Food and Agriculture Organization of the United Nations and other international economic institutions that are supposed to be confronting the crisis in the global food regime. He is an accomplished, emotional, eloquent and powerful speaker that can captivate an audience. In January 2009, he said:

> We've never lived a crisis like the present one. And we did not create it. Humanity is threatened, but not by us. On the contrary, we are the ones who guarantee food. Now, however, it is financial capital that controls the harvests. They speculate with them. We are the

ones called to produce when food is missing. The surpluses of the European Union and the United States will not be able to resolve the problem. (Desmarais and Navarro 2009)

It is not only passionate; it is, as I have tried to show, largely correct. When he says, as he has so many times, that "each country should produce its own food" (Osava 2001), this is not done narrowly, to advance the cause of the small-scale peasantry and the global peasant movement of which he is a part. It is done, rather, because

> for us in the Vía Campesina the human aspect is a fundamental principle, so we see the person, man and woman, as the centre of our reason for being and this is what we struggle for — for this family that is at the centre of it all. Common problems unite us ... but what also unites us are great aspirations ... What unites us is a spirit of transformation and struggle ... We aspire to a better world, a more just world, a more humane world, a world where real equality and social justice exist. These aspirations and solidarity in rural struggles keep us united in the Vía Campesina. (La Vía Campesina 2006)

Vía Campesina shows us why we need to build a better food system. It also shows us part of what that food system will look like. For the rest, read on.

9

WHAT
IS TO
BE DONE?

SOLVING THE GLOBAL
SUBSISTENCE CRISIS

Food is the elemental building block of life: without it, we die. For most of our history, people lived in a simple symbiosis with their food. They hunted, they gathered, they ate and they lived — short, harsh, often brutish lives. Only in the last 10,000 years — the wink of an eye in human history — have things changed. People learned how to farm, and with an increasing ability to control the provision of food, and especially produce more food than the community required, people flourished. Life remained hard for the majority — surplus food gave the power of life and death to those who could control it, and human inequality was born. Inequalities and hierarchies were corralled into place with the emergence of the state, which was first built on the capacity to control surplus food (Fraser and Rimas 2010). Surplus food also allowed small-scale peasant farmers to quit farming; some became artisans and people with a trade. Centuries later they became the waged labour force needed for an expanding capitalist manufacturing sector, which developed as the wealth of the countryside was invested by dominant rural classes in industrial capacities and commodities produced with the purpose of being sold under the imperative of competitive market conditions. The modern world — our world — has its beginnings in a set of transformations that commenced in our relationship to food and farming.

In the last hundred years our connection with food and farming has changed beyond recognition. Most of the world's food is now grown to be sold in markets, where it is imperative that it is competitively priced. This overwhelming need to be competitive has benefitted some farmers around the world; but for an absolute majority, who cannot compete with farms and farmers operating under altogether different ecological and technological production conditions that may be half a world away or may be next door, life is becoming steadily and irrevocably harder. Even those who are market-competitive are not the main beneficiaries from the evolving architecture of our global food regime, because supermarkets and agrochemical companies are now able, in historically unprecedented ways, to dominate the conditions that even successful farms face.

The supermarkets that steer the global food regime want huge quantities of food that is standardized, durable, long-lasting and cheap. This is true for meat, vegetables, grains and dairy. This is as true of those large corporations that apply the principles of modern supermarkets to the large-scale retail sales of organic food, however it is defined —companies such as Whole Foods Market, which Michael Pollan (2006) rightly calls "big organic" — as it is of Walmart, the world's largest food retailer. The result in both the conventional and the organic supermarket sector has been a diverse proliferation of an extensive range of complex chemical and nutritional additives that are scientifically added to heavily processed food in order to add shelf life and nutritional content to them (Schlosser 2005). Heavily processed food is also massively reliant on the processed sugars found in high fructose corn syrup, which is added to a bewildering array of all and sundry food to increase the sales of the products because of a singularly unique characteristic that it engenders: it chemically satiates your taste while producing a reaction in your stomach for more. High fructose corn syrup begets food that is satisfyingly vacant (Tirman 2006, Patel 2007).

The global food regime is distressingly dysfunctional: a third of the planet is underfed while a third of the planet is overfed. Many who produce food are increasingly marginal to the global food regime, while the gargantuan corporations that shape our tastes and food aspirations feed us empty calories so that their bottom line is improved and their shareholders are kept happy. All the while, though, the ecological footprint of our oil-intensive meat-obsessed global food regime is broadening and intensifying, warming the planet and creating the preconditions of a global catastrophe that would be without precedent in the history of our species (Weis 2007).

I think that the stories of the people we have met in this book reveal a lot about the history of and conditions facing the world's farmers and the food that we eat. Noor Mohammed, Haji Shahrukh Khan, Jessica Carson, Grace Muchengi, Sam Naimisi, Qing Youzi, John Hrudy, Abdul Hussain, Bob Miller, Maxime Auxiliare and Ganesh Prasad all offer partial and incomplete glimpses into how we have arrived at this place: a global food regime that underfeeds and overfeeds too many at the same time. It is a regime that cannot last and that has catastrophic consequences for people; it is an absurd affliction on our common humanity.

In the last chapter I tried to show how the World Bank and Vía Campesina have a vision for the future of food and farming. But the two are simply incompatible, being based on radically opposing if not inimical inspirations. One sees agrarian capitalism unleashed; as emerging industrial capitalist agriculture in developing capitalist countries feeds the boundless appetites of the apparently uncaring of the world, those that are dispossessed through enclosure-induced displacement and the differentiation generated by market imperatives end up on the margins of a planet that increasingly resembles a vast slum populated by people that seem to be surplus to requirements. The other sees small-scale peasant and family farming resurrected and sustained, an attractive vision but one that does not consider some of the contradictory complications that arise from that resurrection: that not all small-scale peasant and family farmers share a common set of interests, and indeed, for small-scale peasant and family farmers to thrive they must be able to exclude their neighbours from using their land or seizing their farm production (Hall, Hirsch and Murray Li 2011). In conditions of untrammelled market imperatives the coercion of the need to be competitive must, sooner or later, unleash new exclusionary tensions within small-scale peasant and family farming, both within and between communities, tensions that will threaten to tear communities asunder.

What I have learned is that any new food system must address the simultaneous and mutually-reinforcing tensions found in the visions of both the World Bank and Vía Campesina. The World Bank's inevitable and inescapable reality of market imperatives under the sway of increasingly globalized capital, a reality that has shaped the development of our food for four centuries, must be addressed head on: market imperatives must be disciplined. The appealing counter-vision of food sovereignty must be re-tooled so that the contradictory and plausibly neopopulist tensions in it are also addressed so as to ensure that a reconfigured food system is socially and economically sustainable. The need for sustainability also suggests disciplining market imperatives.

I believe that a first, tentative step in addressing these tensions is to have food become what economists call a "public good": the consumption of food by one should not reduce food consumption by others, and no one should be excluded from being able to get food. Public goods are not inevitably immutable but vary across time, space and place because they are conceived, created and nurtured within and between communities that have identified the needs of a community or its members (Wuyts 1992). Such communities have organized themselves toward meeting those needs through some form of collective action that enhances human security.

The collective action of communities of people to define public goods can result in them being provided by the state, but this need not be so; organizations within communities can seek to change the way public goods are provided, most notably by trying to supply them through the community and the household rather than the state or the market. Such an effort has implications for the character of our food: some food would not be produced to be bought and sold; some food provision could instead become a kind of "commons" — an area outside the exclusive and untrammelled sway of the market, available to all as a basic right of citizenship. Thus, defining food as a public good brings with it the implication that people have a right to food.

This may sound revolutionary, but it is not. In fact, it's a return to the past. For most of our history, being the member of a community has brought with it a right to an elementary amount of food; this has been true for even very poor communities. It is only in the past four centuries that food slowly became something to be bought and sold to the highest bidder, commodification eroding this right to the point where it no longer holds even though it is enshrined in the United Nations Universal Declaration on Human Rights, agreed to more than sixty years ago. The consequence of this violation of our most basic rights — famine — is predominantly associated with the modern world, our world, and not the ancient world (Ó Gráda 2009).

Those who believe that public goods cannot be created by engaged citizens have failed to read their more recent history: the development of mass education and, in most developed capitalist countries, access to a certain level of health care is an outcome of popular and prolonged struggles by engaged citizens to create public goods available to all without a direct market-based charge. Turning food into a public good is if anything pragmatic, resurrecting and sustaining what we have lost so that we can continue, for we cannot continue as we have. It is at the same time radical, in the sense that turning food into a public good explicitly rejects the food architecture of the present, suggesting that we must present a vision of the future that is very much at odds with the way the world currently works. So a new food system, based upon a more sharply defined idea of food sovereignty — agrarian sovereignty, if you like — is if anything an example of "radical pragmatism" (Akram-Lodhi 2005a): underscoring "the fierce urgency of now" (Carson and Shepard 2001) by identifying what needs to be done along with the practical matters of how it might be done.

In order to unearth and then pull together the ways in which agrarian sovereignty could be built, there are three people that must be introduced: Saturnino M. ("Jun") Borras Jr. from the Netherlands by way of the Philippines; the late Hans Singer from Britain by way of Germany; and Stephen Alexander from Canada by way of Australia. Together, these three men offer glimpses into a future of how the planet can farm the food it needs in a way that provides the dignity of daily bread and work for all.

The Philippines is a country with the most extreme inequality in the countryside; as a consequence of a prolonged colonial history, landlords control huge tracts of land, while small-scale land-poor and landless peasants try to survive on the margins, selling rice and vegetables in markets increasingly dominated by cheaper foreign-grown farm products (Borras

Jr. 2007). Maxime Auxiliare would recognize it: the global food regime has coldly crushed the lives of many Filippinos that produce food, like his father, and in a land of plenty many have to go without. Jun Borras grew up in an unjust land, and like Rafael Alegría he spent most of the 1980s involved in organizing small-scale land-poor and landless Filippino peasants so that they could question and challenge their lack of access to land, mostly by defiantly confronting the power of their landlords in order to receive a measure of social justice. A short, modest man with closely cropped curly hair, an infectious laugh and a ready smile that beams when he hears Bob Dylan, Borras became, as a result of his pro-peasant activism, involved in a series of cross-border small-scale peasant farmer initiatives toward the end of the 1980s, travelling extensively in order to learn from the organizational and associational experience of others. So when Vía Campesina was founded in 1993 he became part of its International Coordinating Committee and was deeply involved in its actions against the inclusion of agriculture into the procedures and processes of the World Trade Organization, created in 1995 on the foundations of the earlier General Agreement on Tariffs and Trade. When he left that committee in 1996, at the behest of a friend he knew from his activist circles he applied to do a master's degree in rural development, which is where I met him: he was a student where I was teaching.

Jun Borras has become, in the past decade, perhaps the quintessential activist-academic in international rural development studies, a partisan scholar whose scholarship — which is exceptionally good — is about trying to figure out the necessary and sufficient conditions in which a better world for the small-scale land-poor and landless farmers of developing capitalist countries could be built. His ambition: to contribute to the construction of those conditions. For Borras, currently editor of the Journal of Peasant Studies, the violent and degrading circumstances facing many of the world's small-scale peasant farmers, which he has witnessed first-hand because of his scholarly and activist work, represent an affront, the gravest injustice that he has spent his life trying to address, any way that he can.

Hans Singer was born in Germany in 1910 and died in England in 2006. He had intended to follow his father and become a medical doctor, but while at Bonn University he attended a lecture by economist Joseph Schumpeter and was so inspired that he switched to the study of economics (Shaw 2002). With the rise to power of the Nazis he fled Germany in 1933, the same year as Fritz Haber; in 1934, on the advice of Schumpeter, John Maynard Keynes agreed to accept Singer as one of his first Ph.D. candidates. Singer was one of the few people to study under both Schumpeter and Keynes, two of the great liberal economists of the twentieth century.

Singer's first job after receiving his doctorate in 1936 was a two-year study on the long-term impact of unemployment; like Norman Borlaug he became deeply aware of the conditions facing the marginalized, many of whom were hungry. This awareness was reinforced by his own identity as a Jew growing up in a predominantly Catholic area of a Protestant country and as a refugee in England. His subsequent passion for social justice in an unjust world was borne of these conditions and put him in an exceptionally good position when, in 1947, he became one of three economists to join the economics department of the United Nations, where he saw, all too often at first-hand, the problems facing developing capitalist countries. Singer remained there until 1969, when he began working at the Institute of Development Studies at the University of Sussex.

Singer's most enduring and influential intellectual and policy intervention was to provide the evidence that demonstrated that the benefits of international trade were systemically maldistributed between the countries that imported agricultural commodities and those that exported them, to the disadvantage of the exporters, who were principally poorer developing capitalist countries (Singer and Gray 1988). The international market system, Singer demonstrated, was rigged against the poor of the planet, and only public action by the state and the international community could ensure that the unjust vicissitudes of the system did not bear down heavily on those least able to cope.

I count myself fortunate to have met Hans Singer once, in 1986, and was struck by him. A short, balding man of considerable energy, he was, of course, famous, of which I was respectful. But Singer also had a quiet integrity that was buttressed by an almost meek gentleness, warmth and a deeply-felt, profoundly human concern for people. Strikingly, Singer really was a man who believed that we could collectively make the world a far, far better place if we put our minds to it, being interested, more than anything else, in a socially-just global distribution of goods, services and opportunities, and the institutional modes and mechanisms that could offset the rigged character of the world trading system and deliver the social justice that he so wanted to see.

Stephen Alexander lives a life that is a world away from that of Jun Borras or Hans Singer and would, I think, shy away from being described, like them, as someone who is part of a global movement for social justice. Such a movement would be, in his eyes, political, and he eschews politics. Yet what he does is profoundly political but in a way that is different to the activism of Jun Borras or the scholarship of Hans Singer. Stephen Alexander is a leader in Canada in the local sourcing and selling of meat in a way that tries to benefit farmers, consumers, communities and, of course, his own business. A third-generation butcher, when he emigrated to Canada Alexander found that people were so disconnected from the meat they were buying that they were disinterested: they did not know where it was raised, how it was raised or how cuts of meat could be used. People were alienated from their food, and this was reflected in the quality of the meat that was available, which was terrible compared to that with which he was most familiar, the meat that he had eaten growing up in Australia, where you could taste in the meat you ate where and on what the animal had been raised. Stephen Alexander came head to head with the global food regime and did not like what he saw.

In the late 1990s Stephen Alexander began in a small way to challenge people's understanding of meat. Knowing that small- and large-scale family farmers producing mass-market, commoditized meat were doing so not out of a free choice but because of the way the market imperative operated and because it was what they knew how to do, he bought a family farm, raising livestock to meet his own demanding standards of breeding, grazing, feeding and animal care. With some modest success, Alexander began establishing very close partnerships with a number of large- and small-scale family farmers across southern Ontario, farmers who were prepared to meet the same standards for their animals and then exclusively sell on to him at contractually-agreed better than market prices: call it contract farming plus. He also established a close relationship with a select number of abattoirs that understood the moral implications of killing an animal for meat: that in killing an animal people had a duty to ensure that as little as possible of the animal was wasted.

Alexander wanted to make sure that every animal he had reared or purchased, and so every piece of meat he sold, could be personally guaranteed by him to have been raised on feeds that did not have hormones, drugs or chemical enhancements and in an environment with light and space, so that the quality of the meat came through. These days this approach is called "farm-to-fork" (Hladik 2012). Alexander is not organic, but he has adopted an approach that significantly reduces the ecological impact of raising livestock and better maintains the welfare of the animals until they are slaughtered (Weis 2007).

Alexander is also an educator, working with his wholesale customers in the up-market restaurant trade and his retail consumers to show them that far too much good meat is wasted by Canadian food preferences for a narrow range of cuts of meat, a preference that is based on ignorance and the limited choice offered by supermarkets. Encouraging his customers to try lower-cost "off-cuts," Alexander offers less well known but higher quality meat that can compete with the supermarkets. So Alexander has been instrumental in his local food culture in democratizing people's ability to buy low-impact locally-sourced meat that can compete on price with supermarket meat.

Borras, the activist, Singer, the scholar, and Alexander, the entrepreneurial capitalist, are all part of the answer to the world's agrarian question. The actions of the three have deep implications for the future of farming and the food system: all three in their professional lives have demonstrated reasons why the politics and economics of the global food regime cannot be sustained over time, and all three have, unbeknownst to them, demonstrated a practical commitment to radical pragmatism. In the slipstream of their radical pragmatism we can not only see that change is inevitable, and soon, but can also see the type of change that is necessary to create agrarian sovereignty.

A starting point to create agrarian sovereignty is to go back to the future, to land reform. As I have shown, for most of the twentieth century state-sponsored land reform was used by rural elites to capture more land from the land-poor and the dispossessed. More recently, attempts by the World Bank and the U.S. Agency for International Development to construct "market-led land reform," in which "willing" buyers of land are brought together with "willing" sellers of land, have floundered: the amount of land transferred has been small; it has often been of poor quality; in some cases rural dominant classes have used it to increase their holdings of land; and even when the land-poor get land they incur a large liability to repay the debt they have taken out to obtain the land, without actually owning the land that they have received because they have not paid for it (Borras Jr. 2009). Yet despite these clear failures Jun Borras is right: pro-poor redistributive land reform that ensures that more land is taken from the better off, and without adequate financial compensation, than that which is taken from the worse off, thereby transferring rural wealth from the rich to the poor, remains, worldwide, an urgent necessity for the small-scale land-poor and the landless.

Pro-poor redistributive land reform is needed because scarce access to deficient quantities of land for the small-scale land-poor and the landless is the result of a history of violent dispossession, whether it be from: coerced extraction of crops and labour from small-scale peasants to governing bureaucracies in East Asia (Phongpaichit and Baker 1998); the genocidal extermination of indigenous peoples in the western hemisphere by the arriving colonizers (Crosby 2003); the induced famines arising from enforced rural change in South Asia (Davis 2001); the artificial creation of property rights in land and the establishment of a class of large-scale export-oriented settler-farmers in sub-Saharan Africa (Reid 2012); or the enforced enclosure of communally-held lands by the powerful, which has happened around the world (Hall, Hirsch and Murray Li 2011). The establishment of a global capitalist economy, and a global food regime, has been based upon an extensive, thorough and degrading marginalization of small-scale peasant farmers that has turned many of them into a relative surplus population that is not functional to the working of the global food regime: and these are the families that, as a consequence of a long history of injustice, now struggle to construct a tenacious livelihood in ever more tenuous circumstances. Land reform is restitution for past injustices that continue to reverberate through to the modern day.

It is argued, in the World Bank, international think-tanks and states, that land reform is passé. They say that state-directed land and agrarian reform in the 1950s and 1960s: was overly centralized, bureaucratized and undemocratic; was too driven by the demands of small-scale land-poor peasants and landless workers; was too expensive; was too market-distorting; and so was, as a result of all of these factors, inefficient in the strict economic terms of ensuring as much as possible was produced on marginal pieces of land (Akram-Lodhi, Borras Jr., Kay and McKinley 2007). This kind of argument, which remains very widely held, is quite fundamentally wrong.

State-led land and agrarian reform in the 1950s and 1960s was centralized in the halls of the state apparatus because when it was undertaken the state was the only institutional mechanism capable of challenging the authority of rural dominant classes; certainly, effectively marginalized small-scale land-poor and landless peasants could not challenge the rural elite unless they took up arms, as Emiliano Zapata and the peasant wars of the twentieth century demonstrated. Also, land reform was not necessarily undemocratic. Where democracies existed and freedom to exercise the right to vote was genuine — admittedly, a minority of places — small-scale peasants consistently voted for political parties that advocated land and agrarian reform, because such reform was in their interest, the interest of the rural majority. Where democracy was sublimated to the dictates of dominant classes, land reform may not have been introduced as a result of elections, but the commonplace enclosure of land by rural elites over a prolonged period of time was not based upon any kind of democracy but rather upon the force of the state. Small-scale land-poor and landless peasants want land reform; it is, for them, the basis of collective and individual human rights and thus the basis of democracy because it is the foundation of economic, as opposed to political, democracy.

State-led land and agrarian reform was expensive, but that was because in most instances land reform programs were introduced that had, as a defining principle, expropriation with compensation being paid to the elite. This not only resulted in costs that states often could not bear; where they could bear it, it often resulted in states paying more than was necessary to the rural elite for lesser-quality land that was made available in inadequate quantities. In this way, expropriation with compensation was part and parcel of the mechanism by which land and agrarian reform in the 1950s and 1960s resulted in a redistribution of wealth from the poor to the rich. Pro-poor redistributive land reform can only be achieved if the compensation that accompanies any expropriation is limited to amounts that are less than the value of the land that is expropriated so that, in net terms, a real and meaningful transfer of wealth from the rich to the poor actually takes place, a redistribution that can be justified in terms of restitution.

The argument that state-led land and agrarian reform distorted the working of the market assumes that left to its own devices markets work for the benefit of all. But the everyday operation of markets forces upon market participants the need to be competitive if they are to sell their products and their labour, which means the need to continually strive to lower costs and increase quality. This is not a free choice; the coercive impulse foisted upon market participants by competition results in markets rewarding winners, who become the economically stronger, and penalizes losers, who become the economically weaker. It is this core coercive impulse that produces economic efficiency, an outcome that is based upon rewarding the strong and penalizing the weak. As we have seen, unregulated markets result in the appropriation of the land, labour-power and other resources of the weak by the strong as their quest for increased competitiveness continues. For land and agrarian reform to work in the interests of the marginalized, market imperatives must be disciplined: the ability of the strong to dispossess the weak must be limited. The only institution capable of governing the market in the interests of the weaker is, for all its flaws, the state.

I would say that the need for land and agrarian reform should not be placed within the language of improved economic efficiency. Economic efficiency is an outcome of a Darwinian struggle for survival in which some are better equipped than others to win because of their relatively greater social power. Whether or not a pro-poor redistributive land reform results in increased economic efficiency is not a technical question rooted in the purported "inverse relationship" between size of holding and productivity per unit of land, a relationship that suggests that smaller farms are more productive per unit of land than bigger farms. Whether an inverse relationship is present cannot be abstracted from the prevailing set of social and economic conditions under which farm and food production takes place. It is the ensemble of social and economic conditions that will determine whether a land and agrarian reform results in increases in farm and food production per unit of land, so the issue is whether this ensemble of social and economic conditions is one based upon social justice in access to and control over land or whether it is based upon the historical injustices that have resulted in existing distributions of land.

The case against land reform is weak. The case for land reform is, most fundamentally, about definitively transforming social and economic conditions so that a more just outcome that overturns historical injustices is created and the foundation by which individual and collective human rights can be realized is established. But the lessons of the past are that land reform, even if it is pro-poor in its redistributive outcome, will not be adequate if the redistribution of land from the elite to the poor is not accompanied by a raft of supporting measures necessary to increase rural farm production (Akram-Lodhi, Borras Jr., Kay and McKinley 2007). The small-scale land-poor and landless peasants cannot be expected to simply receive land and immediately increase their food and agricultural production, generating larger surpluses and so increasing their incomes. They need broader support than just land: they need access to appropriate water, seed, fertilizer, pest management and farm equipment technologies that sustain the agroecology in which they farm; they need credit to buy the things they need when they do not have the cash; they need the trucks and barges that will physically shift their crops to places where they can be distributed; they need to get their crops out of the village and to the people that will buy them in ways that do not produce insecure and unstable incomes for them while at the same time conferring disproportionate control to those that make the markets work. Farming is not just about the terms and conditions of getting food from the land; it is also about the terms and conditions by which food is obtained by those that need it, and in this sense land reform requires much broader agrarian reform to support the possibilities created by pro-poor redistributive land reform if the pro-poor redistributive land reform is to succeed.

It is clear that a precondition of the success of pro-poor redistributive land reform requires limiting the capacity of markets to produce negative outcomes for the already marginalized. A critical means by which this can be achieved is by placing strict limits upon markets in land (Kay 2002, Wade 1990). Left unencumbered, land reform establishes the foundations by which land can be redistributed to those that succeed in their response to the market imperative from those that do not succeed in their response to the market imperative. So land will be redistributed through land markets to successfully-differentiating richer peasants and emerging rural capitalists away from the less successful. The only way this process of market-led appropriation can be tempered is by restricting the operation of land markets and the capacity of people to sell or mortgage land, while at the same time installing the conduits through which emerging rural capitalists can direct their economic success into non-farm activities. It is not the unsuccessful that should be encouraged to leave farming; it is the successful. Social and economic conditions in the countryside need to be established that protect the small-scale suppliers of food and agricultural products while encouraging emerging rural capitalists to find new non-farm outlets for their energies.

This suggests another component of a successful land and agrarian re-form. There is a need to see where rural development and change fits within wider transformational impulses in societies. Food and agriculture has usually been an afterthought in development strategies, where it has been thought of at all. This is a mistake (de Janvry 1981). If emerging rural capitalists are to find new non-farm activities on which to unleash their entrepreneurial energy, these will, in the first instance, likely have a close connection to their agrarian origins. There is a need to look for synergies between agricultural and non-agricultural manufacturing and service activities that are simultaneously complementary and self-reinforcing. It is not that food and agriculture lay the foundations of industry and services, although it has in the past in some places; it is that food and agriculture, industry and services develop and change over time together. The current course of that change deepens poverty processes in developing capitalist countries and results in widespread food insecurity. That course has to be changed to be channelled by the state in a way that clearly confronts, reduces and eventually eliminates poverty in both town and country.

If markets are to be disciplined, and if food and agriculture, industry and services are to be developed in mutually-reinforcing poverty-eliminating ways, the role of the state in transforming the food system is going to be magnified. Some might argue that the state is inherently incapable of undertaking this task; but while states can reinforce hierarchy and status they need not necessarily do so, while undisciplined markets are mechanisms that certainly reinforce inequality and hierarchy. The history of the developed capitalist countries shows that the state is capable of guiding the development process if close attention is paid to the needs of the marginalized and the dispossessed: addressing their needs can bring about a more just outcome. The issue is not whether the state can take up this role; it is whether the type of state is capable of taking up this role and, if not, how the state can be reconstituted to take up the role of guiding development for the benefit of the marginalized and the dispossessed.

Capitalist states homogenize social relations in order to "render legible" the capacity to govern (Scott 1999). Nonetheless, rather than a monolithic leviathan the state must be seen as a contested space in which the agendas and interests of the marginalized and the excluded can and must be actively advocated, both from within, so that change is set in motion, and from outside, so that there is no backtracking on change. This approach can be said to be one which is both "in and against" the state: "in" in the sense that it engages with the people in the state, finding those that are sympathetic and if necessary, entering into the state, working from within, in order to pragmatically advance a radical agenda; and "against" in the sense that the predatory possibilities of the state and its functionaries must always be confronted (Akram-Lodhi 2005b). By being "against" the state in order to advance the interests of those "in" the state, a development strategy can be produced that promotes the complementary and interconnected development of agriculture, industry and services by governing the market in order to produce improvements in human security and social justice.

Vía Campesina's daunting demand for food sovereignty gets part way to an answer about the future of food and agriculture. But there is a need to recognize that the social and economic preconditions of increased inequality could be put in place through food sovereignty unless disciplines are placed upon rural elites and markets so that tendencies inherent in the market system are disciplined by a state sympathetic to the needs of the marginalized because of the active role of the marginalized in directing the activities of the state. So part of the agrarian sovereignty agenda must be to seek out those in the state that can be brought on board, rather than treating the state with uniform and unremitting hostility.

If Jun Borras is right, though, truly pro-poor redistributive land and agrarian reform cannot be introduced in isolation from the broader forces at work in the world. The global architecture by which we get our access to food is dominated by agro-food transnational supermarket and agrochemical companies, forms of globalized capital that exist by squeezing value out of emerging rural capitalists and discarding rural and urban populations that are surplus to their needs. The ability of agro-food transnational corporations to do this is reinforced by the power of the World Trade Organization, which creates the playing field on which the squeezing of value becomes possible because it is dedicated to reinforcing the power of the market imperative. Faced with this land and agrarian reform in one country stands little chance, given how interconnected the world is as a result of decades of food globalization.

Hans Singer was able to demonstrate, with vivid and emotive clarity, the way in which international trade between unequal countries, in terms of their level of economic development, can generate unequal outcomes, with the benefits going to the already wealthy and the costs going to the already poor. Singer said that there was a need to create global institutions that would offset this process. Vía Campesina argues that the WTO must get out of agriculture, because food is different (Rossett 2006). This is correct but is not enough. It is not enough because the withdrawal of agriculture from the WTO will result in the WTO still being able to shape the contours and character of the global playing field in a way that is consistent with the corporate interests of capital, and this will continue to affect the operation of farming on a world scale. So the issue is not that the WTO affects agriculture but rather that the WTO deepens the power of the market imperative, and it is this imperative that must be confronted if the operation of food and agriculture is to be made pro-poor rather than pro-rich.

Challenging the power of the market imperative on a global scale cannot just be done by pro-poor redistributive states; it requires a pro-poor redistributive global institution that, by regulating the impact of the market imperative, reduces its influence on the poor relative to its impact on the rich. It was Hans Singer who taught me this on the single occasion that I met him. The WTO must be replaced by a new International Trade Organization (ITO) that one of Singer's mentors, Keynes, attempted to create in 1944 but to which the U.S. objected (Borgwardt 2005).

An ITO that would have satisfied Singer, and by implications Keynes, would still reduce trade barriers between countries but would place the attempt to lower trade barriers within the broader context of the investment and employment generation implications of trade restrictions. In order to ensure that investment and employment were maintained in a world of lowered trade barriers, the ITO would have to have the capacity to tax balance of payments surpluses (i.e., when various sources of money flowing into the country exceed various sources of money flowing out of the country) as a means of sustaining full employment. It would also strictly control flows of speculative capital — the IMF has this power but does not use it. The ITO would, critically, enforce interventionist actions against the restrictive business practices systematically conducted by transnational corporations, including those involved in the global food regime, and so decisively regulate the market imperative in order to sustain full employment. Finally, and importantly, the ITO would develop a global agro-food commodity policy that had, as its core principle, the need to stabilize global food and agriculture prices through a mutually-agreed set of international commodity agreements (Shaw 2002, 2007, 2009). In other words, the ITO at a global level would govern the market in the way the national state does at the country level, complementing the activity of the pro-poor redistributive state by dampening the power of the market imperative on a global scale. Singer would have approved.

Pro-poor land and agrarian reform and the creation of a market-dampening and price-stabilizing ITO creates the preconditions for a transformation in the food system, most particularly by setting in place the foundations of a possible shift from a global to a local food system because agro-food transnational corporations and food markets would be subject to discipline. Here, though, Stephen Alexander's capitalist impulse is right: restricting the operation of the market for food and agricultural produce on its own will solve nothing. Food should be a public good for those that lack it, but beyond that, people should have the freedom to choose; it is the current domination of food and agricultural markets by agro-food transnational corporations that restricts this freedom. But as Raj Patel has said to me, the act of buying and selling will not change the world; expressing choice in an unequal world is a recipe for further inequality. There is instead a need for those of us who, individually and collectively, express choices to reflect on the strictures of the market imperative. We must change ourselves if the world is to change. There must be a form of personal perestroika.

Our tastes must be transformed. We must reject high fructose corn syrup-based calorie- and chemical-intensive processed foods and our excessive love of meat, which together are the cornerstone of the inappropriate and unsustainable food consumption patterns and obesity found in the developed capitalist countries. As Michael Pollan (2008) so succinctly puts it, we must "eat food. Not too much. Mostly plants." Changing our tastes means thinking about the food we eat and how it has been produced and prepared, whether that is by us or for us. It means thinking about the care, or lack of care, that goes into the food we eat; is it assembled, or is it crafted? Care is reflected in the tastes that we sense and savour: food historically has been a source of pleasure and of social integration.

A cultural revolution in food has much to learn from the slow food movement, which seeks to preserve the cultural cuisine within a place and its space, along with the associated food plants, domestic animals, farming systems, food preparation methods and food folklore found in the region (Petrini 2006). Slow food is nothing more than a reaffirmation of what constitutes good food and nutrition, placing the local and the low-impact at a centre that celebrates local produce and cuisines and seeks to increase knowledge of local food systems through education.

In transforming our tastes we must resurrect the seasonal and the local at the expense of the year-round and the global. It means thinking about the oil-, water-, chemical- and machine-intensity of the food we eat and trying to reduce it, largely by producing and eating with a greater respect for the landscapes in which farming takes place: we must produce and eat agroecologically (Altieri 1995).

Agroecology involves understanding the complex interactions between plants, animals, humans and the environment in agricultural systems and is premised on the fact that ecosystems and agricultural systems are context- and site-specific. Paying close attention to the productivity, stability, sustainability and equity of farm production within a specific context, the purpose of farming and eating agroecologically is to maintain a productive agriculture that sustains crop yields, optimizes the sustainable use of local resources and minimizes the negative ecological and socio-economic consequences of modern seed, fertilizer and mechanical farm technologies. As we have seen, yield-maximizing high-input and high-impact farming technologies and products do not usually serve the needs of farmers, consumers and the environment and have resulted in the creation of large numbers of poor farmers. This has set the stage for the farm and food crisis, a crisis that can only be solved by considering farm production in light of the technologies that it uses and its social and environmental impacts, paying close attention to the complexities of local agriculture and evaluating farm performance on the basis of ecological sustainability, food security, economic viability, natural resource conservation and social equity, as well as food production.

Promoting agroecological farming is not the same as suggesting a shift to organic farming: organic food production has already been captured by transnational supermarkets and is commonly very oil- and water-dependent. Agroecological practices instead suggest that we eat food with a far, far lower ecological impact, farming with nature rather than against it, farming in order to sustain soils and ecologies rather than degrading them, farming to match the aspirations of a particular community rather than homogenizing the tastes of the global elite, consistent with place, space and season (Patel 2007). It means supporting local food businesses that pay a living wage under reasonable terms and conditions of employment while avoiding the "big box" stores, whether organic or inorganic, that want uniformity, sterility and volume. It means, in a sense, taking Stephen Alexander's business model and using it as the basis of a new food system that can be built now from the floorboards up but with profound implications for the future direction of farming and food.

A new food system must seek to resurrect and then sustain what we have seemingly lost so that we can continue and in that sense is pragmatic in its aspirations. Its radicalism comes from its recognition that we must present a vision of the future that is achievable while being very much at odds with the way the world currently works. So the new food system identifies what needs to be done along with the practical matters of how that might be done. But agrarian sovereignty will not emerge without collective action by concerned citizens to bring it about.

Challenging the power of the market imperative thus needs more than pro-poor redistributive states and global institutions: it requires pro-poor redistributive social coalitions that coalesce around food and farming; it requires, in the evocative phrase of Eric Holt-Giménez (2011), that "food movements unite." Agroecological principles need to be promoted locally and globally, in both farm production and eating, and this requires farmers and consumers mobilizing for healthier, locally-sourced food. In order for agroecological principles to be introduced systemically there needs to be a new appreciation for small-scale farming in both developed and developing capitalist countries, and this appreciation requires comprehensive pro-poor redistributive land and agrarian reform that gives small-scale peasant farmers the tools they need to do the job they want to do. This too requires mobilization by food movements, working within Vía Campesina and outside it, both to reconstruct food as a public good and to work with elements in the state that are capable of propelling forward a different vision of the future of food and agriculture. Only the state can discipline the market in the ways that are necessary to make agroecological agrarian sovereignty work. Only the state can work with broad coalitions of concerned citizens united as a food movement to push for reform at the global level, most notably through the creation of the ITO.

ENDNOTES

Chapter 1

1. Although the project did reclaim farmland, it did not reduce rural poverty. For a complete account, see Freedman and Akram-Lodhi (2001).
2. The Pakhtuns dominate not only Khyber Pakhtunkhwa but also much of Afghanistan. The best understanding of Pakhtun social relations that I have read is Lindholm (1996), but see also Akram-Lodhi (2001b).
3. On sharecropping, see Byres (1983).
4. All dollar figures are in U.S. currency, unless otherwise indicated.

Chapter 2

1. The cash values in this story are drawn from Oxfam (2002) and are all in U.S. currency.
2. A more analytical account of the circumstances facing Manitoba's farmers can be found in Honey and Oleson (2006).
3. The best biography of Engels is without doubt that of Hunt (2009). For Marx, Francis Wheen's (2000) is superb.
4. Here, I paraphrase my colleague Jacqueline Solway, a formidable political economist.
5. The best recent biography of Lenin is by Service (2000).
6. Remarkably, the most recent biography of Kautsky is that of Geary (1987).

Chapter 3

1. The account here draws heavily on the ever-excellent Darling (1947).

Chapter 4

1. A rock-hard, deliciously sweet sugar.
2. The definitive biography of Zapata remains Womack Jr. (1970).

REFERENCES

Abbott, Elizabeth. 2011. *Haiti: A Shattered Nation*. New York: Overlook Press.

___. 1988. *Haiti: The Duvaliers and Their Legacy*. New York: McGraw-Hill.

ActionAid International. 2005. "Power Hungry: Six Reasons to Regulate Global Food Corporations." At <actionaid.org.uk/_content/documents/power_hungry.pdf>.

Akram-Lodhi, A. Haroon. 2012. "Contextualizing Land Grabbing: Contemporary Land Deals, the Global Subsistence Crisis and the World Food System." *Canadian Journal of Development Studies* 33, 2.

___. 2005a. "Vietnam's Agriculture: Processes of Rich Peasant Accumulation and Mechanisms of Social Differentiation." *Journal of Agrarian Change* 5, 1.

___. 2005b. "Neo-Conservative Ideology, the State and Democracy." In A. Haroon Akram-Lodhi, Robert Chernomas and Ardeshir Sepehri (eds.), *Globalization, Neo-Conservative Policies and Democratic Alternatives: Essays in Honour of John Loxley*. Winnipeg: Arbeiter Ring Publishing.

___. 2001a. "'Like an act of God': Land, Water and Social Power in Northern Pakistan." *Contemporary South Asia* 10, 3.

___. 2001b. "Attacking the Pakhtuns." At <theglobalsite.ac.uk/justpeace/110akram.htm>.

___. 2001c. "'We earn only for you': Peasants and 'Real' Markets in Northern Pakistan." *Capital and Class* 74.

___. 1997. "Structural Adjustment and the Agrarian Question in Fiji," *Journal of Contemporary Asia* 27, 1.

Akram-Lodhi, A. Haroon, and Cristóbal Kay (eds.). 2009. *Peasants and Globalization: Political Economy, Rural Transformation and the Agrarian Question*. London: Routledge.

Akram-Lodhi, A. Haroon, Saturnino M. Borras Jr. and Cristóbal Kay (eds.). 2007. *Land, Poverty and Livelihoods in an Era of Globalization: Perspectives from Developing and Transition Countries*. London: Routledge.

Allen, Weslynn M. 2009. *Traces: Our Connection to the Past*. Mustang, OK: Tate Publishing and Enterprises.

Altieri, Manuel. 1995. *Agroecology: The Science of Sustainable Agriculture*. Boulder, CO: Westview Press.

Anseeuw, Ward, Liz Alden Wily, Lorenzo Cotula and Michael Taylor. 2012. *Land Rights and the Rush for Land: Findings of the Global Commercial Pressures on Land Research Project*. Rome: International Land Coalition.

As They Saw It. 2012. "1965: Agriculture." At <astheysawit.info/8741-1965-agriculture.html>

Atwood, Margaret. 2008. *Payback: Debt and the Shadow Side of Wealth*. Toronto: House of Anansi Press.

Bagchi, Amiya Kumar. 2009. "Nineteenth-century Imperialism and Structural Transformation in Colonized Countries." In A. Haroon Akram-Lodhi and Cristóbal Kay (eds.), *Peasants and Globalization: Political Economy, Rural Transformation and the Agrarian Question*. London: Routledge.

Bailey, Joseph Cannon. 1971. *Seaman A. Knapp: Schoolmaster of American Agriculture*. New York: Arno Press.

Baines, Dudley. 1994. "European Emigration, 1815–1930: Looking at the Emigration

Decision Again." *The Economic History Review* 47, 3.

Barclay, Kate. 2010. "History of Industrial Tuna Fishing in the Pacific Islands: A HMAP Asia Project Paper." University of Technology Sydney Asia Research Center Working Paper no. 169. At

Barclay, Kate, and Ian Cartwright. 2007. *Capturing Wealth from Tuna: Case Studies from the Pacific*. Canberra: Asia Pacific Press.

___. 2006. "Capturing Wealth from Tuna: Key Issues for Pacific Island Countries." At <uts.academia.edu/KateBarclay/Papers/862903/Capturing_Wealth_from_ Tuna>.

Barker, Randolph, and Robert W. Herdt with Beth Rose. 1985. *The Rice Economy of Asia*. 2 vols. Washington: Resources for the Future.

Barrett, Christopher B., and Daniel G. Maxwell. 2005. *Food Aid After Fifty Years: Recasting Its Role*. London: Routledge.

Barros, Geraldo. 2009. "Brazil: The Challenges in Becoming an Agricultural Superpower." In Lael Brainard and Leonardo Martinez-Diaz (eds.), *Brazil as an Economic Superpower: Understanding Brazil's Changing Role in the Global Economy*. Washington: The Brookings Institution.

Bell, Beverly. 2002. "Social Movements and Economic Integration in the Americas." Citizen Action in the Americas Discussion Paper, November. At <cipamericas. org/archives/1051>

Berry, Albert, and William Cline. 1979. *Agrarian Structure and Productivity in Developing Countries*. Baltimore: The Johns Hopkins University Press.

Bevan, Judi. 2006. *Trolley Wars: The Battle of the Supermarkets*. London: Profile Books.

Binswanger, Hans P. 1978. *The Economics of Tractors in South Asia: An Analytical Review*. New York and Hyderabad: Agricultural Development Council and International Crops Research Institute for the Semi-Arid Tropics.

Binswanger, Hans P., and W. Graeme Donovan. 1987. *Agricultural Mechanization: Issues and Options*. Washington: The World Bank.

Blackburn, Robin. 1997. *The Making of New World Slavery: From the Baroque to the Modern, 1492–1800*. London: Verso.

Blythman, Joanna. 2007. *Shopped: The Shocking Power of British Supermarkets*. London: Harper Perennial.

Borgwardt, Elizabeth. 2005. *A New Deal for the World: America's Vision for Human Rights*. Cambridge: Harvard University Press.

Borras Jr., Saturnino M. 2009. *Competing Views and Strategies on Agrarian Reform, Volume I: International Perspectives*. Manila: Ateneo de Manila University Press.

___. 2008. "La Vía Campesina and its Global Campaign for Agrarian Reform." *Journal of Agrarian Change* 8, 2 & 3.

___. 2007. *Pro-Poor Land Reform: A Critique*. Ottawa: University of Ottawa Press.

Borras Jr., Saturnino M., M. Edelman and C. Kay (eds.). 2008. *Transnational Agrarian Movements Confronting Globalization*. Oxford: Wiley-Blackwell.

Borras Jr., Saturnino M., Cristóbal Kay and A. Haroon Akram-Lodhi. 2007. "Agrarian Reform and Rural Development: Historical Overview and Current Issues." In Akram-Lodhi, Borras Jr. and Kay (eds.). 2007. *Land, Poverty and Livelihoods*. London: Routledge.

Bread. 2011. "Number of Hungry Americans Remains at Record High." At <bread. org/media/releases/hungry-americans.html> September 7.

Bremen, Jan and Sudipto Mundle (eds.). 1991. *Rural Transformation in Asia*. Delhi:

Oxford University Press.

Brown, James. 2005. "An Account of the Dolphin-Safe Tuna Issue in the UK." *Marine Policy* 29, 1.

Buckland, Jerry. 2004. *Ploughing Up the Farm: Neoliberalism, Modern Technology and the State of the World's Farmers.* Winnipeg: Fernwood Publishing.

Burbach, Roger, and Patricia Flynn. 1980. *Agribusiness in the Americas.* New York: Monthly Review Press.

Bush, Ray. 2007. "Mubarak's Legacy for Egypt's Rural Poor: Returning Land to the Landlords." In Akram-Lodhi, Borras Jr. and Kay (eds.), *Land, Poverty and Livelihoods.* London: Routledge.

Byres, T.J. (ed.). 1983. *Sharecroppers and Sharecropping.* London: Frank Cass.

Byres, T.J., Ben Crow and Mae-Wan Ho. 1983. *The Green Revolution in India.* Milton Keynes: Open University Press.

Cain, P.J., and A.G. Hopkins. 1993. *British Imperialism: Innovation and Expansion, 1688–1914.* London: Longman.

Campbell, Hugh. 2005. "The Rise and Rise of EurepGap: European (Re)Invention of Colonial Food Relations?" *International Journal of Sociology of Food and Agriculture* 13, 2.

Canadian International Development Agency. 2009. "Micronutrients." At <acdi-cida. gc.ca/acdi-cida/acdi-cida.nsf/eng/FRA-4422402-563> August 7.

Canegrowers. 2012. "Sugarcane: An Important Rural Industry for Australia." At

Carney, Judith Ann. 2001. *Black Rice: The African Origins of Rice Cultivation in the Americas.* Cambridge, MA: Harvard University Press.

Carpenters Fiji Group. 2012. "A Proud Tradition." At <carpenters.com.fj/index. php?option=com_content&task=view&id=18&Itemid=35>.

Carson, Clayborne, and Kris Shepard (eds.). 2001. *A Call to Conscience: The Landmark Speeches of Dr. Martin Luther King, Jr.* New York: Hachette Book Group.

Cary, S.L. 1899. "Southwest Louisiana Up to Date, Omaha edition (Southwestern Louisiana on line of the Southern Pacific) At <ereserves.mcneese.edu/depts/ archive/FTBooks/cary.htm>.

Charles, Daniel. 2005. *Master Mind: The Rise and Fall of Fritz Haber, the Nobel Laureate Who Launched the Age of Chemical Warfare.* New York: Ecco.

ChartsBin. 2011. "Worldwide Rice Production." At <chartsbin.com/view/1009>.

Chernomas, Robert, and Ian Hudson. 2007. *Social Murder and Other Failings of Conservative Economics.* Winnipeg: Arbeiter Ring Publishers.

Clapp, Jennifer. 2011. *Food.* London: Polity Press.

Cline, W. Rodney. 1970. "Seaman Asahel Knapp, 1833–1911." *Louisiana History* 11, 4.

Cochrane, William W. 1993. *The Development of American Agriculture: A Historical Analysis* 2nd ed. Minneapolis: The University of Minnesota Press.

Congressional Budget Office. 1983. "Agricultural Export Markets and the Potential Effects of Export Subsidies." Staff Working Paper. At <cbo.gov/sites/default/ files/cbofiles/ftpdocs/50xx/doc5024/doc03-entire.pdf> June.

Cornwell, John. 2003. *Hitler's Scientists: Science, War and the Devil's Pact.* Harmondsworth: Penguin Press.

Cox, Ronald. 1997. "Private Interests and US Foreign Policy in Haiti and the Caribbean Basin." In David Skidmore (ed.), *Contested Social Orders and International Politics.* Nashville, TN: Vanderbilt University Press.

Cronon, W. 1991. *Nature's Metropolis: Chicago and the Great West.* New York: W.W. Norton.

Crosby, Alfred. 2003. *Ecological Imperialism: The Biological Expansion of Europe, 900–1900*. New ed. Cambridge: Cambridge University Press.

Daniel, Pete. 1986. *Breaking the Land: The Transformation of Cotton, Tobacco and Rice Cultures Since 1880*. Champaign, IL: University of Illinois Press.

___. 1984. "The Crossroads of Change: Cotton, Tobacco and Rice Cultures in the Twentieth-century South." *The Journal of Southern History* 50, 3.

___. 1981. "The Transformation of the Rural South: 1930 to the present." *Agricultural History* 55, 3.

Darling, Malcolm Lyall. 1947 [1928]. *The Punjab Peasant in Prosperity and Debt*. Lahore: Vanguard.

Dasgupta, Biplab. 1984. "Sharecropping in West Bengal: From Independence to Operation Barga." *Economic and Political Weekly* 19, 26.

Davis, Mike. 2006. *Planet of Slums*. London: Verso.

___. 2001. *Late Victorian Holocausts: El Niño Famines and the Making of the Third World*. London: Verso.

Davis, Paul K. 1999. *100 Decisive Battles: From Ancient Times to the Present*. Oxford: Oxford University Press.

de Janvry, Alain. 1981. *The Agrarian Question and Reformism in Latin America*. Baltimore: Johns Hopkins University Press.

Desmarais, Annette Aurélie. 2007. *La Via Campesina: Globalization and the Power of Peasants*. Halifax: Fernwood Publishers.

Desmarais, Annette Aurélie, and Luis Hernandez Navarro. 2009. "Feeding the World and Cooling the Planet." *Briarpatch*. At <briarpatchmagazine.com/articles/view/la-via-campesinas-fifth-international-conference> January.

Dethloff, Henry C. 1970. "Rice Revolution in the Southwest, 1880–1910." *The Arkansas Historical Quarterly* 29, 1.

Dusinberre, William. 2000. *Them Dark Days: Slavery in the American Rice Swamps*. Athens, GA: University of Georgia Press.

Dyer, Geoff. 2007. "Agribusiness May Reap Profits and Problems for China." *Financial Times*, April 3.

Eastwood, R., M. Lipton and A. Newell. 2009. "Farm Size." In P. Pingali and R. Evenson (eds.), *Handbook of Agricultural Economics Volume 4*. Amsterdam: Elsevier.

Economist (The). 2008. "Jack Simplot." June 12.

___. 2007. "Business by Numbers: Consumers and Companies Increasingly Depend on a Hidden Mathematical World." September 13.

Ellickson, Paul. 2011. "The Evolution of the Supermarket Industry: From A&P to Wal-Mart." Simon School Working Paper (series no FR 11-17). At <papers.ssrn.com/sol3/papers.cfm?abstract_id=1814166##>

Emberson-Bain, 'Atu, dir. 2001. *In the Name of Growth — Fiji: A Story of Fisheries Development, Indigenous Women and Politics*. Suva: Infocus Productions.

Engels, Friedrich. 1950 [1894]. "The Peasant Question in France and Germany." In Karl Marx and Friedrich Engels, *Selected Works*. Vol. 2. London: Lawrence and Wishart.

Environmental Working Group. 2011a. "Rice Subsidies in the United States Totaled $12.9 Billion from 1995–2010." At <farm.ewg.org/progdetail.php?fips=00000&progcode=rice>.

___. 2011b. "Rice Subsidies in Acadia Parish, Louisiana, Totaled $323 Million from 1995–2010." At <farm.ewg.org/progdetail.php?fips=22001&progcode=rice&p

age=conc&regionname=AcadiaParish,Louisiana>.

Feder, Gershon, Richard E. Just and David Zilberman. 1985. "Adoption of Agricultural Innovations in Developing Countries: A Survey." *Economic Development and Cultural Change* 33, 2.

Feinberg, Richard E. 2003. "The Political Economy of United States' Free Trade Arrangements." *The World Economy* 26, 7.

Fishman, Charles. 2007. *The Wal-Mart Effect: How an Out-of-Town Superstore Became a Superpower*. Harmondsworth: Penguin Books.

Food and Agriculture Organization. 2011. "The State of Food Insecurity in the World 2011." Rome: Food and Agriculture Organization. At <fao.org/docrep/014/i2330e/i2330e00.htm>.

___. 2002. "Organic Agriculture, Environment and Food Security." At <fao.org/docrep/005/y4137e/y4137e04.htm>.

FoodFirst. 1998. "12 Myths About Hunger." At <foodfirst.org/pubs/backgrdrs/1998/s98v5n3.html> February 8.

Fraser, Evan D.G., and Andrew Rimas. 2010. *Empires of Food: Feast, Famine and the Rise and Fall of Civilizations*. New York: The Free Press.

Freedman, Jim, and A. Haroon Akram-Lodhi (eds.). 2001. *Water, Pipes and People in Pakistan: The Social and Economic Impact of the Salinity Control and Reclamation Project in Mardan, Northern Pakistan*. Lahore: Vanguard Press.

Friedmann, Harriet. 1993. "The Political Economy of Food: A Global Crisis." *New Left Review* 197.

___. 1992. "Distance and Durability: Shaky Foundations of the World Food Economy." *Third World Quarterly* 13, 2.

___. 1982. "The Political Economy of Food: The Rise and Fall of the Postwar International Food Order." *American Journal of Sociology* 88 (supplement).

___. 1978. "World Market, State and Family Farm: Social Bases of Household Production in the Era of Wage Labor." *Comparative Studies in Society and History* 20, 4.

Friedmann, Harriet, and Philip McMichael. 1989. "Agriculture and the State System: The Rise and Decline of National Agricultures, 1870 to the Present." *Sociologia Ruralis* 29, 2.

Friis-Hansen, Esbern. 1995. *Seeds for African Peasants: Peasants' Needs and Agricultural Research — The Case of Zimbabwe*. Uppsala: Nordiska Afrikainstitutet.

Fukuda-Parr, Sakiko (ed.). 2007. *The Gene Revolution: GM Crops and Unequal Development*. London: Earthscan.

Gardner, Bruce L. 1992. "Changing Economic Perspectives on the Farm Problem." *Journal of Economic Literature* 30, 1.

Geary, Dick. 1987. *Karl Kautsky*. Manchester: Manchester University Press.

Ghatak, Maitreesh, Paul Gertler and Abhijit Banerjee. 2002. "Empowerment and Efficiency: Tenancy Reform in West Bengal." *Journal of Political Economy* 110, 2.

Ghosh, Jayati. 1988. "Intersectoral Terms of Trade, Agricultural Growth and the Pattern of Demand." *Social Scientist* 16, 4.

Gibbon, Peter. 1992. "A Failed Agenda? African Agriculture Under Structural Adjustment with Special Reference to Kenya and Ghana." *Journal of Peasant Studies* 20, 1.

Girard, Philippe. 2010. *Haiti: The Tumultuous History — From Pearl of the Caribbean to Broken Nation*. New York: Palgrave Macmillan.

Githinji, Mwangi Wa, and Gebru Mersha. 2007. "Untying the Gordian Knot: The

Question of Land Reform in Ethiopia." In Akram-Lodhi, Borras Jr. and Kay (eds.). *Land, Poverty and Livelihoods*. London: Routledge.

Goodman, David, and Michael Watts (eds.). 1997. *Globalising Food: Agrarian Questions and Global Restructuring*. London: Routledge.

Green America. 2009. "Coffee Industry." At <greenamerica.org/programs/responsibleshopper/industry/coffee.cfm>.

Hall, Derek, Philip Hirsch and Tania Murray Li. 2011. *Powers of Exclusion: Land Dilemmas in Southeast Asia*. Singapore: NUS Press.

Hallam, David. 2003. "Falling Commodity Prices and Industry Responses: Some Lessons from the International Coffee Crisis." Food and Agriculture Organization Corporate Document Repository. At <fao.org/docrep/006/y5117e/y5117e03.htm>.

Harvard Law School. 2009. "Holding Nations Accountable to the Developing World: A Profile of Robert Zoellick '81." At <law.harvard.edu/news/spotlight/public-service/related/zoellick.html>.

Hatanaka, Maki, Carmen Bain and Lawrence Busch. 2006. "Differentiated Standardization, Standardized Differentiation: The Complexity of the Global Agrifood System." *Research in Rural Sociology and Development* 12.

Heldman, Dennis R., and Paul Nesvadba. 2010. "Frozen Food: History." In Dennis R. Heldman and Carmen I. Moraru (eds.), *Encyclopedia of Agricultural, Food and Biological Engineering* 2nd ed. London: Routledge.

Herring, Ronald (ed.). 2008. *Transgenics and the Poor: Biotechnology in Development Studies*. London: Routledge.

Hesser, Leon F. 2006. *The Man Who Fed The World: Nobel Peace Prize Laureate Norman Borlaug and His Battle to End World Hunger — An Authorized Biography*. Dallas: Durban House Publishing Company.

Hildebrand, Clive. 2002. "Independent Assessment of the Sugar Industry 2002. Report to the Hon. Warren Truss MP, Australian Government Minister for Agriculture, Fisheries and Forestry." At <apec.org.au/docs/06_TP_Sugar/04_report.pdf>.

Hladik, Maurice J. 2012. *Demystifying Food from Farm to Fork*. Bloomington, IN: iUniverse.

Hobsbawm, Eric. 1994. *Age of Extremes: The Short Twentieth Century, 1914–1991*. London: Abacus.

Hogan, Michael J. 1989. *The Marshall Plan: America, Britain and the Reconstruction of Western Europe, 1947–1952*. Cambridge: Cambridge University Press.

Holt-Giménez, Eric (ed.). 2011. *Food Movements Unite!* Oakland: FoodFirst Books.

Holt-Giménez, Eric, and Raj Patel with Annie Shattuck. 2009. *Food Rebellions: Crisis and the Hunger for Justice*. Oakland: FoodFirst Books.

Honey, Janet, and Brian Oleson. 2006. "A Century of Agriculture in Manitoba: A Proud Legacy." Sponsored by the Credit Union Central of Manitoba. At <umanitoba.ca/afs/agric_economics/Century/ACenturyofAgriculture.PDF> September 10.

Hooper, Stephen. 2008. "Financial Performance of Australian Sugar Cane Producers, 2005–06 to 2007–08. Australian Bureau of Agricultural and Resource Economics Research Report 08.8 for the Australian Government Department of Agriculture, Fisheries and Forestry." At <daff.gov.au>

Howard, Philip. 1997. "Development-induced Displacement in Haiti." *Refuge* 16, 3.

Humphries, Sally, José Jiménez, Omar Gallardo, Marvin Gomez, Fredy Sierra et al. 2012. "Honduras: Rights of Farmers and Breeders' Rights in the New Globalizing Context." In Manuel Ruiz and Ronnie Vernooy (eds.), *The Custodians of Biodiversity:*

Sharing Access and Benefits to Genetic Resources. London: Earthscan.

Hunt, Tristan. 2009. *The Frock-Coated Communist: The Life and Times of the Original Champagne Socialist*. Harmondsworth: Penguin Books.

Hussain, Akmal. 1988. *Strategic Issues in Pakistan's Economic Policy*. Lahore: Progressive Publishers.

Institute for Agriculture and Trade Policy. 2003. "United States Dumping on World Markets." At <iatp.org/files/451_2_48538.pdf>.

Institute for Policy Studies. 2011. "Robert Zoellick." At <rightweb.irc-online.org/profile/Zoellick_Robert>.

International Fund for Agricultural Development. 2011. *Rural Poverty Report 2011*. At <ifad.org/rpr2011/>.

____. 2001. *Rural Poverty Report 2001*. New York: Oxford University Press.

International Rice Research Institute and Agricultural Development Council. 1983. *Consequences of Small-Farm Mechanization*. Manila: International Rice Research Institute.

Jansen, Kees, and Esther Roquas. 1998. "Modernizing Insecurity: The Land Titling Project in Honduras." *Development and Change* 29, 1.

Johnson, Vernon Webster, and Raleigh Barlowe. 1954. *Land Problems and Policies*. New York: McGraw-Hill.

Kaimowitz, David. 1996. *Livestock and Deforestation in Central America in the 1980s and 1990s: A Policy Perspective*. Jakarta: Center for International Forestry Research.

Kay, Cristóbal. 2002. "Why East Asia Overtook Latin America: Agrarian Reform, Industrialisation and Development." *Third World Quarterly* 23, 6.

Kautsky, Karl. 1988 [1899]. *The Agrarian Question*. London: Zwan Publications.

Kelsey, Jane. 2007. "Going Nowhere in a Hurry: The Pacific's EPA Negotiations with the European Union." *Victoria University Wellington Law Review* 87.

Kipple, Kenneth F. 2007. *A Moveable Feast: Ten Millennia of Food Globalization*. New York: Cambridge University Press.

Kloppenburg, Jack. 2004. *First the Seed: The Political Economy of Plant Biotechnology, 1492–2000*. Madison, WI: The University of Wisconsin Press.

Ladejinsky, Wolf. 1977. *Agrarian Reform as Unfinished Business: The Selected Papers of Wolf Ladejinsky*. Edited by L.J. Ladejinsky. Oxford: Oxford University Press.

Lal, Brij V. (ed.). 2004. *Bittersweet: The Indo-Fijian Experience*. Canberra: Pandanus Books.

Lamont, James. 2009. "Ambitions Dimmed but Not Abandoned." *Financial Times*, January 30.

Latham, A.J.H. 1998. *Rice: The Primary Commodity*. London: Routledge.

La Vía Campesina. 2012. "Food Sovereignty and Trade." At <viacampesina.org/en/index.php?option=com_content&view=category&layout=blog&id=21&Itemid=38>.

____. 2006. "United in the Vía Campesina." At <viacampesina.org/en/index.php?option=com_content&view=article&id=251:united-in-the-vcampesina&catid=33:3-bangalore-2000&Itemid=55>.

Leckie, Jacqueline. 2000. "Women in Post-Coup Fiji: Negotiating Work Through Old and New Realities." In A. Haroon Akram-Lodhi (ed.), *Confronting Fiji Futures*. Canberra: Asia Pacific Press.

Lee, Christopher M. 1996. "The American Rice Industry's Organization for a Domestic Market: The Associated Rice Millers of America." *Louisiana History* 37, 2.

Leonard, Thomas. 2011. *A History of Honduras*. Santa Barbara, CA: Greenwood Press.

Levi-Strauss, Claude. 1969. *The Raw and the Cooked: Introduction to a Science of Mythology* Vol 1. Translated by John and Doreen Weightman. New York: Harper Torchbooks.

____. 1963. *Totemism*. Boston: Beacon Press.

Lindholm, Charles. 1996. *Frontier Perspectives: Essays in Comparative Anthropology*. Karachi: Oxford University Press.

Lindstrom, Martin. 2008. *Buyology: Truth and Lies About Why We Buy*. New York: Crown Business.

Lipton, Michael. 2009. *Land Reform in Developing Countries: Property Rights and Property Wrongs*. London: Routledge.

Lipton, Michael, and Longhurst, Richard. 1989. *New Seeds and Poor People*. Baltimore: The Johns Hopkins University Press.

Livezey, Janet, and Linda Foreman. 2004. "Characteristics and Production Costs of US Rice Farms." United States Department of Agriculture Economic Research Service Statistical Bulletin number 974-7.

LSU AgCenter. 2012. "Acadia Parish." At <lsuagcenter.com/en/our_offices/parishes/Acadia/>.

Lynch, David. 2005. "Structure, Chance and Choice." At <asianreflection.com/structurechancechoice.shtml>.

Maddison, Angus. 2005 [1971]. *Class Structure and Economic Growth: India and Pakistan Since the Moghuls*. London: Routledge.

Mahadevan, Renuka, and John Asafu-Adjaye. 2010. "The Implications of European Union Sugar Price Cuts, Economic Partnership Agreeement, and Development Aid for Fiji." *Contemporary Economic Policy* 28, 1.

Malthus, Thomas. 1993 [1789]. *An Essay on the Principle of Population*. Oxford: Oxford University Press.

Mandel, Ernest. 1976. Introd. to *Capital Volume 1,* by Karl Marx. Translated by Ben Fowkes. Harmondsworth: Penguin Books.

Mann, James. 2004. *Rise of the Vulcans: The History of Bush's War Cabinet*. New York: Viking.

Martin, Douglas. 2008. "J.R. Simplot, Farmer Who Developed First Frozen French Fries, Dies at 99." *New York Times*, May 28.

Marx, Karl. 1976 [1867]. *Capital Volume 1*. Harmondsworth: Penguin Books.

____. 1967 [1852]. *The Eighteenth Brumaire of Louis Bonaparte*. Moscow: Progress Publishers.

Marx, Karl, and Friedrich Engels. 2012 [1848]. *The Communist Manifesto*. London: Verso.

Mazoyer, Marcel, and Laurence Roudart. 2006. *A History of World Agriculture: From the Neolithic Age to the Current Crisis*. Translated by James H. Membrez. New York: Monthly Review Press.

McClenahan Jr., William M., and William H. Becker. 2011. *Eisenhower and the Cold War Economy*. Baltimore: The Johns Hopkins University Press.

McMichael, Philip. 2012. "The Land Grab and Corporate Food Regime Restructuring." *The Journal of Peasant Studies* 39, 3 & 4.

Mikesell, Raymond F. 2009. *The Economics of Foreign Aid*. Piscataway, NJ: Aldine Transaction.

Millet, Donald J. 1964. "The Economic Development of Southwest Louisiana, 1865–1900." Unpublished Ph.D. dissertation, Louisiana State University. At <ereserves.mcneese.edu/depts/archive/FTBooks/millet.htm>.

Mosher, Arthur Theodore. 1966. *Getting Agriculture Moving: Essentials for Development and Modernization*. Westport, CT: Praeger Publishers.

Mosley, Paul, Jane Harrigan and John Toye. 1995. *Aid and Power: The World Bank and Policy-Based Lending*, Vol 1, 2nd ed. London: Routledge.

National Centre for Agricultural Economics and Policy Research. 1996. "Impact of Tenancy Reforms on Production and Income Distribution: A Case Study of Operation Barga in West Bengal. National Centre for Agricultural Economics and Policy Research Annual Report 1995–1996." At <ncap.res.in/upload_files/annual_report/1995-96/chap3.htm>.

Nolan, Peter. 1988. *The Political Economy of Collective Farms: An Analysis of China's Post-Mao Rural Reforms*. Cambridge: Polity.

___. 1982. "De-collectivization of Agriculture in China, 1979–1982: A Long-Term Perspective." *Economic and Political Weekly* 18, 33.

___. 1976. "Collectivization in China: Some Comparisons with the USSR." *Journal of Peasant Studies* 3, 2.

Ó Gráda, Cormac. 2009. *Famine: A Short History*. Princeton: Princeton University Press.

Osava, Mario. 2001. "World Social Forum: Peasants Speak Out Against Food Imports." *IPS News*. At <ipsnews.net/print.asp?idnews=89719>.

Oxfam. 2002. "Mugged: Poverty in Your Coffee Cup." At <oxfam.org.uk/resources/policy/trade/downloads/mugged.pdf >.

Patel, Raj. 2011. "Can the World Feed 10 Billion People?" *Foreign Policy*. At <foreignpolicy.com/articles/2011/05/04/can_the_world_feed_10_billion_people> May 4.

___. 2010. *The Value of Nothing: How to Reshape Market Society and Redefine Democracy*. London: Picador.

___. 2007. *Stuffed and Starved: Markets, Power and the Hidden Battle for the World's Food System*. London: Portobello Books.

Perdikis, Nicholas, and Robert Read (eds.). 2005. *The WTO and the Regulation of International Trade: Recent Trade Disputes Between the European Union and the United States*. Cheltenham, UK: Edward Elgar.

Perlez, Jane. 1991. "Naivasha Journal: Dutch Flowers? In Name Only. Ask the Kenyans." *New York Times*, February 2.

Petras, James, and Henry Veltmeyer. 2005. *Social Movements and State Power: Argentina, Brazil, Bolivia, Ecuador*. London: Pluto Press.

Petrini, Carlo. 2006. *Slow Food Revolution: A New Culture for Dining and Living*. New York: Rizzoli International Publications.

Phongpaichit, Pasuk, and Chris Baker. 1998. *Thailand's Boom and Bust*. Chiang Mai, Thailand: Silkworm Books.

Polanyi, Karl. 1957. *The Great Transformation: The Political and Economic Origins of Our Time*. Boston: Beacon Press.

Pollan, Michael. 2008. *In Defence of Food: An Eater's Manifesto*. New York: Penguin Press.

___. 2006. *The Omnivore's Dilemma: A Natural History of Four Meals*. New York: Penguin Press.

Population Reference Bureau. 2011. "2011 World Population Data Sheet." At <prb.org>.

Post, Lauren C. 1940. "The Rice Country of Southwestern Louisiana." *Geographical Review* 30, 4.

Prasad, Satendra, and A. Haroon Akram-Lodhi. 1998. "Fiji and the Sugar Protocol: A Case for Trade-based Development Cooperation." *Development Policy Review* 16.

Prescott, John. 2001. "Taste Hedonics and the Role of Umami." *Food Australia* 53, 12. At <aseanfood.info/Articles/11009445.pdf>.

Project for the New American Century. 2001. "Gulf War Anniversary." At <newameri-cancentury.org/defense-20010116.htm>.

Provost, Claire. 2012. "Global Hunger: Do the Figures Add Up?" The Guardian Poverty Matters Blog. At <guardian.co.uk/global-development/poverty-matters/2012/jan/26/global-hunger-fao-figures-add-up> January 26.

Ragatz, Lowell Joseph. 1960. *The New United States: America in the Postwar Era.* Tokyo: Fukuinkan-Shoten.

Rahman, Atiur. 1986. *Peasants and Classes: A Study in Differentiation in Bangladesh.* London: Zed Books.

Rajan, Jyotishma. 2005. "Gilt-edged Packet or Economic Straightjacket? A Case Study of Cannery Workers in Levuka, Fiji Islands." In Irene Novaczek, Jean Mitchell and Joeli Veitayaki (eds.), *Pacific Voices: Equity and Sustainability in Pacific Island Fisheries.* Suva: Institute of Pacific Studies.

Ratuva, Steven. 2000. "Addressing Inequality? Economic Affirmative Action and Communal Capitalism in Post-Coup Fiji." In Akram-Lodhi (ed.), *Confronting Fiji Futures.* Canberra: Asia Pacific Press

Reid, Richard J. 2012. *A History of Modern Africa: 1800 to the Present.* 2nd ed. Oxford: Wiley-Blackwell.

Richards, John F. 1993. *The Mughal Empire.* Cambridge: Cambridge University Press.

___. 1965. "The Economic History of the Lodi Period: 1451–1526." *Journal of the Economic and Social History of the Orient* 8, 1.

Roberts, Wayne. 2008. *The No-Nonsense Guide to World Food.* Oxford: New Internationalist Publications.

Robin, Marie-Monique. 2010. *The World According to Monsanto: Pollution, Corruption and the Control of Our Food Supply.* New York: The New Press.

Ross, Eric B. 1998. *The Malthus Factor: Poverty, Politics and Population in Capitalist Development.* London: Zed Books.

Rossett, Peter. 2006. *Food is Different: Why We Must Get the WTO Out of Agriculture.* London: Zed Press.

Rossett, Peter, Robert Rice and Michael Watts. 1999. "Thailand and the World Tomato: Globalization, New Agricultural Countries (NACs) and the Agrarian Question." *International Journal of Sociology of Agriculture and Food* 8.

Rothermund, Dietmar. 1969. "Government, Landlord and Tenant in India, 1875–1900." *The Indian Economic and Social History Review* 6, 4.

Rowthorn, R.E. and J.E. Wells. 1987. *De-industrialization and Foreign Trade.* Cambridge: Cambridge University Press.

Roy, Kaushik. 1997. "Recruitment Doctrines of the Colonial Indian Army: 1859–1913." *The Indian Economic and Social History Review* 34, 3.

Ruddle, Kenneth. 1989. "The Organization of Traditional Inshore Fishery Management Systems in the Pacific." In Philip Neher, Ragnar Arnason and Nina Mollett (eds.), *Rights Based Fishing.* Dordrecht: Kluwer Academic Publishers.

Sarris, Alexander. 1990. "Guidelines for Monitoring the Impact of Structural Adjustment Programmes on the Agricultural Sector." Food and Agriculture Organization of the United Nations *Economic and Social Development Paper* no 95.

Schlosser, Eric. 2005. *Fast Food Nation.* New York: Harper Perennial.

Schonhardt-Bailey, Cheryl. 2006. *From the Corn Laws to Free Trade: Interests, Ideas and Institutions in Historical Perspective.* Cambridge, MA: MIT Press.

Schultz, Theodore W. 1960. "Value of US Farm Surpluses to Underdeveloped

Countries." *Journal of Farm Economics* 42, 5.

Scott, James C. 1999. *Seeing Like A State: How Certain Schemes to Improve the Human Condition Have Failed.* New Haven: Yale University Press.

___. 1976. *The Moral Economy of the Peasant: Rebellion and Subsistence in Southeast Asia.* New Haven: Yale University Press.

Sen, Amartya. 1983. *Poverty and Famines: An Essay on Entitlement and Deprivation.* Oxford: Oxford University Press.

Service, Robert. 2000. *Lenin: A Biography.* London: Pan MacMillan.

Shaw, D. John. 2009. *Global Food and Agricultural Institutions.* London: Routledge.

___. 2007. *World Food Security: A History Since 1945.* Basingstoke: Palgrave Macmillan.

___. 2002. *Sir Hans W. Singer: The Life and Work of a Development Economist.* Basingstoke: Palgrave Macmillan.

Sheeran, Josette. 2009. "One Year On from the Food Crisis." Keynote address to the United Kingdom Department for International Development Annual Conference. At <wfp.org/eds-centre/speeches/%E2%80%9Cone-year-food-crisis%E2%80%9D-dfid-annual-conference> March 10.

Sheingate, Adam D. 2001. *The Rise of the Agricultural Welfare State: Institutions and Interest Group Power in the United States, France and Japan.* Princeton: Princeton University Press.

Shiva, Vandana. 1993. *Monocultures of the Mind: Perspectives on Biodiversity and Biotechnology.* London: Zed Press.

___. 1989. *The Violence of the Green Revolution: Third World Agriculture, Ecology and Politics.* London: Zed Press.

Simms, Andrew. 2007. *Tescopoly: How One Shop Came Out on Top and Why It Matters.* London: Constable and Robinson.

Simplot. 2012. "2012 J.R. Simplot Company Sustainability Summary." At <simplot.com/fileUploads/sustainability_report.pdf>.

Sinclair, Upton. 2003 [1906]. *The Jungle.* Tucson: Sharp Press.

Singer, Hans W., and Patricia Gray. 1988. "Trade Policy and Growth of Developing Countries: Some New Data." *World Development* 16, 3.

Sivramkrishna, Sashi, and Amalendu Jyotishi. 2008. "Monopsonistic Exploitation in Contract Farming: Articulating a Strategy for Grower Cooperation." *Journal of International Development* 20, 3.

Smil, Vaclav. 2004. *Enriching the Earth: Fritz Haber, Carl Bosch, and the Transformation of World Food Production.* Cambridge, MA: MIT Press.

___. 2000. *Feeding the World: A Challenge for the Twenty-first Century.* Cambridge, MA: MIT Press.

Smith, C. Wayne, and Robert H. Dilday (eds.). 2003. *Rice: Origin, History, Technology and Production.* Hoboken, NJ: John Wiley and Sons.

Smith, Julia F. 1991. *Slavery and Rice Culture in Low Country Georgia, 1750–1860.* Knoxville, TN: University of Tennessee Press.

Smith, Richard Saumarez. 2004. "Mapping Landed Property: A Necessary Technology of Imperial Rule?" In Huri Islamoglu-Inan (ed.), *Constituting Modernity: Private Property in the East and West.* London: I B Tauris.

___. 1996. *Rule By Records: Land Registration and Village Custom in Early British Panjab.* Delhi: Oxford University Press.

Snyder, C.S., and N.S. Slaton. 2001. "Rice Production in the United States: An Overview." *Better Crops* 85, 3.

Sporting Pulse. 2012. "Fiji Hockey Federation: Sponsor Information — Morris Hedstrom." At <sportingpulse.com/assoc_page.cgi?c=2-1417-0-0-0&sID=14303>.

Stonich, Susan C., and Billie R. DeWalt. 1996. "The Political Ecology of Deforestation in Honduras." In Leslie E. Sponsel, Thomas N. Headland and Robert C. Bailey (eds.), *Tropical Deforestation: The Human Dimension.* New York: Columbia University Press.

Street, Anne M. 2004. *Haiti 2004: A Nation in Crisis.* London: Catholic Institute for International Relations.

Sunderlin, William D. 1997. "Deforestation, Livelihoods and the Preconditions for Sustainable Management in Olancho, Honduras." *Agriculture and Human Values* 14, 4.

Sutherland, William. 2000. "The Problematics of Reform and the 'Fijian' Question." In Akram-Lodhi (ed.), *Confronting Fiji Futures.* Canberra: Asia Pacific Press

Swain, Nigel. 1985. *Collective Farms Which Work?* Cambridge: Cambridge University Press.

Teubal, Miguel. 2009. "Peasant Struggles for Land and Agrarian Reform in Latin America." In Akram-Lodhi and Kay (eds.), *Peasants and Globalization.* London: Routledge.

Thanassoulis, John. 2009. "Supermarket Profitability Investigation." At <economics.ouls.ox.ac.uk/14356/>.

Thompson, Laura. 1949. "The Relations of Men, Animals and Plants in an Island Community (Fiji)." *American Anthropologist* 51, 2.

Thompson, Lyndal, Michelle Young, Max Foster, Arlene Bury, Sophie Cartwright, Patty Please, James Tyson, Bill Binks and Anna Carr. 2010. "A Report on the Impacts of the Sugar Industry Reform Program (SIRP): 2004 to 2008." Australian Bureau of Agricultural and Resource Economics and Sciences for the Australian Government Department of Agriculture, Fisheries and Forestry. At <daff.gov.au>.

Thomson Reuters. 2012. "Aramark Corp/DE 10-Q Quarterly Report Persuant to Sections 13 or 15(d)." At <phx.corporate-ir.net/phoenix.zhtml?c=130030&p=irol-sec> February 8.

Tiefer, Charles. 2004. *Veering Right: How the Bush Administration Subverts the Law for Conservative Causes.* Los Angeles: University of California Press.

Tirman, John. 2006. *100 Ways America is Screwing Up the World.* New York: Harper Perennial.

Toussaint-Samat, Maguelonne. 1992. *A History of Food.* Oxford: Blackwell Publishing.

United Nations Conference on Trade and Development. 2009. *World Investment Report 2009: Transnational Corporations, Agricultural Production and Development.* Geneva: United Nations Conference on Trade and Development.

United States Agency for International Development and International Rice Research Institute. 1986. *Small Farm Equipment for Developing Countries.* Manila: International Rice Research Institute.

United States Department of Agriculture.2011. "Rice." At <ers.usda.gov/Briefing/Rice/>.

___. 2004. *Rice: Situation and Outlook Yearbook.* Washington: Market and Trade Economics Division, Economic Research Service, US Department of Agriculture.

___. 2002. "Farm Bill 2002." At <usda.gov/farmbill2002/>.

Veitayaki, Joeli. 1995. *Fisheries Development in Fiji: The Quest for Sustainability.* Suva:

Institute of Pacific Studies.

von Braun, Joachim. 2007. "The World Food Situation: New Driving Forces and Required Actions." Washington: International Food Policy Research Institute. At <ifpri.org/pubs/fpr/pr18.pdf>.

Wade, Robert. 1990. *Governing the Market: Economic Theory and the Role of Government in East Asian Industrialization*. Princeton: Princeton University Press.

Walden, Michael. 1996. "Ridin' High with J.R. Simplot." *The Oregonian* June 30.

Warriner, Doreen. 1969. *Land Reform in Principle and Practice*. New York: Oxford University Press.

Watts, Michael. 2009. "The Southern Question: Agrarian Questions of Land and Labour." In Akram-Lodhi and Kay (eds.), *Peasants and Globalization*. London: Routledge.

___. 1998. "Recombinant Capitalism: State, De-collectivization and the Agrarian Question in Vietnam." In J. Pickles and A. Smith (eds.), *Theorising Transition: The Political Economy of Post-Communist Tranformations*. London: Routledge.

Weis, Tony. 2007. *The Global Food Economy: The Battle for the Future of Farming*. London: Zed Press.

Welsman, Sandra. 2011. "Australian Sugar Industry RD&E Reform." At <canegrowers.com.au/page/Search/>.

Wheen, Francis. 2000. *Karl Marx: A Life*. New York: WW Norton.

Wikinvest. 2012. "Monsanto Company." At <wikinvest.com/stock/Monsanto_Company_(MON)>.

Wolf, Eric. 1999. *Peasant Wars of the Twentieth Century*. Norman, OK: University of Oklahoma Press.

Womack Jr., John. 1970. *Zapata and the Mexican Revolution*. New York: Random House.

Wood, Ellen Meiskins. 2009. "Peasants and the Market Imperative: The Origins of Capitalism." In Akram-Lodhi and Kay (eds.), *Peasants and Globalization*. London: Routledge.

Woodgate, Mary and Jo Matthews. 2010. "Food for Thought." Accenture Development Partnerships blog, at <accenture.com/us-en/blogs/accenture-development-partnerships/archive/2010/10/04/food-for-thought.aspx> October 4.

World Bank. 2011. "Global Food Crisis: At a Glance." At <web.worldbank.org/WBSITE/EXTERNAL/NEWS/0,,contentMDK:21928797~menuPK:34480~pagePK:64257043~piPK:437376~theSitePK:4607,00.html>.

___. 2010a. "Extreme Poverty Rates Continue to Fall." At <data.worldbank.org/news/extreme-poverty-rates-continue-to-fall> June 2.

___. 2010b. "Financial Information." At <web.worldbank.org/WBSITE/EXTERNAL/EXTABOUTUS/EXTANNREP/EXTANNREP2010/0,,contentMDK:22626599~menuPK:7115719~pagePK:64168445~piPK:64168309~theSitePK:7074179,00.html>.

___. 2008. "The World Bank Annual Report 2008." At <siteresources.worldbank.org/EXTANNREP2K8/Resources/YR00_Year_in_Review_English.pdf>.

___. 2007. *World Development Report 2008: Agriculture for Development*. New York: Oxford University Press.

___. 1967. *Experiences with Agricultural Development in Tropical Africa, Volume II: The Case Studies*. Baltimore: Johns Hopkins University Press.

World Food Programme. 2012. "Who Are the Hungry?" At <wfp.org/hunger/who-are>.

World Health Organization. 2011. "Obesity and Overweight Factsheet no 311." At <who.int/mediacentre/factsheets/fs311/en/>.

Wuyts, Marc. 1992. "Deprivation and Public Need." In Marc Wuyts, Maureen Mackintosh and Tom Hewitt (eds.), *Development Policy and Public Action*. Oxford: Oxford University Press.

Zoellick, Robert. 2002. "Unleashing the Trade Winds." *The Economist* December 5.

___. 2000. "Campaign 2000: A Republican Foreign Policy." *Foreign Affairs* at <foreignaffairs.com/articles/55632/robert-b-zoellick/campaign-2000-a-republican-foreign-policy> January 1.

INDEX